Parish Ministry in a Hispanic Community

Parish Ministry in a Hispanic Community

Charles W. Dahm, OP

Paulist Press
New York/Mahwah, N.J.

Cover art is by Jeff Zimmerman. The mural is entitled *Increibles las cosas que se ven (Incredible, the Things We See)*. Used by permission.

Cover design by Diego Linares
Book design by Lynn Else

Library of Congress Cataloging-in-Publication Data

Dahm, Charles W.
    Parish ministry in a Hispanic community / Charles W. Dahm.
        p.   cm.
    ISBN 0-8091-4272-4 (alk. paper)
    1. Church work with Hispanic Americans. 2. Hispanic Americans—Religion. 3. Hispanic Americans—Social conditions. 4. Christian sociology—Catholic Church. 5. Hispanic American Catholics—History. I. Title.

BV4468.2H57D34 2004
259'.089'68073—dc22

                                                                          2004006597

Published by Paulist Press
997 Macarthur Boulevard
Mahwah, New Jersey 07430

www.paulistpress.com

Printed and bound in the
United States of America

Contents

Introduction

María and José spent their first night in Chicago sleeping in the waiting area of Cook County Hospital's emergency room. Three months earlier, the young couple had left their home in Guadalajara, Mexico, where José had worked as a truck driver until the company he worked for folded. Unable to find work or stay with relatives poorer than themselves, the couple headed north with their three-year-old son. In Laredo, Mexico, they paid a coyote (smuggler) to take their child across the border. The $850 fee exhausted their savings. María's brother-in-law retrieved the boy in San Antonio, Texas, and took him to his home in Rock Island, Illinois, to await the arrival of his parents. Over the next three months, María and José made fifteen attempts to cross the Rio Grande. Each time they were caught by the border patrol and returned to Mexico. After each failed effort, José worked a few days at odd jobs to earn enough money to pay for food and a room before their next attempt.

Before stepping into the river, María and José prayed to the Virgin of Guadalupe for protection. Because she could not swim, María cried out in fear when the water rose to her chin and the current turned treacherous; in her desperation, she clung to José. After their successful crossing, María and José walked 150 miles in six days to reach San Antonio, where they caught a freight train to the Midwest. María was terrified, but José assured her everything would be all right. When they arrived in Pueblo, Colorado, a railroad engineer gave them food and guided them to a train bound for Chicago. Seven days later, they arrived in the City of Big Shoulders (Chicago) and were directed to St. Pius V parish to seek help.

When I welcomed them to the parish, José slid down into his chair and exclaimed, "I feel like shouting for joy." After selecting some clothing at the parish secondhand store and eating a hearty meal at the parish soup kitchen, they showered at the priests' apartment while I officiated at a wedding. Upon returning, I found them fast asleep on the sofa.

Refreshed from a good night's rest, they accompanied me to Sunday Mass and then enjoyed a hot bowl of menudo (tripe) soup with the parish community in the church basement. Before boarding the bus for Rock Island, they hugged me warmly and promised never to forget St. Pius V parish.

The journey of María and José has been repeated hundreds of times during the eighteen years (from 1986 to 2004) I have served as pastor of St. Pius V. Some immigrants become active at the parish, enriching the community, while others, like María and José, continue their journey to other cities where family, friends, or jobs await them. This book provides a picture of a church community not unlike an increasing number of others from Denver to Minneapolis, from Salt Lake City to Charlotte, from Omaha to Rockville Centre. Although a study of a predominantly Mexican immigrant parish, this book also speaks to parishes that encounter Mexican immigrants as a minority ethnic group by illuminating the history, challenges, and religious and cultural strengths of this group. St. Pius V is presented not as a model parish but as a community of Mexican immigrants that feel at home in their church, enthusiastically celebrating its faith and culture.

This book, which relates experience to the literature about Hispanic ministry, is less about Hispanic theology or Mexican popular religiosity than about ministry in a Mexican immigrant community today. At its core, is the frequent story of impoverished immigrants fleeing their native land to seek a better life for themselves in a new and rather resistant world, and also the story of generosity and hospitality of family, friends, and community who welcome and assist newcomers despite their own poverty. Immigrant families react differently to their new world: some readily assimilate new customs, jettisoning the old; others struggle to preserve fundamental Mexican values and traditions, and still others strongly resist what they perceive as a threat to their Mexican identity. This book describes those most recently arrived and, consequently, less influenced by American culture. They best reflect the cultural traditions Mexicans offer our country and church, and they are more likely to recognize and react to the differences between life and culture in Mexico and the United States. Thus, observations in this book may not apply as adequately to some first-, many second-, and especially third-generation Mexicans.

The population of the Pilsen neighborhood in Chicago is ninety percent Hispanic, and ninety percent of the Hispanics are of Mexican origin. The majority are immigrants who arrive filled with hope but all too often with mistaken notions about how easy their lives will be in the new land. From rural areas, with little concept of life in a large city, they come with no money, speaking no English, with limited education, and lacking skills to find well-paying jobs. Many are illiterate. Yet these immigrants are a people of profound faith, strong work ethic, festive spirit, and loving commitment to family and community who enrich the nation as well as the Catholic Church.

The words *Hispanic* and *Latino* are inappropriate to describe people of Latin American origins because both refer originally and more properly to European groups than to people of indigenous American heritage. Nevertheless, both words have become commonplace in referring to people from the Western Hemisphere's southern continent. I have chosen *Hispanic* because it is more commonly used by Mexicans at St. Pius V.[1] I use the word *Mexican* rather than *Mexican American* partly because most parishioners are immigrants, and partly because it is awkward to say *Mexican Americans* at every turn. When it is important to distinguish between immigrants and first- and second-generation Mexicans, *Mexican American* will be used.

In the 1960s and 1970s, St. Pius V changed from a Euro-American parish to a predominantly Mexican community as one ethnic group left the neighborhood and the new group arrived. Because the neighborhood became predominantly Hispanic so rapidly, the parish had to shift gears quickly, refocusing to incorporate a new population into its community life. There were many stops and starts, as some parishioners resisted change. But step by step, program by program, dedicated lay leaders and an able staff created multifaceted institutional structures and ministries to respond to the material, emotional, and spiritual needs of its new parishioners. In the process, the staff also changed from predominantly clerical and Euro-American to lay and Hispanic.

Forming community and celebrating faith and life with Mexican immigrants has been a deeply rewarding experience for all involved. Working together, the parish helped transform the voiceless victims of an immigrant community into powerful advocates for themselves, their families, their community, and their church. Moreover, non-Hispanics have also been transformed by a new culture that has enriched the way we believe, hope, and love in community. But our ministry remains a work in progress.

The first priority for a parish serving an immigrant community is meeting their immediate needs of food, clothing, shelter, and jobs. Thus, St. Pius V established a soup kitchen, shelters for homeless men and women, a secondhand clothing store, affordable housing, day-care centers, and more. To address long-term problems of transition, the parish instituted a panoply of programs ranging from marriage counseling to parenting classes, from violence prevention to youth empowerment, from legal aid to educational guidance, from community organizing to economic development. And to integrate immigrants more fully into the life of the church, St. Pius V broadened the participation of parishioners by enhancing their understanding of the Bible, liturgy, sacraments, and popular religiosity and facilitating their involvement in diverse ecclesial ministries.

No Hispanic ministry is complete if it ignores Hispanics' festive spirit. Celebrations are endemic to their culture, flowing out of the people and into the church, enriching it in the process. In many ways, life moves from one fiesta to another; thus, incorporating celebration into Hispanic community and ministry is essential for fashioning a church where Mexicans feel at home. Building community with them is a joyful experience.

Finally, Hispanic ministry must be guided by principles of social justice. Hispanics are attracted to Jesus Christ because he, like they, is an innocent victim of injustice. He is also their savior, triumphing over sin and despair, discrimination and death. They expect their church to succor the poor, feed the hungry, welcome the immigrant, and defend the defenseless as he did. They are most proud of the Catholic Church when it works to transform the world into God's reign of justice and peace. The success of St. Pius V has been its broad-based, structural approach to its ministry, while including its parishioners in developing responses to their problems and incorporating Hispanic values, traditions, and gifts into parish life. The following principles guide its pastoral ministry:

1. Recognize the strength and wisdom of immigrants and members of an ethnic minority in dealing with the challenges facing them.
2. Provide, through all parish programs, instruction in the faith that is doctrinally substantive, spiritually motivating, relevant to the contemporary world, and practically useful.
3. Respect and preserve people's cultural traditions and values, including the Spanish language and the celebration of all aspects of parish and family life, from liturgies to meetings, always with special attention to the sharing of food.
4. Create parish structures to foster multiple human relationships as the foundation for family and community, faith and love, justice and service.
5. Further lay ecclesial ministry by employing lay staff and preparing lay leaders for a wide variety of ministries.
6. Challenge and empower people to act on their faith in their church and in their social and civic worlds by enhancing their self-esteem and strengthening their human relations skills.
7. Instill the vision of sharing in community at all levels of life—family, neighborhood, church, and world.

God's Spirit led me to Hispanic ministry. I grew up in a Chicago suburb and attended Catholic schools. After my ordination as a Dominican priest in 1964, I was assigned to Bolivia, which was entering a period of military dictatorships. The Catholic Church was also changing dramatically. The Second Vatican Council had just concluded, and in 1968, Latin American bishops gathered in Medellín, Colombia, to write documents that guided the Latin American Church in a new direction of lay involvement, small Christian communities, preferential option for the poor, and radical transformation of unjust social and economic structures. The subsequent involvement of the church in political and economic affairs sparked brutal government repression of progressive church leaders, reaping intimidation, persecution, and death for thousands of church ministers throughout the continent. In the midst of this turmoil, Bolivians, kind and gentle, introduced me to a new way of looking at the world, faith, and religion. After returning to the United States in 1970 and completing a doctorate in political science with a concentration in Latin American politics, I researched the political conflicts between Chicago clergy, inspired by Vatican II, and their recently installed archbishop, John Cody, who was committed to preserving authoritarian structures in the church. I then helped establish and worked in a Catholic center for peace and justice for twelve years. The desire to return to Hispanic ministry, however, kept pulling at my heart, and in 1986, I was appointed pastor of St. Pius V.

I hesitated to write this book because I thought it inappropriate, if not risky, for a non-Hispanic to comment on Hispanic ministry. Over the years, however, I have often been asked to share my experiences—both the difficulties and the opportunities of Hispanic ministry. The increasing number of non-Hispanic priests and pastoral ministers being called to serve this burgeoning community of faith, and the dearth of written material available about concrete, practical efforts in Hispanic ministry, eventually led me to put pen to paper. I hope that the personal joy, enrichment, and fulfillment I have received as a pastoral minister in a Mexican community will encourage others to join this deeply rewarding ministry. I can attest, without reservation, that there is no better life for a priest. Mexicans love and respect their church and their priests and pastoral ministers, showering them with support and affection.

I would not have begun this book without encouragement from a gentle and wise colleague, Sister Mary Jo Maher, IHM. I would not have been able to finish this book without the understanding, patience, and editorial advice of Mary Hawkins and the support and prodding of my Dominican brother, Thomas F. O'Meara, OP, who provided invaluable editorial and theological guidance. I thank them as well as my family and friends who suffered my lack of attention as I focused on this book. But most of all, I thank Hispanic immigrants, especially Mexicans, who through their personal struggles, unshakable faith, heartfelt compassion, commitment to family, love of community, and festive spirit have sustained and nourished my faith and life.

Notes

1. Ada María Isasi-Díaz notes, "'Latina/o' does not have a more politicized or radical connotation than 'Hispanic' among the majority of our communities. In my experience it is most often those outside our communities who insist on giving Latina/o such a connotation." Ada María Isasi-Díaz, "Pluralism," in Allan Figueroa Deck, Yolanda Tarango, Timothy M. Matovina, eds., *Perspectives: Hispanic Ministry* (Kansas City, MO: Sheed & Ward, 1995), 22–23.

1.

A Mexican Church in the United States

This book has a single topic: pastoral ministry in a predominantly Mexican Catholic parish, a community at prayer and in service, a community of faith that celebrates life even as it struggles for a better life for its people. After a brief overview of weekly parish activities, this chapter reviews the journey of Mexican immigrants as they wend their way to Chicago, arrive in the Pilsen neighborhood, and emerge as an ethnic parish, St. Pius V.

A Profile of a Christian Community

Like most Catholic parishes, St. Pius V spans a specific geographic territory, fourteen blocks long, eight blocks wide, within which eight Catholic "ethnic parishes" are located. Many of its parishioners, however, live beyond these borders. More than 4,000 families, mostly Mexican immigrants, are registered members, while hundreds more come regularly for both religious and social services. Approximately 3,000 people attend Mass each Sunday, and hundreds are involved in some form of parish ministry.

St. Pius V is a religious community of families, husbands and wives, single mothers and young adults, elderly and large numbers of children. It encompasses many different kinds of people: recently arrived immigrants and longtime residents, working-class laborers and some from the middle class, people who are mentally ill, social reformers, people striving to get ahead, and others locked in poverty, chemical addictions, and gangs. Each brings diverse talents, unique challenges but singular hopes and aspirations. While Sunday Mass is central to Catholic life, forming and living church in today's Catholicism involves much more.

1

Life and grace flow out of Sunday Mass not only into sacramental celebrations of baptism, confirmation, and matrimony but also into typically Mexican celebrations, such as Our Lady of Guadalupe, the Christmas *posadas*, the Day of the Dead, the *via crucis* of Good Friday, as well as into many social ministries conducted inside and outside the parish complex of buildings.

Parish creates community among people sharing a common Christian faith. Community requires its members to know and trust one another, share with and help one another—a daunting challenge in a large, densely populated, inner-city neighborhood riddled with violence and populated by undocumented immigrants. Yet the local church gathers parishioners to worship together, serve one another, celebrate their lives together; there, people are not only formed in the faith and trained in various ministries but socialize at parish dances and street festivals; there, people find new acquaintances and friends, frequently their future spouses, and children develop friendships while participating in religious education. Gathering people to share and celebrate their faith and life in community is the most important mission of a parish.

Creating community in an inner city, Mexican parish demands a sensitive and generous response to its people's many and diverse needs. A review of a week at St. Pius V illustrates the multifaceted approach required to meet those needs. On *Monday* morning, after the daily 8:00 a.m. Mass in Spanish, a number of people in search of clothing come to the parish office to obtain vouchers for the parish secondhand store. Others arrive asking for letters of recommendation to obtain jobs or identification cards *(la matrícula)* from the Mexican consulate. Encouraged by the Sunday sermon, women abused by their husbands often seek advice from the priests or pastoral counselors. At noon, the soup kitchen in the church basement serves hot meals to more than a hundred people, mostly homeless men. In the evening, Christian Base Communities gather in homes to reflect on biblical themes, share their faith, and plan activities. At night, a shelter for the homeless opens to care for forty-five men, many of whom are recent immigrants traveling across country looking for work.

On *Tuesday* afternoon, the pastoral and administrative staff of twenty-five gathers for its weekly luncheon meeting to pray and support one another, as well as to discuss ministerial issues and plan activities. In the late afternoon, social service volunteers open the emergency food pantry for families in crisis. That night and other nights of the week, parish committees, such as social service workers, the Guadalupe group, and the liturgy committee, meet to develop and implement their programs.

On *Wednesday* morning, a mother brings her teenage son for counseling because he is dropping out of school and entering a gang. That afternoon teenage catechists prepare a lesson they will offer smaller children in the Christian Base Communities the following Monday. Teachers in the parish elementary school, serving 265 children, participate in a faculty meeting to fine-tune their curriculum and respond to the special needs of their immigrant students. At Casa Juan Diego, the parish youth center, the staff receives one hundred children and teenagers in a daily after-school program aimed at gang prevention that includes tutoring and computer learning, educational games, arts and crafts, music, sports, martial arts, and photography. In the evening, adults attend a variety of classes, such as English as a second language, Spanish literacy, and parenting skills, and block clubs meet to improve conditions in their vicinity. A lay pastoral associate conducts classes in personal growth and community leadership, while the pastoral family counselor leads a group counseling session for struggling married couples. In the church basement, the charismatic renewal group conducts classes on evangelization for people interested in deepening their prayer life.

On *Thursday* morning, parenting classes are offered for mothers and fathers working at night. In the afternoon, a group of women with chemically dependent spouses meets with a pastoral counselor to find support and develop strategies for dealing with their husbands' behavior. That night, the English and Spanish choirs practice in church, and two other important groups meet: first, the elected members of the parish council and, second, parish representatives to the board of directors of the local community organization and economic development corporation.

The approaching weekend marks the climax of the week. *Friday* finds the church celebrating both a funeral and a few rehearsals for Saturday weddings. After school, fifty teens and smaller children meet with their mothers, victims of domestic violence, to strengthen their family bond. At night in the parish offices, twenty-five catechists gather to prepare their classes for Saturday and Sunday mornings, and fifteen men who have abused their wives meet to learn how to deal with their anger and violence.

On *Saturday* morning, baptismal catechists conduct classes for parents and godparents preparing to baptize their children. In the parish youth center, a program involving sports, community service, Bible study, and sessions on personal development prepares teenagers for the sacrament of confirmation and Christian leadership. After the daily English Mass at noon, baptism of twenty babies is followed by two weddings or Masses for *quinceañeras* (fifteen-year-old girls). In the church basement, either the Guadalupe or St. Jude Thaddeus group is preparing for a Sunday breakfast of *menudo*, while other parishioners are decorating the church hall for a dance to raise money to support parish ministries. At night in the church, after an hour of confessions, the charismatic renewal group conducts its weekly circle of prayer. At the parish youth center, a family of parishioners has rented the hall to celebrate a baptismal party for its newest member.

On *Sunday*, the first of six Masses (two in English and four in Spanish) begins at 7:45 a.m. From 8:00 a.m. to 3:00 p.m., parishioners enjoy a brunch of hot *menudo* served in half of the church basement. After the Masses, children gather in the other half of the basement for the Liturgy of the Word following their catechism classes in the school building. Across the street, adults meet to study the Catholic faith in preparation for the sacraments they did not receive as children. In the afternoon, children with disabilities gather for classes in religious education in a room specially designed for their use, while young adults assemble to support one another and plan their group's activities.

While considering all this activity, this book highlights important Mexican values and traditions. It details different aspects of creating and celebrating community, such as forming small Christian communities, incorporating people and their traditions into sacramental celebrations, serving basic human needs for food, clothing, and education, and organizing people to participate in

4

rebuilding their neighborhood community. Before examining this community of faith, let us review how Mexicans arrived in Chicago's Pilsen neighborhood and in St. Pius V parish.

Mexicans in What Became the United States

The history of Mexicans in the United States is a story of determination and hope in the face of physical hardship, racial prejudice, and social injustice. Unlike European immigrants, Mexicans have only to cross the Rio Grande to reach the land of their dreams. Some even trace their roots to families living within the current confines of the United States before 1848, when the territory belonged to Mexico. Mexican immigration from south of the current border has been continual, with sudden rushes during periods of crisis. Like most European immigrants, Mexicans left poverty and/or persecution to seek political freedom and economic opportunity. Whereas Europeans saw their dreams realized relatively rapidly, Mexicans, as a whole, not only arrived poor but continued in poverty for generations. Many European immigrants were treated as second-class citizens, but unlike Mexicans, they assimilated relatively quickly in language and appearance and so avoided persistent discrimination.[1]

Strangers in Their Own Land

Under the Treaty of Guadalupe Hidalgo, which ended the Mexican American War in 1848, local Mexican residents became United States citizens and were guaranteed specific civil rights and land titles.[2] The ink on the treaty was hardly dry, however, when the United States began to disregard many of its provisions. Former Mexican citizens and their Mexican American descendants became second-class citizens in what was once their own land; many fell victims to extreme violence. Moises Sandoval, a historian of Mexican immigration, notes: "According to some estimates, between 1865 and 1920, more Mexicans were lynched in the Southwest than blacks in the old South."[3] Mexican Americans were often not allowed to vote, forced off their lands, and dealt injustice by the judicial system.

Over the years, most Catholic Church leaders and Euro-American Catholics played an ambivalent role for Mexican immigrants, at times defending them against exploitation and at other times resisting their inclusion into the Catholic fold as equal brothers and sisters. The history of this ambivalent response sets the stage for understanding the importance of parishes like St. Pius V in welcoming Mexican immigrants into their communities. Frequently, bishops remained silent while Mexicans were subjected to gross injustice. Some bishops and priests joined others in blaming them for their poverty, embracing stereotypes of the immigrant as "childlike, ignorant, improvident, long-suffering, indifferent to the education of their children, and having a claim only on the Church's charity."[4] Some priests decried the Mexicans' failure to obey church rules and mores, such as regular attendance at Sunday Mass and financial support of the church, and labeled their religious beliefs and practices superstitious, pagan, and even demonic.[5]

Undoubtedly, the lack of Mexican and Spanish clergy contributed to the hierarchy's lack of appreciation for Mexican Catholics. After the Mexican American War, some Mexican priests remained in the United States to serve Mexican Catholics, and some Mexican bishops sent priests as missionaries to minister here. In time, however, the influx of Mexican clergy diminished to practically nothing, largely because of the discrimination they suffered at the hands of their Euro-American brother priests and bishops.[6] By the end of the nineteenth century, Mexicans and Mexican Americans lacked native clergy and, consequently, defenders of their culture, religious traditions, and civil rights. In 1900, all but one of the eight dioceses in the West and Southwest were headed by bishops born in Europe, most of whom were intent on building a European-style church.[7] Although in the late 1920s a minuscule effort to promote priestly vocations among Hispanics developed in New Mexico, discrimination against Mexicans remained the general rule in seminaries well into the 1960s.[8]

While not welcoming Mexicans, the Catholic Church did not totally neglect them. Some priests traveled to remote *ranchos* to administer the sacraments and provide religious instruction. In some instances, the church offered schooling and health care and helped people assimilate into the broader American society. The growing number of Mexicans caused some bishops to establish parishes specifically for them. Unfortunately, this policy mirrored and sanctioned the segregation of Mexicans in civil society and, ironically, heightened Mexican identity. Some clergy encouraged Mexicans to form their own organizations, namely *cofradías*, *sociedades*, and *apostolados*, to help them minister to one another both spiritually and materially and preserve their culture.[9]

By the 1920s, some bishops and clergy made notable efforts to respond more positively to Mexicans. Bishop John L. Cantwell of Los Angeles countered the racist ideology and practice dominating the American hierarchy by spending more than half the archdiocesan budget for social welfare benefiting Mexican Catholics. In the 1940s, a small group of bishops formed the Bishops' Committee for the Spanish-Speaking, which launched its first program in four urban dioceses with large Mexican populations to educate Hispanics in their faith, improve their educational and economic opportunities, and eliminate discrimination and prejudice.[10]

Before examining Mexicans' entry into Chicago and the Pilsen neighborhood, it will be helpful to review the arrival of their predecessors, European immigrants, who developed the area where Mexican immigrants later entered.

First Immigrants to the Pilsen Neighborhood

In the mid-nineteenth century, two adjacent neighborhoods, the Near West Side and Pilsen, together encompassing approximately three square miles, were founded in an area of swamps and truck farms. The population growth in the area exploded after 1848, the year the Illinois-Michigan Canal opened, forming the southern boundary of Pilsen. Soon both banks of the canal were lined with lumber and brickyards, a limestone quarry, and industry of all kinds.[11] With the development of manufacturing, stockyards, and railroads, steady jobs were created, attracting newly arrived European workers. Around the turn of the century, the new Chicago Sanitary and Ship Canal opened alongside the Illinois-Michigan Canal, enabling barges to travel between Chicago and the Mississippi River. The increased demand for labor in the area lured Lithuanians, Croatians, Germans, Swedes, and Italians, who joined the earlier Irish, Polish, Bohemian, and Slovak immigrants.

In Pilsen, the immigrants lived in small enclaves. They formed ethnic leagues to defend their interests and serve their needs, founding social institutions, such as credit unions, publishing houses, insurance companies, and community centers where ethnics celebrated and preserved their culture, and organized parties and rituals to mark their national holidays.[12] By 1910, over twenty-six different ethnic groups lived in Pilsen, which reached its peak population of 85,680 residents in 1920.[13] The last group to arrive were Mexicans, coming first to the Near West Side in the 1920s and later moving southwest into Pilsen in the late 1950s and early 1960s.

Catholics residing within the geographical boundaries of a local parish traditionally "belong" to that parish and participate in it. Parishes thus become social anchors in their neighborhoods, community centers as much as places of worship, where people meet not only to pray but also to seek help, recreate, and celebrate life. As Catholic ethnics flooded into Chicago neighborhoods, they demanded their own churches and schools staffed by priests and religious sisters from their respective homelands. To placate their demands and assure their fidelity to the Catholic Church, bishops allowed them to establish national, or ethnic, parishes with no territorial limits within the specific geographical boundaries of territorial parishes.[14] These parishes welcomed and integrated immigrants into American society, preserving and fostering their language and culture, music and humor, understanding and solidarity. While they served as links to the homeland, they also conferred a sense of identity and belonging to immigrants in a strange land and fostered a sense of dignity in people often unwelcomed in their new country. They built magnificent churches, symbols of national pride, constructed with hard-earned donations from working-class people. All operated schools where ethnic language and culture were taught to the next generation, and some even founded their own financial institutions and orphanages. Ethnic parishes were first created by German immigrants in 1846. They flourished in Chicago during Archbishop James Quigley's tenure (1903–1915), which saw the creation of 113 ethnic parishes. With obvious pride, people came to identify themselves as belonging to a particular parish, and many in Chicago still describe their place of residence not by their neighborhood or street but by their local parish. Thus, parishes humanized the city for immigrants, transforming it from an alien to a familiar place.[15]

In 1874, exactly two hundred years after Father Jacques Marquette, the famous Jesuit missionary and explorer, wintered in the heart of the Pilsen neighborhood, Irish immigrants from Holy Family parish in the Near West Side founded St. Pius V and Sacred Heart as the first two parishes in Pilsen and the twelfth and thirteenth in Chicago.[16] Shortly thereafter, Bohemian immigrants inaugurated St. Procopius parish just five blocks from St. Pius V. Four years later, St. Procopius opened a mission, St. Vitus parish, closer to St. Pius V, and in 1906 established yet another, St. Joseph, to serve Slovak Catholics. St. Adalbert parish was founded in 1874 to serve Polish families, who worked for years raising funds to build a majestic church seating 1,500 people. As the Polish community expanded, St. Ann church was founded in 1906, just five blocks to the west. Two years later, forty German families inaugurated St. Paul parish when they purchased a stable and turned it into a church just four blocks south of St. Ann. St. Stephen parish, constructed in 1898 six blocks from St. Pius V and three blocks east of St. Paul, was the first Slovenian Catholic Church in the Midwest. In 1903, Italians established St. Michael parish near St. Paul. In 1904, on Pilsen's east side, Lithuanians founded Providence of God parish, where services were celebrated only in Lithuanian until the 1940s. Because the Lithuanian population grew so rapidly, two years later, a second parish, Our Lady of Vilna, was founded in southwestern Pilsen. Croatians founded Holy Trinity parish in 1915 in the heart of Pilsen, just three blocks from St. Pius V.[17] Thus, by the 1930s, the Pilsen neighborhood, an area of just two square miles, was home to fourteen ethnic Catholic and two territorial parishes.

When Mexicans arrived in the 1960s, they changed the face of the neighborhood, gradually introducing for the first time a solid ethnic homogeneity. Most parishes continued to exist as Mexicans replaced their European predecessors, creating the premier Mexican area of Chicago, the principal port of entry for neighbors from south of the border.

Mexicans in Chicago

In the two decades following its revolution in 1910, Mexico experienced an economic, political, and religious upheaval, which pushed many Mexicans north into the United States. The Mexican government's revolutionary violence and economic reorganization displaced hundreds of thousands of farmers, virtually destroying the hacienda system. Those immigrating to the Midwest consisted mainly of displaced small farmers, skilled artisans, and merchants, predominantly from Mexico's central states. They leapfrogged over states in northern Mexico and followed a northeasterly path through Texas and Kansas to Chicago. Economic growth, fueled by World War I, attracted thousands desperately looking for employment.[18] The military draft heightened the demand for replacement labor, as did the exodus of American farm workers from rural to urban areas.[19] Mexicans were readily available to fill the labor gap, and an expanded railroad network facilitated their arrival to the Midwest. Low-cost Mexican labor helped employers not only secure a plentiful workforce in a tight labor market but control wages and contain labor activism. Between 1910 and 1925, the United States admitted 660,000 Mexicans, and an estimated 300,000 more entered illegally, since entry was virtually uncontrolled until the United States Congress created the border patrol and began restricting immigration in 1924.[20]

Arriving in Chicago, Mexicans encountered the same problems experienced by previous immigrant groups. At first, they were clustered in labor camps or colonies, rat-infested areas

10

plagued by pollution, overcrowding, and disease. Later, they lived primarily in three neighborhoods out of which they ventured with caution. Unskilled Mexicans recruited from Texas and Mexico to work on the railroads moved into the Near West Side, while those contracted by the steel mills made South Chicago their home. Others soon began working in the slaughterhouses in Back of the Yards, an area graphically described in Upton Sinclair's novel *The Jungle*. Gradually Mexican immigrants found employment in factories and service industries in other areas of the city. They were relegated to the lowest-paying jobs, and their employment was tenuous because employers fired them with impunity. They were excluded from certain restaurants, barbershops, movie houses, and businesses, and their Spanish-speaking children were discriminated against in neighborhood schools. Unquestionably, the difficulties of language rendered their integration into local communities and parishes a serious challenge.[21]

Like other immigrant groups, Mexicans formed mutual aid societies *(mutualistas)* which raised money for church buildings, formed leaders, extended economic assistance, located jobs, preserved culture, and strengthened ethnic ties.[22] Early Mexican immigrants, however, unlike the Polish and Irish, never developed a collective political response to deal with their common problems in Chicago. The first citywide organizations, like the Mexican Civic Committee, founded in 1943, and the Mexican American Council, founded in 1951, addressed some issues common to Mexicans but failed to develop the political clout necessary to defend the interests of Mexicans increasingly dispersed throughout the city.[23]

The Mexican population in Chicago undulated like waves responding to the winds of economic change. In 1910, the census listed 1,672 foreign-born Mexicans in Chicago. In the prosperous aftermath of World War I, Mexicans were brought in by the trainloads so that by the end of the 1920s, the city had the fourth largest population of Mexicans in the country, approximately 25,000.[24] In the wake of the Depression, however, federal, state, and local governments cooperated with industry in sending back nearly half the Mexicans in the United States.[25] In Chicago, the "repatriation" of Mexican workers assumed a coercive and nativist dimension as federal immigration officials and state and local welfare agencies organized "relief programs," a euphemism for campaigns that herded whole families on special trains bound for the border.[26]

The economic expansion generated by World War II once again pulled Mexicans into the Midwest. In 1942, the State Department permitted the entry of Mexican contracted workers *(braceros)* initially as seasonal agricultural workers and later as industrial labor. By 1950, the number of Mexicans in Chicago had risen to 24,000, and by the mid 1950s, the tide turned against them once again.

In 1954, Congress reacted to an economic slowdown by approving Operation Wetback, a program that deported thousands of undocumented Mexican immigrants from Chicago. The population decline, however, was less severe than during the Depression because many Mexicans had become either legal residents or citizens, because the deportation program lacked unity and organization, and because the *bracero* program continued to actively recruit contract labor from Mexico.[27]

By 1964, when Congress discontinued the *bracero* program, 5.2 million Mexican workers had entered the United States, as well as hundreds of thousands of illegal immigrants. By 1960, the Mexican population in Chicago had risen to 55,597 and by 1980 to 368,981.[28] While Mexicans continued in their traditional areas of employment, namely, steel mills, railroads, farming, and factories, they also expanded into new areas, such as the service industries of restaurants, hotels, and landscaping.[29]

Since the 1960s, Hispanics have been the fastest-growing ethnic group in the United States. Between 1990 and 2000, the Hispanic population increased by 58 percent nationally (from 22.4 million to 35.5 million), by 69 percent in Illinois, and by 39 percent in Chicago. In Chicago, the Hispanic population grew from 247,343 in 1970 to 753,644 in 2000, constituting slightly more than one of four persons in the city.[30] By 2005, one of every three Chicagoans is expected to be Hispanic. Hispanics are also the youngest ethnic group in the city, with an average age of 25.9 years, compared with 35.3 years for the overall population. Since 1960, they account for 71 percent of national Catholic growth, currently constituting more than one third of the Catholics in the United States. At this rate, by the year 2050, 86 percent of American Catholics will be Hispanic. Between 1990 and 2000, the number of Hispanics living in the Archdiocese of Chicago jumped 60 percent, from 732,764 to 1.2 million, making Hispanics more than half the Catholics in the archdiocese. Mexicans are by far the largest and fastest-growing segment of this Hispanic population. The 2000 census recorded 530,565 Mexicans in Chicago, accounting for 70.4 percent of Hispanics in the city and making Chicago the city with the second-highest number of Mexicans after Los Angeles.[31] By the 1980s, Mexicans had dispersed throughout most areas of metropolitan Chicago, and many new Mexican immigrants were arriving directly to the suburbs without passing through traditional ports of entry in the central city, making several suburbs home to large numbers of Mexican families.[32]

In 1994, amid virulent anti-immigrant sentiment in the United States, Congress approved Operation Gatekeeper, an effort to seal the Tijuana-San Diego border area against illegal immigration. The government spent multi-millions of dollars to build a triple wall of steel and add massive numbers of Border Patrol officers at the most frequently crossed border in the world. As expected, the crossing of undocumented people in this zone diminished considerably, but to the dismay of government officials, nationally the entrance of undocumented people from Mexico increased. Because the North American Free Trade Agreement between the United States and Mexico is likely to continue to reap economic hardship on the majority poor in Mexico, it is estimated that Mexicans will continue immigrating, no matter what barriers are created. In 1998, the Northeastern Illinois Planning Commission estimated that by 2020 one million more Mexicans would enter the six-county area of Northeastern Illinois.[33]

The Catholic Church and Mexican Immigrants

During and after World War I, American bishops counteracted anti-Catholicism by trying to convince Americans that Catholics were loyal to their new country. Thus, they encouraged assimilation and discouraged the preservation of ethnic cultures in national parishes precisely when Mexican immigrants were arriving.[34] In Chicago, the Catholic Church failed to welcome them as warmly as it had previous European immigrants. Church leaders remained largely silent about racial attacks against Mexicans, as well as about their massive deportation during the Depression, which some even supported.[35]

Although George Mundelein, Archbishop of Chicago from 1915 to 1939, pursued his own policy of Americanization, he feared that dismantling ethnic parishes might push some ethnic groups toward schism. Thus, he refrained from closing them and simply made it difficult to erect new ones.[36] Nonetheless, because the Mexican population was increasing so rapidly and because Euro-American parishes generally refused to welcome the new immigrants, he permitted the formation of two Mexican-national parishes and contracted Claretian priests from Spain to staff them. In 1925, the Spanish priests began their ministry in a small chapel in South Chicago, and three years later built Our Lady of Guadalupe church, almost exclusively with Mexican money and labor. In the Near West Side, St. Francis of Assisi Church, originally a small German and then Italian parish, became the second Mexican parish. During the late 1930s, the Claretians began celebrating Sunday Masses in storefront chapels in the Back of the Yards neighborhood, where eventually, in 1947, they constructed the mission church Immaculate Heart of Mary.[37] Apart from the Spanish Claretians working in these three churches, no Hispanic priest occupied a pastorate or a position of authority in the Archdiocese of Chicago until the late 1980s.

Two Mexican-national parishes and one mission church hardly met the religious needs of the burgeoning Mexican population, largely unwelcome in other archdiocesan parishes. It was not uncommon that Mexican parents visiting the nearest Catholic church to arrange a baptism were directed by the English-speaking pastor to "the Mexican parish," possibly miles away in a strange neighborhood. Ironically, as authorities complained that Mexicans were not integrated into mainstream Catholicism, they did little to assist their assimilation.

Mexicans Arriving in Pilsen and at St. Pius V Parish

In the late 1950s, Mexicans and Mexican Americans began moving into Pilsen as they were displaced from the adjacent Near West Side neighborhood, pushed out first by the construction of the Eisenhower Expressway, and then in 1961 by the development of the University of Illinois in Chicago. Mexicans from South Chicago and Back of the Yards, as well as other areas in and around Chicago, also moved to Pilsen because there they found low-cost housing, a monolingual environment, stores with Mexican products, a broad range of services for new immigrants, and community organizations focused on Mexican issues. So in the 1960s, Pilsen became the new port of entry for Mexicans in Chicago and the city's largest Hispanic settlement. The 1970 census reported that 106,000 Mexicans lived in Chicago, nearly 25 percent of them in Pilsen.[38] By 1990, Hispanics constituted 89 percent of 49,000 Pilsen residents, 88.4 percent identifying themselves as Mexican. The constant influx of new immigrants from Mexico not only converted the neighborhood from the most diverse ethnic area in Chicago to a culturally homogenous community but also ensured that the Mexican flavor of the area was constantly replenished. As Mexicans filled Pilsen, they spilled over into the adjacent neighborhood of Little Village, where the Hispanic population increased from 6,972 in 1960 to 67,000 in 1990. Together, Pilsen and Little Village became one of the largest solidly Hispanic, and mostly Mexican, communities in the United States.

Hispanics again encountered resistance as they moved into Pilsen. In her study of the area, Louise Año Nuevo Kerr cites a source describing their experience:

> Schools were making only conciliatory gestures to the large non-English-speaking school-age population. Churches were going through an agonizing transition as the predominantly Catholic Mexican population sought to replace Polish and Slovak Masses with Spanish Masses. The politics of the Daley machine proceeded on course, neither affecting nor affected by Chicano needs and concerns. Streets were unswept and garbage remained uncollected as the Italian alderman responded to the bidding of a far off constituency; police harassed residents, immigration officials made periodic raids searching for illegal migrants, and urban renewal threatened the integrity of the community.[39]

In response, Hispanic adults developed organizations and a loose coalition of volunteer groups to serve their needs, while Mexican and Puerto Rican youth formed clubs and gangs to defend themselves against Euro-American gangs. Catholic parishes responded slowly to the new population. Ethnic parishes, despite declining membership resulting from the departure of their parishioners to outlying neighborhoods and suburbs, were reluctant to welcome Hispanics. St. Stephen, a Slovenian parish, refused to schedule a Sunday Mass in Spanish as late as 1997, when 97 percent of the students in its parish school were Hispanic. Parishes that did not open their doors to Hispanics eventually closed for lack of sufficient parishioners and funds.[40]

St. Pius V parish had witnessed two prior waves of immigrants. By 1920, many of the original Irish families had moved out of the area and were replaced predominantly by Polish immigrants. In 1925, Dominican priests accepted responsibility for the parish, where, after the stock market crash of 1929, they founded a shrine honoring St. Jude Thaddeus, which attracted thousands of people for special devotions to the "patron of hopeless cases." For the next 30 years, the parish became a hub of activity as parishioners active in neighborhood politics worked to better their community.[41] When Hispanics began arriving in large numbers, St. Pius V became the first parish in Pilsen to offer Mass in Spanish in 1963. But this change was not easy. For years, on Sundays, Euro-American ushers had stood at the front door to head off Hispanics coming to church, directing them to "their parish," St. Francis of Assisi, about a mile away. At first, the Mass in Spanish was held in the church basement, a common practice deeply offensive to Hispanic Catholics in parishes first opening their doors to them. Although Margarita Menchaca was pleased when she could attend Mass in Spanish at St. Pius V, her husband refused to participate until Mass was moved into the church proper.

Prior to Vatican II, all pastoral and liturgical ministry was performed by priests. In the 1950s and 1960s, more than ten priests staffed St. Pius V, some working specifically for the Shrine of St. Jude. They officiated at many daily Masses, distributed communion, heard confessions, and spent hours making communion calls (home visits) to sick and elderly Euro-American parishioners. They conducted the religious education program for children, directed youth activities, and attended to the needs of the poor. After Vatican II, the priests began to involve laity in liturgical and pastoral ministries, and a Spanish-speaking social worker was hired to develop social services, including a food pantry. Pastors gradually trained liturgical ministers for communion, lectoring, and commentating and prepared others for youth ministry and religious education for children and adults.

As the 1960s progressed, St. Pius V developed an increasing openness to Hispanics.[42] More Masses in Spanish were added, and the parish sponsored English classes for Mexican children, developed activities for youth, initiated social programs aimed at helping newly arrived immigrants to find housing, jobs, and community, and formed numerous parish groups, including a Mexican musical group, *Cursillos de Cristiandad,* and a Guadalupe Society.[43] In 1972, a Mexican American associate pastor attracted many Mexicans by installing a beautiful shrine to Our Lady of Guadalupe in the church. In the early 1970s, the parish actively participated in the successful effort sponsored by the local community organization, now largely Hispanic, to build the first high school in the neighborhood and endow it with a Mexican name, architecture, and direction. In 1974, St. Pius V received its first bilingual pastor, Thomas Moore, who was convinced that Mexican immigrants were not only equal members of the parish but undoubtedly its future. He organized the painting of an enormous mural honoring St. Jude and Our Lady of Guadalupe on a parish building. The next pastor, Gerard Cleator, a fine preacher, also focused the parish on the newly arrived Hispanics, promoting with them the Catholic Charismatic Renewal. The parish's development of new ways of responding culturally and pastorally to its predominantly Mexican people won their long-lasting affection. For years afterward, Mexican parishioners who moved from the area still considered St. Pius V their parish, returning often for services.

The following chapters examine the ways in which St. Pius V welcomed Mexican immigrants and transformed itself into a vibrant Mexican parish. It also looks at the wealth of culture and enthusiasm for the faith that Mexicans bring to the Catholic Church.

Notes

1. Timothy M. Matovina, "No Melting Pot in Sight," in Allan Figueroa Deck, Yolanda Tarango, Timothy M. Matovina, eds., *Perspectives: Hispanic Ministry* (Kansas City, MO: Sheed & Ward, 1995), 35–39.

2. Moises Sandoval, *On the Move: A History of the Hispanic Church in the United States* (New York: Orbis Press, 1990), 25. The author provides a concise history of this period.

3. Wayne Moquin with Charles van Doren, eds., *A Documentary History of Mexican Americans* (New York: Praeger Publishers, 1971), 181, cited in *Ibid.*, 26. Sandoval notes, "From 1908 to 1925, as many as 5,000 civilians—the exact number will never be known—died in lawlessness so widespread that a federal official warned the governor of Texas that action would have to be taken to protect the victims." *On the Move*, 50.

4. Gilberto M. Hinojosa, "Mexican-American Faith Communities in Texas and the Southwest," in Jay P. Dolan and Gilberto M. Hinojosa, *Mexican Americans and the Catholic Church, 1900–1965* (Notre Dame, IN: University of Notre Dame, 1994), 45.

5. When Father Dominic Manucy was appointed head of the Vicariate Apostolic of Brownsville, Texas, in 1874, he wrote to his superior, "I consider this appointment...the worst sentence that could have been given me for any crime. The Catholic population is composed almost exclusively of Mexican greasers—cattle drivers and thieves." For more on discrimination suffered by Mexicans, see David A. Badillo, "The Catholic Church and the Making of Mexican-American Parish Communities in the Midwest," in Dolan and Hinojosa, *op. cit.*, 249.

6. The disciplining and removal of some Mexican priests who protested unfair treatment taught other clergy how to survive: keep quiet and mind your own business. Sandoval states that Jean Baptiste Lamy, the first archbishop of New Mexico, "killed the tradition of priesthood that had begun to develop during the Mexican period by failing to develop an effective seminary and relying so heavily on European clergy and religious. It would be five generations and five French bishops later before an Anglo American bishop would try to revive it." Sandoval, *op. cit.*, 32.

7. Many bishops considered Mexicans unworthy of priesthood, an attitude that constrained the emergence of Mexican American priests for nearly a hundred years (Hinojosa, *op. cit.*, 30). In 1918, the Archbishop of Guadalajara visited Chicago in an effort to support his country's immigrants, but he was unable to supply them with any priests (Badillo, *op. cit.*, 251).

8. Virgil Elizondo has described the discrimination he and other Hispanic seminarians suffered while studying for priesthood in Texas in the mid-twentieth century. Virgil Elizondo, *The Future Is Mestizo: Life Where Cultures Meet* (Boulder, CO: University of Colorado, 2000), 21.

9. Sandoval, *op. cit.*, 43.

10. *Ibid.*, 48.

11. William J. Adelman, *Pilsen and the West Side* (Chicago: Illinois Labor History Society, 1983), 2. See also The Chicago Fact Book Consortium, ed., *Local Community Fact Book 1990* (Chicago: Chicago Fact Book Consortium, 1995), 115.

12. Edward R. Kantowicz, "The Ethnic Tangle," in Edward R. Kantowicz, *Corporation Sole* (Notre Dame, IN: University of Notre Dame, 1983), 65–83.

13. The population of Pilsen dropped precipitously by almost 20,000 in the 1920s and by 8,000 during the Depression. Losses in the next thirty years averaged about 4,500 per decade so that in 1970 the population stood at approximately 49,000. *Local Community Fact Book, loc cit.*

14. Andrew Greeley, "Catholicism in America: A Personal Interpretation," *The Critic* (Summer, 1976), 42. Parishes usually began with lay people seeking a priest from the old country.

15. E. Skerrett, E. Kantowicz, et al., *Catholicism, Chicago Style* (Chicago: Loyola University, 1993), 8. Between 1870 and 1920, thirteen parishes were founded in Pilsen alone, only two of which were territorial. After World War I, bishops stiffened their opposition to the proliferation of ethnic parishes, whose sheer number and severe ethnocentricity made it difficult for bishops to manage them. Ethnic parishes and their corresponding leagues evolved into powerful fiefdoms that fought bishops for their own autonomy. Bishops also worried that the post-war, pro-American spirit would further fuel an already strong anti-Catholic sentiment in the country.

16. With a congregation of nearly twenty thousand persons, Holy Family was then the largest English-speaking and most westerly parish in the Archdiocese, located only ten blocks west of State Street, the heart of the city (Skerrett, *op. cit.*, 39). See also Charles Shanabruch, *Chicago's Catholics: The Evolution of an American Identity* (Notre Dame, IN: University of Notre Dame, 1981), 17.

17. For a history of Chicago parishes, see Harry C. Koenig, *A History of the Parishes of the Archdioceses of Chicago*, I & II (Chicago: Archdiocese of Chicago, 1980).

18. Badillo, *op. cit.*, 237. See also Paul S. Taylor, *Mexican Labor in the United States: Chicago and the Calumet Region* (Berkeley, 1932), 52, cited in *Latinos in Metropolitan Chicago: A Study of Housing and Employment* (Chicago: The Latino Institute, 1983), 11.

19. During World War I, companies hungry for cheap labor in Chicago expanded recruitment into the midwestern hinterland and the border areas of Texas and contracted with the Mexican government to supply workers. Around 1915, large midwestern corporations growing and processing beet sugar hired Mexicans *(betabeleros)* to replace European immigrants as cheap labor. The 1917 Immigration Act set a legislative precedent for establishing quotas for newcomers from certain European countries, but the fear that economic growth in the nation's heartland would wither and die without farmworkers moved Congress to exempt Mexicans from quota restrictions on immigration in the 1921 and 1924 Quota Acts. Louise Año Nuevo Kerr, "Chicano Settlements in Chicago: A Brief History," *Journal of Ethnic Studies* (Winter 1975): 22–32. Kerr provides excellent data and analysis of Mexicans arriving in Chicago. See also Kerr, *The Chicano Experience* (Chicago: University of Illinois at Chicago Circle, diss., 1976). See Rita Arias Jirasek and Carlos

Tortolero, *Mexican Chicago* (Chicago: Arcadia, 2001) for an excellent photographic history of Mexican family, social, and working life in Chicago.

20. Sandoval, *op. cit.*, 49.

21. *Latinos in Metropolitan Chicago*, 14.

22. Eunice Felter, "The Social Adaptations of the Mexican Churches in the Chicago Area" (master's thesis, University of Chicago, 1941). See also Badillo, *op. cit.*, 241, and Felix M. Padilla, *Latino Ethnic Consciousness: The Case of Mexican Americans and Puerto Ricans in Chicago* (Notre Dame, IN: University of Notre Dame Press, 1985), 28. Settlement houses like Jane Addams' Hull House on the Near West Side supported these organizations.

23. Padilla, *op. cit.*, 30–31.

24. The 1850 U.S. census reported 52 Mexicans living in the state of Illinois. In 1930, the U.S. census recorded 20,963 Mexicans living in Chicago while other reports show the Mexican population to be 25,211. Jorge Casuso and Eduardo Camacho, "Hispanics in Chicago: The Mexicans," *Chicago Reporter*, no date, 1.

25. Hinojosa, *op. cit.*, 34. See also Badillo, *op. cit.*, 271.

26. Badillo, *op. cit.*, 268.

27. *Latinos in Metropolitan Chicago*, 15. With the entry of Cuban refugees after 1959, and finally Central Americans in the 1980s, Chicago's Hispanic population became very diverse. The largest group, however, remained Mexican.

28. Casuso and Camacho, *op. cit.*, 1.

29. The INS reported that in the 1950s, 53 percent of all legal immigrants in the United States were from Europe, with only 22 percent coming from Latin America. Conversely, in the 1980s, only 10 percent of legal immigrants came from Europe, whereas 47 percent were from Latin America. Puerto Ricans migrated to Chicago mainly after World War II. Before 1946, there were a reported 86 Puerto Ricans in Chicago, but after that year, which marked the beginning of their entry as contract labor, their numbers swelled dramatically, increasing to nearly 8,000 families by 1950 and to 12,000 families by 1952. In 1960, 32,371 Puerto Ricans resided in Chicago, 7,162 of whom settled in the Near West Side. Ten years later, the number of Puerto Ricans in Chicago more than doubled to 78,963, nearly a third of the city's Hispanic population, and by 1990, they increased to 121,000. While many came as contract laborers, others entered Chicago via New York City, where the job market became saturated in the 1960s. *Latinos in Metropolitan Chicago*, 14–15. Puerto Ricans generally settled apart from Mexicans, developing their own church-based organizations. In 2000,

Puerto Ricans were the second largest Hispanic group in Chicago, the second largest Puerto Rican population after New York City.

30. *LatStat: Latino Statistics and Data* (Chicago: Latino Institute, October, 1997), nos. 8, 4, 7. In the late 1990s, the U.S. Census Bureau projected that by 2010, Hispanics would be the largest minority in the nation (a position reached in 2002), with 42 million people, and that by 2050 the mainland Hispanic population would reach 88 million, or 20 percent of the total population. In the 1990s, the United States was the fifth largest Hispanic country in the world, trailing Mexico, Spain, Argentina, and Columbia.

31. Abdon M. Pallasch, "Changing Mix of Cultures, Neighbors: Mexican Immigrants Displace Puerto Ricans," *Chicago Tribune* (September 6, 1998), Sec. 4, 1–2; At the national level, Mexicans account for 58.5 percent of the Hispanic population. Yanira Hernández Cablya, "Aumenta el Número de Mexicanos: Conforman el 75.5 por Ciento de la Población Hispana en Illinois," *Exito* (May 17, 2001), 8.

32. For example, Cicero, Chicago's closest western suburb, saw its Hispanic residents, mostly Mexicans, jump from 9 percent of the population in 1980 to 77 percent in 2000. In the decade after 1980, the Hispanic population in Elgin, 35 miles west of Chicago, increased to 18 percent, in Aurora to 22 percent, and in Waukegan, bordering Wisconsin, to 23 percent. Dan Mihalopoulos, "Immigrants Bypassing City for Suburbs," *Chicago Tribune* (September 12, 2000), Sec. 2, 1–2, and *Bordering the Mainstream: A Needs Assessment of Latinos in Berwyn and Cicero, Illinois* (South Bend, IN: University of Notre Dame, Institute of Latino Studies, 2002). The U.S. Census Bureau reported in 2003 a nearly even split between the city and suburbs among people moving into the Chicago area from foreign countries from 1995 to 2000. See John McCormick, "City Losing Immigrants to Suburbs," *Chicago Tribune* (August 25, 2003), Sec. 2, 1.

33. Because undocumented immigrants now must cross the border at more dangerous points, fatalities among those attempting the crossing are rising. Immigrants desperately swim across the Rio Grande, jump from bridges or freight trains, run through traffic along highways, and trudge hungry and thirsty through the desert. Between 1998 and 2000, the Mexican Ministry of Foreign Relations counted 1,186 deaths along both sides of the two-thousand-mile Mexican border, while the U.S. Border Patrol counted 861 deaths on the United States side alone. Moises Sandoval, "Borderline Christianity," *U.S. Catholic* (June 2001), 12.

34. *Ibid.*, 255. Fitzpatrick counters their arguments: "Actually, far from hindering adjustment to American life, the immigrant community

and the immigrant parish gave immigrants the stability and strength that enabled them to move gradually and with confidence into the mainstream of American life." Joseph P. Fitzpatrick, "The Poor in a Middle-Class Church," Deck et al., *op. cit.*, 10–11. The codification of Catholic canon law completed in 1918 further complicated the establishing of ethnic parishes by requiring the Vatican's permission to erect them.

35. Badillo, *op. cit.*, 270 and 241.

36. Skerrett, *op. cit.*, 25. Between 1916 and 1929, he approved the foundation of 42 new parishes, only nine of which were national.

37. Badillo, *op. cit.*, 254–56, 278, and Skerrett, *op. cit.*, 26. In 1925, the Claretians also served a mission for 500 Mexicans in the far northern Illinois city of Waukegan.

38. By the 1980s, most Euro-American residents had moved to higher-income neighborhoods and suburbs to find better housing and less crowded schools, but some returned for Sunday Mass.

39. Kerr, *The Chicano Experience*, 196.

40. Sacred Heart was merged with Providence of God in 1959 after a fire destroyed its church. St. Joseph was also merged with Providence of God in 1968. In 1970, the schools of St. Paul and Our Lady of Vilna were combined, and in 1985, Our Lady of Vilna parish was closed. St. Vitus was closed in 1990, and St. Stephen in 1996, although it remained open as an oratory under the care of Jesuit priests who began using the parish and school buildings for their new Cristo Rey Jesuit High School, founded in 1997. In 2004, only seven parishes remained in Pilsen. Although all the parishes had operated parochial schools, all but four had closed by 2002 because of rising costs and decreasing enrollments.

41. Parishioners organized dances for all sorts of occasions, and in warm weather, outdoor carnivals; men promoted boxing events, and parents renovated the church basement to accommodate a roller rink for their children that operated nightly from September through May. In the early 1960s, St. Pius V became the lead parish in the recently founded Saul Alinski–style community organization, Pilsen Neighbors Community Council, which organized neighborhood residents to better the quality of life in their community.

42. Soon after Alex Kasper's installation as pastor in 1968, the Dominicans assigned two Spanish Dominicans and a Mexican American Dominican, Bartolome Joerger, OP, to assist him.

43. Thomas G. Kelliher, *Mexican Catholics and Chicago's Parishes, 1955–1976* (Notre Dame, IN: Cushwa Center for the Study of American Catholicism, Working Paper Series, 1993), 22.

2.

Mexican Families in an American City

This chapter profiles Mexican immigrants at St. Pius V parish. Their housing, education, health, family structure, and immigration status reveal how they live in a large American city today, how God's grace works in them, and the challenges faced by the Catholic Church in ministering among them.

The *Barrio* Is a Village

The Pilsen neighborhood is a small world. Its geographical area is limited, less than two square miles, but it is also small because many residents know every street and corner and live much of their lives within its borders. Many people live in the *barrio* just as they did in Mexico. Spanish is spoken everywhere, the first language of the area. Local stores supply Mexican goods, especially food, including a wide array of chilis, *nopales* (cactus leaves), *achiote*, yuca, and plantains. Four tortilla factories guarantee a ready supply of hot tortillas at any time of day.

In Pilsen, one encounters a charming, lively, even thriving *barrio*, with streets lined with *taquerias* (taco restaurants), *panaderias* (bakeries), street vendors, and brightly painted brick buildings nestled closely together. On nearly every block, colorful murals depicting Mexican heroes, saints, landscapes, and values brighten up an otherwise dreary cement city. Though outsiders may fear entering the community, local residents generally feel safer here than any other place. Saturnina commented that when riding the bus home from work, she is often anxious and tense until she passes under the railroad viaduct, the northern border of Pilsen; then she breathes a sigh of relief because she is home. Although most immigrant residents work outside the neighborhood, many shop, go to school, attend church, and socialize within the community.

Some lack the transportation, courage, or desire to venture outside the area. Some live for years in Pilsen without ever seeing Lake Michigan, just one mile east. Many make trips to malls and visit homes of relatives in other neighborhoods, but they take little advantage of the many museums, parks, entertainment centers, and architectural sites that attract so many tourists to Chicago.

The children of Mexican immigrants, once grown and with families of their own, help their parents break out of the *barrio* to discover the vast expanses and exciting diversity of Chicago. Nevertheless, even though Mexican stores started to spread throughout the Chicago metropolitan area during the 1980s, many former Pilsen residents return to the *barrio* periodically to purchase their favorite chilis or meats and to experience the familiar welcoming atmosphere of the old Mexican neighborhood. The *barrio* will always be their home.

One reason immigrants, and especially first-generation Mexican immigrants, love their neighborhood, poor as it may be, is that they feel respected there. In the wider society, they commonly experience discrimination, a serious cause of concern, frustration, and anger. When Virgil Elizondo asked Mexican immigrants how they experienced institutions in the United States, "responders used, over and over again, such terms as 'patronized,' 'silenced,' 'powerless,' 'alienated,' 'ignored,' 'not wanted,' 'merely tolerated.'"[1] Elizondo found that the only social institutions mentioned consistently in a positive way were the *familia* and the *barrio*.

At the Bottom

People living in Pilsen are poor. More than 70 percent live below the poverty line, and more than 85 percent of the children qualify for free or reduced-price lunches in schools.[2] According to the 1990 census, the median per capita income in Chicago was $12,070, but for Hispanics in Pilsen it was only $5,680 (47 percent of the city's median). When adjusted for inflation, both household and per capita income in Pilsen between 1980 and 1990 actually declined. Many immigrant Hispanic families live on even less because they send part of their income to more needy family members back in Mexico. Their ability to survive on little is extraordinary. Many earn minimum and sub-minimum wages for years. In 2003, families applying for Christmas food baskets at St. Pius V reported weekly incomes averaging $275. Nevertheless, Mexican immigrants see their economic standard of living improve in the United States, albeit for many, not as fast as the cost of living. The more successful ones generally move upward economically and out of Pilsen, while the thought of returning to more severe poverty in Mexico motivates others to continue to struggle to survive in the *barrio*.

Before God, No One's Illegal or Alien

Conservative calculations estimate one-third of Pilsen residents lack legal documentation.[3] Many families are divided, the parents and some children lacking immigration "papers," while other children born in the United States are American citizens. These immigrants resent being labeled "illegal aliens" because they consider themselves neither "illegal" nor "alien"; they prefer the term "undocumented." For them, no one is an alien; borders created by governments and patrolled by military force cannot change the fact that human beings are all brothers and sisters in God's family. They see themselves as ordinary people struggling to survive, and their need convinces them of their right to be in this country, no matter what laws declare them illegal. According to current immigration law, most of them are ineligible for legal residency because they lack either the professional skills or the family relationships with legal residents to qualify.

After arriving in the United States illegally, immigrants live in constant fear of being detected and deported by the Immigration and Naturalization Service (INS), renamed the Bureau of Citizenship and Immigration Services (BCIS) in 2002, which Mexicans pejoratively refer to as the *migra*. At different times over the past twenty-five years, the BCIS has conducted raids or roundups within the immigrant community. In the 1980s, it swept up residents at bus stops, factories, and even in front of St. Pius V church on Sunday. In 1994, five St. Pius V parishioners were caught in a BCIS raid that netted twenty-five workers at a nearby wholesale flower shop.

The undocumented immigrants responded in very different ways. Teresa opted to be "voluntarily deported." She took the bus to Laredo, Texas, where, upon leaving the United States, she obtained the necessary exit stamp on her deportation papers. Within days she re-entered the United States using her sister's legitimate tourist visa and returned to Chicago to rejoin her family and look for a new job. Jorge and Elena decided they could not leave their children alone in Chicago to make such a trip, so they simply disobeyed their order of "voluntary departure" and hid from the BCIS by moving to a new address. Because of limited personnel, the BCIS rarely searches for delinquent undocumented immigrants.[4]

Rosario, the third arrested worker, was a hard-working single mother of three, who, after consulting lawyers at St. Pius V, filed for a suspension of deportation based on several arguments. First, she had lived uninterruptedly in the United States for eleven years. Second, not only had she never applied for welfare, but she had worked steadily at a variety of assembly, packaging, and housecleaning jobs. Third, she had never committed a crime, and fourth, she and her children would suffer "extreme hardship" if deported because she had no family in Mexico. A fifth argument proved decisive. Over the years, Rosario had volunteered in the parish soup kitchen, and other volunteers had not only befriended her but depended on her work. When the judge pronounced his decision to lift the deportation order and grant her permission to work while she applied for permanent residency, she, her son, the lawyer, and I all burst into tears and embraced one another.

The community clearly understands the threat of arrest as well as the trauma of deportation, and people respond compassionately to anyone who has fallen victim to the snares of the BCIS. In 1986, Socorro, a mother of six, was arrested by immigration officers at her work. After being detained several days in downtown Chicago, where, of course, she could not attend to her children, she was deported. Meanwhile, the community prayed for her and assisted the father with childcare. She was deported to Mexico. After crossing the border and having her papers stamped in Mexico, proving that she had indeed left the United States, she immediately crossed the border again and returned to Chicago. At Mass the following Sunday, when the priest asked her to stand to be recognized, the congregation applauded enthusiastically for her courageous commitment and resolve.

When Congress passed the Immigration Reform and Control Act of 1986 (IRCA), undocumented people with a long history in the United States were able to obtain legal residency. Vicente Rodriguez, however, like many, feared that the so-called amnesty offered by IRCA was a trick to surface undocumented immigrants. Although he had worked as a farm worker since the 1960s, his fear of BCIS kept him from applying for legalization and caused him to lose his only opportunity to acquire it.

During the early 1990s, years marked by community protests, numerous legal battles (some involving legal residents deported as undocumented people), and a vibrant American econ-omy, the government moderated its heavy-handed tactics of arresting people. Nevertheless, most undocumented immigrants continued to live in fear as the BCIS rounded up and deported dozens of people in Chicago each week. In the midst of the anti-immigration frenzy sweeping the country in 1996, Congress passed new legislation that reduced public welfare benefits to legal residents and divided families by requiring spouses and children applying for legalization to wait years for approval in Mexico.

Fear of deportation tends to foster a privatism uncommon among Mexicans in Mexico. Those using falsified documents fear someone may discover their status and report them. Most generally keep to themselves, limiting involvement with co-workers and neighbors, wary of others visiting their homes or knowing much about their families. Because Mexicans easily translate their experi-ence of police corruption in Mexico to Chicago, a city notorious for police brutality and corruption, some people believe the police work with the BCIS and, consequently, fear that encounters with police may lead to their deportation. The fact that relatively few police are Hispanic or speak Spanish exacerbates their distrust. Most important, most residents can recount a story of police abuse against them or a family member. When many call for help, police notoriously fail to respond, arrive late, or provide little or no assistance. These fears and insecurities help undermine a traditional Mexican openness to community and willingness to accept the stranger.

"¿Tienes Trabajo?" "Gotta Job?"

Although Mexican immigrants have long come to Chicago to find work, the creation of industrial jobs has not kept pace with their growing numbers. With the flight of manufacturing industries, Pilsen lost 13,000 jobs between 1972 and 1984, forcing residents to look for work outside the neighborhood and often at a great distance. Instead of working in railroad yards, stockyards, and steel mills, most now labor in smaller factories, restaurants, construction, landscaping, and hotels. It is difficult to find a restaurant kitchen in Chicago, whether Italian or Chinese, that does not employ Mexicans as busboys and dishwashers, or a landscaping crew manicuring suburban lawns that is not staffed exclusively by Mexican immigrants. The "day-labor" industry has blossomed with the influx of undocumented Mexicans. In Pilsen, five day-labor offices, called *oficinas,* open at 4:00 a.m. to long lines of workers hoping to be sent to a minimum-wage job for the day. If they are lucky, after two hours of waiting, three hours of transportation, and eight hours of work, and after payroll deductions, they bring home less than $40 for a thirteen-hour day.

Contrary to the stereotype that portrays persons in poverty as lazy, immigrants work long hours for low wages. Because pay is low, Mexican workers generally seek positions offering overtime, albeit at the standard hourly rate instead of time-and-a-half. Some workers are so desperate they work seventy hours a week to make only $350, and usually more than one person must work to support the family. Although many Mexican immigrants are unable to raise themselves out of poverty, once their children grow up, speak English, and find better jobs, even though manual labor, the whole family tends to improve economically.

Frequently, Mexican immigrant workers find themselves on the lowest rung of the labor ladder. Their limited English and rudimentary job skills (many are farm workers) render them vulnerable not only to employers but to fellow workers. Mexicans often complain about abuse from non-Hispanics, but being mistreated by a Mexican boss aggravates them more. Although there is considerable solidarity among Mexican workers, conflict between immigrants and first- and second-generation Mexican Americans sometimes erupts. Because immigrant workers are often the first laid off when a company downsizes and the last rehired after economic recovery, their quest for employment is constant. When factories move away or close down, undocumented workers, who do not qualify for unemployment compensation, are left with nothing but the urgent need to find another job.

In addition to low pay and long hours, immigrant workers, particularly the undocumented, often suffer discrimination and abuse because their employers realize they have little legal recourse. Some unscrupulous employers refuse to pay employees for work performed. Although even undocumented workers can file a complaint with the Illinois Department of Labor, few do because they are too intimidated by or fearful of the government, unwilling to suffer the lengthy bureaucratic delay of two to three years, or lack sufficient documentation to substantiate the abuse. Employers count on this reaction, even fomenting fear in workers by threatening to report them to the BCIS. Because the money to be gained in such cases is generally small, hiring a lawyer makes little economic sense. Aggrieved workers sometimes ask the parish priest to contact the employer, hoping to embarrass him into paying them. Undocumented workers are at the mercy of their employers.[5]

Many Mexican immigrant workers are paid in cash, either because their employers want to avoid paying federal payroll taxes or to accommodate workers lacking valid Social Security numbers. Although, in 1986, Congress mandated heavy fines for employers hiring undocumented workers, making it more difficult for them to find jobs, many employers continue to hire them. Most undocumented workers, however, are paid by check with the proper tax deductions. If they are using false Social Security numbers, they never collect benefits or refunds from the government; their payroll taxes remain a permanent contribution to the national Social Security trust fund.[6] If the Social Security Administration discovers that a particular Social Security number does not match the person's name, it asks the employer to investigate; such notice usually results in the worker's dismissal.[7]

Because Social Security numbers are needed to open checking accounts, undocumented workers generally do not have bank accounts. However, in 2001, the IRS and Mexican consulates began issuing special numbers, Individual Tax Identification Numbers (ITIN), allowing undocumented people to open bank accounts. Without this opportunity, they cash checks at currency exchanges that charge exorbitant fees. Many immigrants able to save money keep their savings under the mattress because they distrust financial institutions. As immigrant families become more economically stable, however, many, usually with the assistance of their adult children, begin trusting banks, opening checking accounts, and using credit cards.

Many Mexican immigrants also use the traditional system of *tanda* to save money. A *tanda* generally consists of eight to fifteen people who deposit the same amount of money each week with a designated member of the group. Each week that person pays the total weekly income to a different member of the group. Thus, if each of ten people deposits $50, over ten weeks everyone takes a turn receiving $500. While no interest is earned in a *tanda*, some people feel their money is safer than in a bank and prefer it because it creates social pressure on them to save from week to week. When Adelina and Armando bought a new house in 1997, Adelina was able to purchase all their new furniture with a *tanda* payout of $2,000.

As hard as life may be for an immigrant family in Chicago, most deem it easier than what they left in Mexico. For many, coming to the United States is a matter of survival. Loreto Garza farmed the land he inherited in a small rural town of one hundred families. Bad weather and declining prices for corn and beans convinced him to come to Chicago to build a better future for himself and his family. He lived in a small room with another man and each month sent money to his wife and twelve children in Mexico. After three years of nothing but work, he brought them to Chicago, all thirteen floating across the Rio Grande on inner tubes. They lived cramped in a small two-bedroom apartment in Pilsen where each night they heard shouting and shooting. They feared for their lives but could find no one willing to rent them a larger apartment with so many children. Although they contemplated returning to Mexico, they realized they would have less opportunity there. Once the children grew older and found jobs, the family bought a home, and their life changed dramatically for the better.

A strong work ethic is characteristic of most immigrants because they are a self-selected group of energetic, adventure-some, and ambitious members of their countries' lower classes. The Latino Institute examined the 1990 census in Chicago neigh-borhoods with large Hispanic populations and found a strong work ethic. More than 80 percent of Hispanic men in Chicago had jobs or were actively looking for work, compared with slightly less than 70 percent of non-Hispanic males. A 1997 study pointed not to traits of national character but to networks of social rela-tionships that give Mexicans an edge over blacks.[8] Because Mexicans have networks of large extended families and friends, not only do their chances of finding jobs increase but they are quickly taught the mundane yet critical techniques for survival in the world of work. Employers in the Chicago area prefer Mexican workers because they are hardworking, honest, docile, respectful, family-oriented, and dedicated; they know that many are desper-ate and vulnerable and, thus, willing to suffer difficult conditions. Mexicans are also a reliable source for recruiting additional reli-able workers; one need only inform them of job openings, and the following day new applicants appear, well instructed on the employer's expectations.

Despite their interest in work, Mexican immigrant workers are burdened with persistent negative stereotypes. Virgil Elizondo writes that the public image of Mexicans is that they are brown, Spanish-speaking, racially mixed, Roman Catholic, dirty, lazy, prolific, and prone to violence.[9] These characteristics go largely unquestioned and seriously damage Mexicans' self-concept. Pedro Martinez, a young parishioner from St. Pius V who gradu-ated from the University of Illinois, observed:

As a teenager I noticed people around my neighborhood had low expectations of themselves. My own self-esteem was really low. I always believed that people of other cultures, mainly Caucasians ("Americans"), were meant to be at a higher level than Hispanics. Nobody ever really told me that, but I learned it. Whenever I went downtown or to the suburbs, I couldn't help but notice that people were white. When I began high school, I had a choice of going to Whitney Young (a magnet school for better students) or Benito Juarez in the neighborhood. Because most Hispanics went to Benito Juarez, I thought maybe Hispanics were not meant to be successful because we are not smart enough to go to college and be professionals. Racism lowers our expectations of ourselves, stops us from dreaming; it imprisons us in our own stereotypes.[10]

Psychological studies by R. Diaz-Guerrero show that one of the greatest needs of Mexican Americans is heightened self-esteem. To compensate for the low self-image drummed into them by "bossism," racism, poverty, and classism, Mexicans sometimes resort to excessive bragging or boasting, a desperate sign of overcompensation and insecurity. Elizondo comments:

As long as Mexican Americans look upon their origin in terms of inferiority, they themselves accentuate what the dominant society has been telling them. But if they can go back to their origins and see it in terms of birth pangs—something painful but full of potential for future life—they will see it not as a curse but as a blessing. The acceptance of *mestizaje* (mixed race) is at the root of reversing the Mexican American inferiority complex.[11]

Danny Arroyo, a guitarist at St. Pius V English liturgies, described his experience as follows:

I was born in Pilsen, a third-generation American with a dark complexion and a foreign sounding surname. I

33

didn't know that I was Mexican until my friend's mother called me one when I was six years old. I will always remember that day. I started hating myself for being Mexican because it made me feel like one of "them" and not one of "us." I called Mexican immigrants "brazers" and tried to separate myself from them. But whites generally did not accept me either. My grandparents sacrificed their language and much of their culture in order to assimilate into the United States society. Now I have to work to recover all they gave up and make up for the injustice that once darkened my own mind.[12]

Mexicans have already made their mark on the economy and will continue to do so in new ways. In 1990, the U.S. Labor Department predicted that by the year 2010, one of every three new workers in the United States will be Hispanic. Moreover, Hispanics are increasingly launching their own businesses. While the number of all American businesses in the five-year period ending in 1992 increased by 26 percent, the number of Hispanic-owned businesses increased by nearly 83 percent.[13] Most of these businesses employ other Hispanics, often because of their commitment to assist their compatriots. Furthermore, as first-generation Hispanics achieve higher levels of education, many non-Hispanic businesses actively recruit them to enhance ethnic diversity in their workforce. This improvement of social class is evident in St. Pius V. In 1986, the parish had few professional members, but by 2003, it was easy to recognize teachers, nurses, computer technicians, accountants, paralegals, office managers, and other mid-level professionals in the congregation.

English as a Second Language

Spanish is clearly the dominant language in Pilsen.[14] Since the late 1960s, it has been spoken in nearly all neighborhood businesses, and by the 1980s, most public schools offered bilingual programs for children arriving from Mexico. Because most adult Mexican immigrants lack formal education in Spanish, learning

English is difficult. Demands of family and work also limit people's ability to meet the rigors of a regular class schedule, usually four nights or mornings a week. Nevertheless, most Mexican immigrant adults try to learn English because they want better jobs. Although there are many opportunities to study English in the neighborhood, classes are generally filled with long waiting lists. As with other immigrant groups, some Mexicans learn English well, others a little, and some despair of ever speaking it. Chicago's Latino Institute found that in 1994 three-fourths of all Hispanics in Chicago "spoke English well," a fact that contradicts the prevailing image of the monolingual Spanish-speaker.[15]

Children of most immigrant groups, on the other hand, not only learn English, but in their desire for social acceptance, soon prefer it to their parents' language. Conversely, many Hispanic immigrants, especially children, begin to lose proficiency in Spanish. Few Hispanic children study it in schools, and few parents take the time or feel they have the proficiency to teach it to their children. Although many children begin kindergarten with almost no English, by fourth grade most are pronouncing English perfectly while speaking Spanish less correctly and perhaps with an English accent. They may never learn Spanish grammar and begin to transliterate from English to Spanish, unconsciously weaving the two languages together in the same conversation.

The political tension over language is largely symbolic, reflecting the real conflict between forcing assimilation on immigrants and embracing cultural diversity. Most Mexican immigrants are not cultural isolationists. They realize they are entering a new world and must create something new, a mixture of their cultural heritage and the life and customs of the United States. The challenge for Mexican immigrant families, and, consequently, their church, is how much of their culture will they jettison and how much will they preserve, however modified it might be. Whatever their response, retention of certain cultural mores and values from the old country is more difficult without the Spanish language. Ada María Isasi-Díaz, a well-known writer about Hispanic ministry, notes:

35

For us, language is the main means of identification here in the United States. To speak Spanish, in public as well as in private, is a political act, a means of asserting who we are, an important way of struggling against assimilation. The different state laws that forbid speaking Spanish in official situations, or militate against bilingual education, function as an oppressive internal colonialism that ends up hurting United States society.[16]

Educated But Unschooled

To call someone *maleducado*, or uneducated, refers more to the person's lack of social graces than to their years of schooling. Although most Mexican immigrants have not had an opportunity to attend much school, they are very *educados*, excelling in courtesy, respect, and graciousness, even to the point of being quite formal with family and friends. But their status in schooling is another matter. A 1990 study by the National Council of La Raza provides this sobering analysis: "Hispanics remain the most undereducated major segment of the U.S. population."[17] In the early 1990s, only 46 percent of Pilsen residents over eighteen years of age had finished primary school (sixth grade) in Mexico. Few men and even fewer women have completed four years of secondary school. This pattern continues once Mexicans reach the United States. A study of the Chicago area in 1990 reported that 68 percent of Hispanics lacked a high school diploma, compared with 40 percent of African Americans and 25 percent of Euro-Americans.[18] Among Hispanics, Mexicans were the least likely to have a high school diploma and Cubans the most likely.[19] In Chicago in 1994, only 9 percent of Hispanics older than twenty four had a university degree, compared with 24 percent of non-Hispanics, a statistic reflecting a decline for Hispanics from 1975.[20]

The low level of education among Mexican adults is most evident in their limited ability to handle written material. Women especially lack functional literacy. If they read, they do so with great difficulty, a reality reflected in the fact that the neighborhood has one of the highest levels of TV-viewing and one of the lowest of newspaper readership in the Chicago area. Nevertheless, many strive to improve their educational level by attending classes at four local adult education centers, where English, computer science, and G.E.D. classes are filled.

Hispanic high school students, soon to become the largest education group in the country, have the highest dropout rate of any ethnic group.[21] Their failure to complete high school has many causes. First, discrimination. A study of Chicago public schools found that in "virtually all cases, Hispanics were overrepresented in situations with negative connotations (conditions) and underrepresented in situations with positive connotations."[22] For example, minority representation on school boards, administrative staffs, and school faculties was low. Hispanic students were also more likely to be placed in classes for the educable mentally retarded and limited-English proficiency rather than in classes for the gifted. Recently arrived immigrant children often remain in bilingual programs throughout their schooling and, consequently, graduate with deficiencies in English. In 2000, a study revealed that magnet schools in Chicago, which serve gifted students from a wide geographical area, are less available to Hispanics than to whites and African Americans.[23]

Second, focus groups of parents meeting at St. Pius V in 1996 identified overcrowding as a major reason for teenage dropouts. Schools in Pilsen are the most overcrowded in the city. Indeed, because Mexican immigrants tend to have large families, wherever they settle, local schools soon become overcrowded and, consequently, unable to give proper attention to students.

Third, inferior teaching, resources, and facilities explain part of Hispanics' poor educational performance.[24] Most teachers are non-Hispanic, and many fail to engage Hispanic students, owing to their ignorance of Hispanic culture or the belief that students should abandon family traditions and assimilate as quickly as possible into American culture. Without adequate resources and support for their culture, Hispanic students easily become disinterested in school.

Fourth, some Mexican immigrants remain unconvinced that a high school diploma will make a difference in their lives. Recently arrived immigrants and their children often presume the youngsters will end up in factory or menial jobs, even if they complete high school. Many with a diploma from a secondary school (ninth grade) in Mexico are uninterested in earning a high school diploma in the United States. Relatively few of those who successfully obtain one, attend college. In 2000, less than 10 percent of the seniors graduating from Benito Juarez, Pilsen's public high school, enrolled in college, a situation explained in part by the fact that undocumented students are ineligible for financial aid for higher education.

Fifth, many Mexican immigrant parents are uninvolved in their children's education, a situation stemming less from a lack of interest than from a variety of other reasons. Many parents believe they should not interfere with the job of the teachers; indeed, some researchers compare parents' respect for teachers with the awe most Americans have for doctors or priests.[25] Many also have a problem understanding the school's rules and regulations, and their limited ability to speak English complicates their communication with their children's teachers. Furthermore, because some parents have had little schooling, they underestimate the value of education for their children, especially for their daughters. Others appreciate the importance of schooling but lack sufficient preparation to help their children with homework.[26] Sixth, economic necessity often dictates that teenage boys work to complement their parents' income and that adolescent girls stay home to care for younger siblings.

Finally, the menacing, violent recruitment by gangs within and around schools convinces some youth to abandon school. Girls are particularly frightened by violence in school hallways and bathrooms, whether it be fighting, brandishing guns, or hurling threats of bodily harm. Teenage boys are more vulnerable to gang recruitment, some succumbing to their pressure and dropping out of school to wander the streets. Still others are like Javier, a twelve-year-old boy who spent an entire year self-confined in his family apartment after being threatened by local gangs. His family solved the problem by moving to another neighborhood.

While too many Hispanics drop out of school, many excel in academics. During the years covered by this book, the number of college graduates active in St. Pius V increased notably. Although they represent a small percentage of the youth in the neighborhood, they exemplify the potential. Nevertheless, most students complain of the lack of preparation and encouragement they receive from their elementary and high school teachers and counselors to seek higher education. Once in college, they find themselves much less prepared than students from non–inner-city or non-minority high schools, and high dropout rates are the rule. In 1990, only 2.7 percent of Hispanics living in Pilsen had completed a bachelor's degree or higher.

Any Room in the Inn?

Although many immigrant communities experience poor housing, the situation in Pilsen is extraordinary. In 1990, 28 percent of the units, housing approximately half of all Pilsen residents, were overcrowded (i.e., more than one person per room), nearly three times the rate for the city as a whole, making Pilsen the most overcrowded community in the Midwest. The large size of Mexican families explains some of the overcrowding. In 1990, the average number of persons per household in Pilsen was 3.76, compared with the citywide average of 2.67. In Pilsen, housing stock is also old; of the 13,869 housing units, 78 percent were built before 1939, compared with 44 percent in all Chicago. To compound the problem, the aging housing has not been well maintained, partly because many buildings are owned by absentee landlords. In 1990, only 22.5 percent of Pilsen housing was owner-occupied, compared with a citywide rate of 37.5 percent. Absentee owners interested in wringing profit from their rental units do not respond favorably to renters' pleas to install a functional heater, fix a leaky roof, repair falling plaster, or remove peeling lead-based paint. Few immigrants report housing code violations because they fear involvement with the government or retaliation from the landlord. Moreover, because few renters sign leases, many are at the landlords' mercy. When owners refuse to fix their apartments, renters generally deal with the problem by moving.

Hispanics nationwide and in Chicago suffer greater racial discrimination than African Americans in renting or purchasing housing.[27] An additional injustice to many Mexican immigrants is the denial of housing to families with many children, an illegal practice difficult to document. Large extended families experience the same problem. In 1996, authorities in the outlying cities and suburbs of Cicero, Addison, and Waukegan passed ordinances limiting the number of extended family members living under the same roof, regardless of the size of the home. These ordinances targeted Hispanics (mostly Mexicans) and reflected the anti-immigrant sentiment of the time. Hispanics successfully challenged the ordinances in court as discriminatory, arguing that the definition of family used by the cities directly conflicted with their own cultural concept of family.[28]

As Hispanics in Chicago improved their incomes in the 1980s and 1990s, they became increasingly interested in purchasing homes. Hispanic homeowners increased from 24.4 percent in 1980 to 31.4 percent in 1990, compared with 48 percent for all non-Hispanics.[29] Because the availability of housing in Pilsen did not keep pace with the growing population, many Mexican families purchased homes outside the area. At the same time, more recently arrived immigrant families struggled to pay even the relatively low rents in the neighborhood because their incomes failed to keep pace with the rising cost of rents. In 1996, rents in Pilsen remained, according to government calculations, technically unaffordable for 58 percent of the residents.[30]

Health at Risk

Because Mexican immigrants as a whole are younger than the average population, statistics concerning certain aspects of their health are positive. In some regards, their diet is healthy, albeit simple. The combination of rice, beans, and tortillas, their daily staples, provides a relatively nutritional fare. On the other hand, Mexicans generally consume too much sugar (in sweet rolls, cakes, and beverages) and excessive fat (in fried pork rinds, called *chicharon*, or tamales made with lard), causing high incidences of diabetes and high blood pressure. Hispanics are nearly two times more likely to have diabetes than the general population, with 10.6 percent of all Mexicans and Mexican Americans suffering from the disease. Although they have a lower rate of obesity than the general population, their rate of increase was the fastest in the nation in the 1990s. Hispanics have the highest rate of asthma and substance abuse in Chicago, and in 2001, they contracted sclerosis of the liver at nearly twice the rate of the national population. On the positive side, Mexican immigrants have healthier babies than the general population, infant mortality in Pilsen being lower than in the city as a whole.[31] However, in 1998, the percentage of Hispanic teenagers giving birth now surpasses that of African American teens, with both groups more than twice as likely as whites to become mothers before age 20.[32]

The overall health of Mexicans in Pilsen would undoubtedly improve if they had better access to health care services. In 1999, the Census Bureau reported that 35.3 percent of Hispanics lacked health insurance, ranking Hispanics the least insured ethnic group in the nation.[33] Some workers receive health benefits for themselves, but their families are frequently not covered. Although children born in poverty are eligible for Medicaid benefits if their parents apply, Mexican immigrants have the lowest rate of enrollment for public aid of any ethnic group in Chicago, partly because the undocumented are ineligible, partly because receiving public aid clashes with their strong desire to support themselves, and partly because many are uninformed about available benefits or discouraged by a bureaucracy unfriendly to non-English speaking people.

The uninsured, notably women and children, usually attend the city's neighborhood clinic for routine examinations and minor health problems, paying a small fee of eight dollars per consultation. In the late 1980s and 1990s, a private low-cost clinic, Alivio Medical Center, opened two facilities, primarily to serve women and children with minor health problems. Other small for-profit clinics are sprinkled throughout the neighborhood. For major health problems, uninsured families go to Cook County Hospital, where, just as at the local city clinic, they face long waits for both appointments and service.[34] Of course, health care provided by these public institutions is not integrated or managed, and since the poor generally do not have a family physician, they often go to the emergency room for care, the most expensive avenue for both major and minor health services. Although undocumented workers qualify for workers' compensation for job-related injuries, they are frequently fired when injured on the job. To obtain compensation, they often must file a claim with the Department of Labor and/or hire a private attorney. Because both options involve much red tape and years of costly delay, few pursue their legal rights.

General health care services in Spanish are available in the community, but mental health care in Spanish is extremely scarce throughout metropolitan Chicago. Mental health services in Pilsen focus almost exclusively on patients discharged from hospital psychiatric wards, providing virtually no psychotherapy for the common problems of anxiety and depression, or counseling for families. Because services in Spanish are so limited, many immigrants come to the churches for help with their emotional stress.

Alcoholic abuse is extremely common in the community. Mexican men often arrive in Chicago alone, leaving their families behind until they are financially ready to bring them. During years of separation, these lonely men while away their evenings drinking in local taverns. Pilsen has the second-highest concentration of taverns per capita in the city. Other men arrive in Chicago already firmly in the grip of alcohol. Drinking may have been a tradition in their family or in their small *ranchos* where hanging around the *cantina* was the principal form of entertainment for men. Because of the severity of the alcoholism problem, several Alcoholics Anonymous groups in Pilsen formed to assist the chemically dependent.

Social services in Pilsen are also severely inadequate. A 1996 survey of service agencies found that not only were residents relatively ignorant of existing services but no agency conducted outreach in the community because all were stretched beyond their capacity with existing clients. Although three agencies operate day-care centers, the young population warrants several more. Some Catholic parishes and the city's Department of Human Services provide limited social services, primarily emergency food, clothing, and referrals to other agencies. St. Pius V founded San Jose Obrero Mission, a shelter for homeless men, while local parishes through their community organization, The Resurrection Project, operate the Casa Maria and Casa Sor Juana shelters for women and children.

In summary, in the area of health, Mexican immigrants are extremely vulnerable.

All in the Family

Families in Pilsen are the largest, youngest, and most rapidly growing in the Midwest. The official average age is twenty-one, and the crude birth rate from 1980 to 1990 was 28.4 per 1000, the highest in the city and three times the city's median rate. Mexicans also bring a strong family fabric to the United States, where it is pulled and stretched and sometimes torn apart. They love their children and work long hours at backbreaking jobs so their children can enjoy opportunities they themselves were denied. For Mexicans, family is always first. They sacrifice mightily to care for them and keep them together. Unlike many American parents, they almost never want their children to leave the nest, whether married or not. They discourage their children from moving away for college, and young couples frequently begin their married lives living not just in the same building as their parents but in a spare bedroom in the same apartment. Of course, they also extend family relations through the institution of *compadrazgo*, creating close relationships with godparents, who are generally treated as family, included in family celebrations, trusted with secrets, and supported morally and financially when in need.

The Mexican family is famous for its warmth and hospitality. "My house is your house" (*Mi casa es su casa*) is a common Mexican expression that captures the flavor of family life. It is rare to visit a Mexican family and not be offered food and drink. Short visits are frowned on. In fact, the principal form of entertainment is visiting family and friends, with visitors often taking precedence over other responsibilities. When people miss a parish event, it is often because they had *una visita* (a visitor). No one ever questions the explanation. Mexican tradition also dictates that families welcome into their home other family members and even friends from their hometowns. In 2000, Mecino Reyes sat down to breakfast in his three-bedroom apartment each morning with his wife and three children, his brother and sister-in-law, his parents, and a handful of nieces and nephews. These relatives arrived from Mexico and needed somewhere to stay while looking for work. They remained within this protective cocoon for months, while learning to navigate

43

in unfamiliar surroundings. Eventually, they struck out on their own, journeying toward self-sufficiency.[35]

The Mexican spirit of hospitality is also evident at parties when hosts offer their guests plates of food to take to those unable to attend or for "your lunch tomorrow." At receptions for baptisms and weddings, hosts deliberately order an enormous cake in order to send leftovers home with guests, a generous gesture of hospitality but also a sign of God's abundant blessings and the host's desire to share with others. Mexican hospitality is also reflected in the people's delight in physical contact. Unlike Americans, they like touching and hugging. At Mass, holding hands while praying the Our Father is a joy, whereas for many Americans it is a painful experience. Mexicans constantly shake hands, both upon entering a room and leaving. Indeed, people are often offended when someone does not shake their hand, even if they might have seen them and shaken it earlier in the day.

Because of the proximity of Mexico, Mexican immigrants can maintain close ties with family left behind. Many dream of saving enough money to return to Mexico, rejoining their family, buying some land, and living out their golden years in their homeland. These dreams rarely become reality. Even if Mexican immigrants save enough money to return home to start afresh, they soon discover they have unwittingly set down roots in the United States. Once their children are grown, speaking English better than Spanish, working a good job, and procreating darling grandchildren, parents are uninterested in returning to Mexico for more than a visit. Often, other family members have also moved here, giving even less reason to return. And once Mexican immigrants learn the fiscal logic of buying rather than renting a home, they or their children eventually purchase one, and their roots grow deeper.

Because Mexican immigrants long for their country and the family left behind, they often spend large sums of money on phone calls to and from Mexico and sacrifice to send money to their families on a regular basis. The Mexican government calculated that remittances from Mexicans living abroad in 1998 totaled $5.5 billion, nearly triple the level recorded annually at the beginning of the decade.[36] Moreover, the strongest organized network of Mexicans in the United States consists of clubs identified with specific Mexican regions that help immigrants maintain contact and express their solidarity with their place of origin by funneling their economic contributions into public works there.[37]

Americans are surprised to see how highly Mexican immigrants value a trip home. Poor families, living in the simplest apartments, with no car, a secondhand wardrobe, and eating meat only a few times a week, sacrifice greatly to return to Mexico because "my father is sick" or "I have not seen my mother in years." Some leave without the security of returning to their job. Without adequate documents, a trip home may require a substantial payment to a *coyote* and another perilous swim across the Rio Grande. The importance of family for Mexicans is born of sacrifices such as these, some of which may seem foolish to Americans.

Some people return to Mexico for more practical reasons. They may have a small piece of land and/or a small business to look after. They may have to participate in the annual harvest or fulfill a promise to join in the annual religious celebration in their village. Because some lack health insurance or are ineligible for Medicaid, they return for relatively inexpensive medical attention. Moreover, for Mexican immigrants and many first-generation Mexican Americans, Mexico is home. They display the Mexican flag, pictures of Our Lady of Guadalupe, family photos, and calendars with pictures of Mexico in their Chicago homes to preserve the sense of being in Mexico. They also extensively videotape family events, such as birthdays and weddings, to send them to Mexico and thus maintain family ties. A large number of people also send the bodies of their loved ones for burial in Mexico. Parishioners often comment how they want their "bones to rest in *mi querido* Mexico." The parish staff officiates at approximately 100 wake services per year for people whose bodies are shipped there.

This attachment to family and the ability to communicate easily with Mexico help explain why relatively few Mexican immigrants became United States citizens until the restrictive immigration legislation of 1996 scared many into applying. Prior to this time, although citizenship brought some political benefits, such as the right to vote, it held little attraction for most Mexicans. The economic benefits, however, especially for the poor, and the greater facility to normalize the immigration status of other family members, convinced many to apply for citizenship.

Although the Mexican family is strong, its life in large urban areas like Chicago is less than idyllic. Economic and social conditions assail their family style of life. Demanding work schedules and cultural clashes involving child rearing and the role of women upset family dynamics and weaken the family fabric. Parents frequently work different shifts and, consequently, see little of each other. If the women work, they often prepare and leave a meal on the stove for reheating when their husbands or children arrive from work or school. Although sharing family meals together is an important custom that helps produce adjusted and academically successful children, family schedules often make it an unattainable goal. Moreover, the small size of dining areas and the lack of a large table and sufficient chairs may make eating together physically impossible.

The main source of entertainment in Mexican immigrant households is television. Many have two TV sets; older members prefer Spanish channels, while younger ones watch English. It is rare to walk into a home and find the TV set turned off. Spanish soap operas (*novelas*) are a major attraction and, unlike their English counterparts, air in prime-time evening hours. Many families use their limited income to purchase cable television because there are no movie theaters showing Spanish-speaking films. Concerts and rodeos attract crowds, but only a fraction of the Mexican community attends. While some young and middle-aged people frequent weekend dances in clubs, for most, the primary sources of entertainment beyond television involve visiting family and shopping at malls and flea markets. While younger family members may be out and about on Sunday afternoons, their parents and younger siblings reserve the time for informal visiting. Food is available on the stove all afternoon, ready for the occasional visitor, with the TV constantly blaring, of course. In the living room, men watch a soccer game telecast from Mexico, while upstairs the children watch a movie, a cartoon, or professional wrestling. The women, more interested in communicating, gather in the kitchen to discuss family concerns.

Parenting Under Fire

Many parents successfully raise loving, responsible children, maintaining a close, affectionate, and respectful relationship with them. They instill a sense of self-esteem that empowers the children to perform well in school, however inferior it may be. They spend time with them, accompanying them to activities and encouraging them to experience new challenges. At the same time, immigrant families encounter specific difficulties stemming from budding cultural differences between parents and children. Parents trying to preserve their native culture clash with their children who want to be Americans. Unresolved issues of communication, authority, discipline, and shared responsibility sometimes result in serious family conflict and teenage delinquency.

Normal communication between the generations is complicated in a number of ways. After a few years in school, children tend to prefer English to Spanish. It is not uncommon for children to respond to their parents' questions in Spanish by answering in English. Parents who understand some English often succumb to this arrangement, further widening the communication gap between themselves and their children. When children speak with friends in English on the phone, parents often have little or no idea what they are discussing. The parents' limited English and minimal understanding of American mores also give their children an advantage. When a non–Spanish-speaker calls or visits the home, from a repairman to a letter carrier, it is not the child who calls the parent for help but the parent who seeks the child's assistance. Children interpret American laws and customs for their parents, and some parents, concerned about fitting into their new homeland, accept their children's far-from-disinterested explanation. This dynamic reverses traditional roles, assigning to children the power customarily belonging to adults. Furthermore, because children experience more of the wider society, they often feel superior to or at least more knowledgeable than their parents, who remain wedded to the "outdated" ways of the past. Thus, a cultural divide develops that weakens parental authority.

Unfortunately, immigrant parents frequently lack good parenting skills to raise their children here. Because some parents experienced strict and even abusive parents, they want to be more understanding and lenient with their children. Sometimes this desire renders them excessively permissive, demanding almost nothing of their children, such as household chores, and thereby depriving them of a sense of belonging achieved through shared responsibility.

Cristina's parents made great sacrifices for her to attend St. Pius V grammar school. Soon after graduating, she flirted with the idea of joining a gang. She complained of not being able to communicate with her mother, an uneducated women still thinking and acting as if she were living in Mexico. When Cristina insulted her mother, calling her ignorant and backward, her mother failed to demand respect. Cristina loved her father, but he never had time for her. He worked ten hours a day, six days a week; when he came home, he wanted to be left alone. Cristina ached for her father's attention and approval. She wanted him to take her out and tell her he loved her, but he never did. At home, Cristina avoided all responsibilities; she did not wash dishes, cook, or clean. Her mother wanted her to enjoy the freedom of her youth and wanted to avoid the conflict that would result if she ordered her to help out. In her junior year, Cristina became pregnant, dropped out of high school, and moved out of the house. Unwittingly, Cristina's parents, trying to provide her the best, deprived her of what was most important: time, responsibility, and a sense of belonging.

Because many parents do not understand the cultural challenges their children face as first-generation Mexican Americans, they fail to adequately confront and affirm, discipline and reward them. Their children may have the run of the house, have few responsibilities, and easily talk themselves out of any discipline. Their struggles and successes might go unnoticed. To compound the problem, parents generally treat their sons more leniently than their daughters.[38] Many parents abdicate their responsibility, placing too much power into their children's hands—for example, allowing them to dominate the selection of TV viewing or the schedule for meals. Sadly, their children are soon out of control.

Racial discrimination also exacerbates internal family conflict because it leads many Hispanic children, like children of previous immigrant groups, to ignore, if not deny, their cultural heritage. Some prefer not to speak Spanish in public even though they are perfectly bilingual. Others insist on being called by the English version of their Spanish name, Joe instead of José. Racism also causes problems of self-identity and self-worth and creates tensions between children and their parents. Parents often complain that their children's lack of knowledge of and appreciation for traditional Mexican culture hinders family communication. Children, on the other hand, complain that their parents are "out of it," do not listen, understand, or trust them. Because parents similarly note that their children do not listen and cannot be trusted, conflicts result, which the children often win.

In focus groups at St. Pius V, many parents commented on the difficulty of parenting in the United States. They are frustrated with the cultural differences and methods of discipline, most notably the laws against corporal punishment. They fear their children are wresting control from them by threatening to report them to governmental agencies if they spank or hit them. Many adults who were disciplined with the belt believe such techniques are still appropriate and effective. Without recourse to physical violence, they are at a loss for what to do, ignorant of alternative methods of disciplining in a firm, consistent fashion, setting limits, and establishing consequences. Their children wear them down by refusing to obey, and as parents realize they cannot put their children in chains, they eventually give up. Because of their jobs, many are unable to take their children to school each morning or to be at home after school. Some parents who work late find it difficult to meet with their children's teachers, and because many teachers are non-Hispanics, they are often unaware of the struggles of cultural identity their students suffer. Furthermore, as mentioned above, because of their own limited educational preparation, many parents feel unable to assist their children with their homework, while their children in turn resent their lack of involvement. Thus, the gulf between parents and children steadily widens.

Flight into Gangs

Pilsen is a community plagued by five major and several smaller gangs. Walking several blocks in any direction almost certainly involves crossing gangland borders. Although no data detail the number of young people involved in gangs, common estimates claim less than 10 percent of teens participate in gang activity.[39] But because young people in gangs are organized, secretive, and violent, their impact far exceeds their numbers. During the years covered by this book, gang violence in Pilsen not only increased, but became a serious threat to public health. Although the number of Hispanic gun owners in the United States is the lowest of any ethnic group, Hispanics are disproportionately affected by gun violence, their firearm homicide rates nearly four times that of whites.[40] Wars between Hispanic gangs leave dead and wounded among innocent people as well as gang members. Between 1987 and 1994, Hispanic gangs in Chicago were responsible for more than 350 deaths, more than 10,000 serious incidents of violence, and 20,000 serious crimes. In Pilsen, the Ambrose gang had 548 violent crimes attributed to it, while its rival, La Raza, was responsible for 537. Between 1994 and 1996, a protracted war between these two gangs left a half dozen members dead and dozens wounded.[41]

Adolescence is normally a period of transition when children separate from parents, associating with peers while seeking self-identity and respect in the larger society. Studies have long identified the desire for belonging as the principal reason for youth gangs. What may have begun as wayward children hanging around street corners, alienated from their families, misunderstood by and uncommitted to schools, and fearful and resentful of police, gradually developed into an organization with a new subculture: the street gang. Gangs commonly thrive among adolescents in poor immigrant or racially marginal populations. Multiple factors, including economic, cultural, and socio-psychological components, contribute to a sense of displacement, isolation, and alienation in many Mexican youth.[42] To flirt with danger, to find loyal companions, to command respect, to flee an irrelevant or abusive home, to find love and acceptance, are all reasons luring teenagers into gangs, and usually it is only age and maturity that convince them to leave the gangs. Instead of parents, schools, and police, gangs provide a substitute structure and culture of caring, sharing, education, and discipline. This shift in socialization from the home to the streets produces a *cholo* street subculture, a mixture of Mexican and Euro-American traits and habits. Gang signs and colors, hairstyles, swaggering, speaking, dressing, and assigning nicknames help create a new identity, with its own values and norms, where youth feel at home. It is no accident that gang members refer to one another as "homeboys." With gang association come mind-altering drugs, hair-trigger weapons, and a *locura* (quasi-controlled craziness) to act out personal aggressions and rage.[43] Acting *loco* (crazy), a respected mode of behavior, is the manly, *macho* way to behave. Conflicts among gangs, including drive-by shootings, usually result from apparently insignificant problems, but in the small world of gang life, flashing a gang sign, crossing into rival gang turf, or disrespecting the rules for drug sales may justify killing the offender. Then the retaliation is always of equal or greater force, and from there, the violence escalates until both sides establish a truce.

Although adults and young children are almost never the target of gang violence, they are infrequently the victims of a stray bullet. Those newly attracted to gangs generally focus on gang camaraderie, minimizing, if not ignoring, the violence the gang inflicts on others. They believe their gang's war is justified to defend its honor against a hostile enemy gang. They accept the violent rites of initiation, often requiring robbery or shooting, as tests of courage and loyalty, and they participate in signing ("tagging") neighborhood walls with graffiti as legitimate markers of the gang's "lawful" territory. In short, their attention focuses not on the gang's violence and crime but on the friendship, loyalty, and honor among gang members. Although it appears incongruous, Mexican gang members are usually religious. Almost all wear a crucifix or an image of Our Lady of Guadalupe, and most respect the church, including its ministers and buildings, seeing little contradiction between their faith and their gang involvement.

Like other teenagers, gang members are interested in sports, courting, fashion, movies, food, and recreation. But when they choose the discipline of the street, they quickly drop out of school, staying out most nights and sleeping during the day. Because their educational level and job skills are low, they cannot find or maintain jobs and prefer to make money through a life of crime—selling drugs, stealing, and extorting. Most have extremely low self-esteem, and bravado behavior serves to mask it. Solidarity among gang members helps reduce the fear and anxiety a life of violent crime normally causes. In reality, many fear leaving the community, applying for a job, or meeting and conversing with adults outside the community. When not involved in their income-producing activities, they simply hang out, drinking alcohol, taking drugs, expressing their aggressive and violent thoughts and feelings, or recruiting new members to the gang. And gang recruiters know how to spot vulnerable youth, those alienated from their parents or easily intimidated by threats of personal harm. However, if teenagers adamantly refuse to join a gang, demonstrating they are more interested in living with their family than running with the gang, the gang eventually leaves them alone.

A few alternative high schools in surrounding neighborhoods encourage dropouts, including gang members, to return to school. But community programs working directly with gang members are rare, not only because they are costly, but they are also extremely difficult to staff. Former gang members are usually hired as outreach workers, but they tend to burn out or return to gang life after a year or two. Schools, parks, youth clubs, and churches usually take the easier route of gang prevention, offering after-school recreation and tutoring, as well as occasional parenting classes for adults.

Macho Men and Abused Women

Machismo, a deeply rooted and destructive element in Hispanic cultures, is unfortunately alive and well in Pilsen. *Machismo*, the ideological foundation of the traditional Hispanic family, claims that because God made men superior to women, they can and should dominate women. This belief deeply permeates the relationship between husband and wife, revealing men's desire for power and control over their spouses. *Machista* men expect their wives to care for the entire household by themselves. Whether women work outside the home or not, they are responsible for shopping, child care, cooking, cleaning, and washing, and they are expected to prepare and serve meals whenever men want them. At family gatherings, men often expect their wives to prepare a plate of food and bring it to them before the women serve themselves. *Machismo* often surfaces when the woman confesses that her husband or fiancé has *celos* (jealousy). Most women understand that jealousy reflects a man's distrust of them, but few recognize it as a form of control.

Luis and Carmen had been dating for a year when they began living together. Pressured by fear that her mother in Mexico would discover she was living with her boyfriend, she and Luis came to St. Pius V to arrange for their marriage. When asked about jealousy, she admitted Luis had a problem. Because he became angry if he thought she was looking at another man, she kept her eyes always forward. He told her what clothes to wear in public to avoid attracting men's attention. He constantly quizzed her about to whom she was talking and what she was saying on the phone. Claiming he did not like her family, he generally refused her permission to visit them. Whenever she went out, he insisted on accompanying her. She naively thought his reactions were a problem of jealousy, but she admitted they had worsened after she moved in with him.

Abusive men have many ways of controlling if not dominating their wives. They usually try to isolate them from outside influences, threatening them if they leave the house without permission, even to walk the children to the park, visit friends or family, or sit on the front porch, where other men might see them. To guarantee their wives' dependence, some husbands do not allow them to learn to drive and refuse to apply for legal residency for them. Frequently, men control all family finances, doling out money to their wives in small portions and demanding strict accountability from them, while keeping them ignorant of how much money they make or spend. Often husbands accompany their wives to the doctor's office, distrusting them alone with the physician, or do the weekly grocery shopping (*hacer el mandado*) simply to control their movement and use of money.

Many Mexican women accept their inferior status as a fact of life. From childhood, many girls learn that a woman's role is to serve men. Their mothers teach them how to give and give until they are nearly empty. Many women abused by their husbands were abused as children, and as a result threw themselves precipitously into marriage. If a marriage begins to fall apart, *machismo* declares the woman at fault. If the husband is an alcoholic and beats his wife, somehow she is to blame. Husbands insist that women deserve or even need whatever treatment they mete out to them, including beatings. Psychological abuse of women is often more devastating than physical violence. Husbands insult and humiliate their wives in order to subdue them, and all too frequently women internalize these deprecations. They believe they are of little worth and learn not to question or object, raise their glance, or look other people in the eye. If only they were better wives, they conclude, their husbands would not be drinking or angry with them.

Women find it difficult to confront or break this pattern of violence. Most have so little self-confidence they cannot imagine themselves surviving economically or emotionally without their husbands. Some are terrified because their spouses threaten to leave them, take away their children, or report them to immigration authorities. Others fear their children will be upset if they leave their fathers. Frequently, because their own parents and siblings expect them to suffer whatever abuse their husbands mete out, they feel they have no one to turn to. Some priests may even counsel them that because marriage is for life, they must accept their husband's abuse—it is God's will that they carry this cross.[44]

Sociological literature suggests that domestic violence services are underused by African American and Hispanic women, even though they encounter a higher incidence of spousal abuse than Euro-American women. Moreover, compared with Anglo women, victims who are racial, ethnic, religious, or linguistic minorities are not only less likely to seek shelter but are more likely to encounter difficulties with shelter providers. Explanations for low levels of social services used by Hispanic battered women focus on four areas: (1) Cultural norms emphasize that family problems are best addressed within the family and are not to be shared with outsiders. (2) Services in Spanish are limited, and those that exist tend to ignore cultural differences in values and norms among a culturally diverse Hispanic population. (3) Most existing services are scarcely accessible because they are outside the minority communities. (4) Economic resources and legal protection are often unavailable to immigrant women because of their undocumented status, for example, welfare benefits enabling women to leave abusive relationships.[45]

Once in the United States, many Hispanic immigrant women gradually learn, each at her own pace, that *machismo* is an evil they need not accept. When they discover that their parish is interested in assisting them in their suffering, confusion, anxiety, or depression, they readily approach the staff. Many discover their own worth and capability, while others fall back time and time again into the culturally inherited mold of codependency. Some never find liberation, but those who escape the web of violence generally need a lot of support from others.

First- and second-generation Mexican American women are much less likely to accept abuse. They already have benefited from the empowerment generated by women's liberation in the United States. Many abusive men are too comfortable in their traditional ways and too supported by a thriving culture of *machismo* to change their behavior even after serious confrontation, but some, when challenged, change for the better, and frequently faith plays an important role in their conversion. Also, many first-generation Mexican American men are more sensitive to the destructiveness of male domination and are more likely to share domestic responsibilities with their wives and to support them in seeking employment outside the home or in pursuing advanced education.

This chapter has described the world of Mexican immigrants in the Pilsen neighborhood. While the *barrio* preserves much of the old world, it helps people create something new. Many forces threaten Mexican culture and family in the United States. Under the onslaught of individualism and materialism, independence and autonomy become more important than commitment to family, and personal comfort supersedes hospitality. Instead of welcoming into their homes family and friends recently arrived from Mexico, some first- and second-generation Mexican Americans begin to view them as a burden and support curtailing the influx of new immigrants. Concerned about their financial situation, newly married couples are less interested in raising a large family than their parents. Possession of materials things, from clothes to cars, from elaborate electronic equipment to multiple homes, takes precedence over developing and sustaining family and personal relationships. Time becomes a commodity to be wisely spent instead of a gift to be shared, and their involvement with the church and the practice of their faith begin to fade. The long, rich tradition of domestic rituals is gradually forgotten. On the other hand, many families struggle to preserve their customs and values and pass them on to their children. A Catholic parish can and should actively support their effort. The following chapters detail how St. Pius V has responded to this challenge.

Notes

1. Virgil Elizondo, *Galilean Journey, The Mexican American Promise* (Maryknoll, NY: Orbis, 1983), 23.

2. In 1995, the median earnings for year-round full-time Hispanic males in the United States was $20,054, or 63.1 percent of the earnings of non-Hispanic whites ($31,765). The poverty rate for Hispanics was 27 percent in 1995, compared with 8.5 percent for non-Hispanic whites and 26.4 percent for African Americans. Dean R. Hoge, "The Demographics of the U.S. Hispanic Presence" (working paper, Catholic University of America, 1998), 2.

3. In 2002, the Pew Hispanic Center estimated 7.8 million undocumented immigrants in the United States, including 4.5 million Mexicans. Oscar Avia, "Illegal Workers Potent Force in U.S.," *Chicago Tribune* (March 22, 2002), Sec. 2, 9.

4. Like many, Jorge and Elena managed to avoid the INS, and five years after their arrest, still undocumented, they bought a house as their children finished high school. If they were ever arrested again or if they ever wanted to obtain legalization in the future, their failure to comply with the voluntary departure would almost certainly lead to a denial of their application.

5. In 1997, the National Academy of Sciences released a study of the economic effects of immigration, concluding that, contrary to popular belief, immigrants produce substantial economic benefits and only slightly reduce wages and job opportunities of low-skilled American workers. No evidence suggested that African Americans are hurt by competition with immigrants. "Immigrants Dampen Wages But Boost U.S. Economy, Panel Finds," *Chicago Tribune* (May 18, 1997), no Sec., 7.

6. Undocumented workers can now file a W-7 form with the IRS to receive a number just to recover their payroll and income taxes and to open a bank account.

7. In 2002, false *(chuecos)* Social Security cards could be purchased readily on the street for $160. Sometimes vendors try to convince prospective buyers that the number is good, that is, belonging to no one else; the price then may rise to $1,500 per card.

8. *LatStat, op. cit.*, 1–2. See also Melita Marie Garza, "Hispanics Work, But They Are Still in Poverty, Study Reports," *Chicago Tribune* (March 8, 1993), Sec. 2, 5.

9. Elizondo, *Galilean Journey, loc. cit.*

10. Interview with Pedro Martinez, December 14, 1998.

11. Elizondo, *Galilean Journey*, 24.

12. Interview with Danny Arroyo, December 15, 1998.

13. Frank James, "Hispanics Start Businesses at the Fastest Pace for Minorities," *Chicago Tribune* (November 19, 1996), Sec. 3, 1.

14. Studies in the 1990s showed that 28 percent of the population in Pilsen spoke only Spanish, 13 percent only English, and 59 percent spoke both languages to varying degrees.

15. *Chicago Tribune* (October 20, 1994), Sec. 2, 8. See also Marcia Farr, "Biliteracy in the Home: Practices Among *Mexicano* Families in Chicago," in D. Spener (ed.), *Adult Biliteracy in the United States* (Washington, DC: Center for Applied Linguistics, 1994), 89–110.

16. Ada María Isasi-Díaz, "Pluralism," in Deck et al., eds., *Perspectives*, 25.

17. Denise De La Rosa and Carlyle E. Maw, *Hispanic Education: A Statistical Portrait* (Washington, DC: National Council of La Raza, 1990), i. Indeed, those who immigrate to the United States probably include Mexicans with the least education. The average Mexican has left school at age fourteen. Kevin Sullivan and Mary Jordan, "Mexico's Dropout Economy," *Washington Post* (November 24, 2003), Sec. A, 1, 15.

18. Alvarez, *op. cit.*, 5.

19. Hoge, *op. cit.*, 2.

57

20. Gary Goldbert, "Ingresos Hispanos, Los Peores de EE.UU.," *La Raza* (February 13, 1997), 8.

21. In 1997, 25.3 percent of Hispanics age 16 to 24 dropped out of high school, compared with 13.4 percent of blacks and 7.6 percent of whites. "Study: Hispanics Are More Likely to Drop Out of School," *Chicago Tribune* (March 16, 2000), Sec. 2, 3, 16.

22. K. J. Meier & J. J. Stewart, *The Politics of Hispanic Education: Un Paso Pa'lante y Dos Pa'tras* (Albany, NY: State University of New York Press, 1991), 162.

23. Kate N. Grosmann, "Magnets Not in Latino Areas: Study," *Chicago Sun-Times* (August 27, 2000), 12. However, as socioeconomic status of Hispanic students increased, "positive placement in classes, lower discipline rates, and greater high school completion rates were recorded."

24. William Claiborne, "Hispanic Education Gap Grows," *Lansing State Journal* (October 14, 1994), 4A. Pilsen's Benito Juarez high school lacked an athletic field for twelve years and is still missing an auditorium and lunchroom twenty-eight years after the school's inception. For years, scheduling students in three overlapping shifts made extracurricular activities nearly impossible.

25. Nancy Feyl Chavkin and Dora Lara Gonzalez, "Forging Partnerships Between Mexican American Parents and the Schools," *ERIC Digest* (October 1995), 2.

26. In 2002, the Tomas Rivera Policy Institute for Latino Education Excellence released a study showing that few Hispanic parents know how to orient their children toward higher education. Ana Beatriz Cholo, "Latinos Lag in College Knowledge," *Chicago Tribune* (December 13, 2002), Sec. 2, 3.

27. Ana Paul—in "Discriminación en la vivienda," *Exito* (November 21, 2002), 9—cites a study by the U.S. Department of Housing and Urban Development, *Discrimination in Housing*, 1989–2000.

28. Tara Gruzen and Steve Mills, "Mexicans Say Tradition at Risk in Housing Fight," *Chicago Tribune* (August 8, 1996), Sec. 1, 16.

29. *LatStat* (Chicago: Latino Institute, March, 1994), 3.

30. Data is based on a study by the Center for Neighborhood and Community Development at the University of Illinois at Chicago. Federal guidelines indicate that no more than 30 percent of a household's monthly income should be spent on rent and utilities; see "Unaffordable Rents in Pilsen," *Extra* (May 23, 1996), 3. In public housing, Hispanics have also suffered discrimination. In 1996, Latinos Unidos, a Hispanic advocacy organization, won a federal lawsuit against the Chicago Housing Authority (CHA) for not conducting outreach in Spanish, thus practically

excluding Hispanics from the waiting list. Thus, the court mandated CHA to integrate thousands of Hispanics in the existing waiting lists for apartments and produce all relevant forms in Spanish. In addition, it ordered the federal agency, Housing and Urban Development (HUD), to issue an additional 500 vouchers to Hispanic families for the federal Section 8 program, which subsidizes rents of poor people in private housing.

31. Infant mortality decreased in Pilsen from a rate of 10.3 in 1982–84 to 6.5 in 1992–1994, while the citywide rate also decreased from 17.5 to 13.1.

32. Hispanics lead the nation in the rate of teenage mothers, with 93 per 1,000 mothers, compared with 50 per 1,000 for non-Hispanics. Sue Ellen Christian and Teresa Puente, "En Contra de la Tendencia: Aumenta el Número de Embarazos entre Adolescentes Latinas," *Exito* (February 8, 2001), 7. See also Babara Vobejda and Amela Constable, "Hispanic Teens Rank First in Birthrate," *Washington Post* (February 13, 1998), A10.

33. "Casi 45 Millones Sin Seguro Médico," *Exito* (October 7, 1999), 10.

34. Cook County Hospital turns no one away, but it does try to collect payment, whether through insurance or private pay. Many are forced to ignore bills they cannot afford, while bill collectors have little success collecting from people with no assets. But most families take their financial obligation seriously, working out a payment plan that often requires years to pay.

35. Gruzen and Mills, *op. cit.*, 16.

36. Joel Millman, "Mexicans Are Home for Holidays, Bearing Gifts for Rural Economy," *Wall Street Journal* (December 30, 1998), A7.

37. Teresa Puente, "Hometown Heroes: Mexicans in U.S. Nourish Their Roots," *Chicago Tribune* (December 23, 1999), no Sec., 6.

38. Teresa Puente, "Culture Clash Complicates Latinas' Teen Years," *Chicago Tribune* (February 28, 1999), Sec. 1, 1.

39. In September 1999, the Chicago Crime Commission released a study indicating that of the estimated 100,000 gang members in Chicago, 16,000, approximately one in six, are girls, many of whom belong to female gangs affiliated with a men's counterpart. Margaret O'Brien, "At Least 16,000 Girls in Chicago's Gangs," *Chicago Tribune* (September 17, 1999), Sec. 2, 5. In 1992, the University of Chicago tested methods of reducing gang violence. They chose to study Pilsen's adjacent neighborhood, Little Village, and used Pilsen as a control group because they believed that Pilsen gangs were too numerous and too violent to achieve measurable success; Pilsen at the time had the highest rate of gang violence in Chicago. Irving A. Spergel and Susan F. Grossman, "The Little

Village Project: A Community Approach to the Gang Problem," *Social Work* 42:5 (September 1997): 456–70.

40. Cynthia L. Orosco, "Hispanics Are Targets for Handgun Violence," *The Tidings* (May 18, 2001), 13.

41. Jorge Oclander, "La Violencia es Una Esquina de Chicago," *La Raza* (November 21 1996), 8.

42. James Diego Vigil, *Barrio Gangs: Street Life and Identity in Southern California* (Austin: University of Texas Press, 1988), 36.

43. James Diego Vigil, *Personas Mexicanas: Chicago High Schoolers in a Changing Los Angeles* (Fort Worth, TX: Harcourt Brace). Quoted in James Diego Vigil, "Learning from Gangs: The Mexican American Experience," *ERIC Digest* (February 1997), 2.

44. Many Catholic churches are actively counteracting the misinterpretation of Catholic teaching. See Kathryn Casa, "Violence at Home: Faith Community New Frontline for Aiding Abused Women," *National Catholic Reporter* (June 29, 2001), 3–6.

45. Anna M. Santiago and Merry Morash, "Strategies for Serving Latina Battered Women," in *Urban Affairs Annual Review*, 42:219–20. This work provides an excellent survey of the literature on services for and involvement of Hispanic survivors of domestic violence.

3.

A Parish That's Building Community

St. Pius V is a community-building community. Community is a motivating concept and a force inspiring the parish. Community is a central theme in its preaching, teaching, and daily life. The parish attempts to implement the ideal of the Acts of the Apostles, which describes early Christians meeting in homes to pray, sharing food and the Eucharist, and reflecting on Christ's teachings. Since many Mexican immigrants already have had strong families, circles of friends, and a history of belonging to local communities, the parish builds on these inherited strengths.

A Catholic Parish, A Safe Haven

Upon arriving in a large urban area like Chicago, some Mexican immigrants are welcomed into extensive networks of family, or *paisanos*, from their hometown. Many, however, feel lost, trusting few, if any, people. Sometimes women slip into depression as they, more than their husbands, remain isolated in their homes. For them and others, the parish is a haven, often their only resource to deal with a myriad of challenges. They may first visit the parish in search of some assistance, whether food, clothing, employment, furniture, or friendship. They may gradually trust a neighbor or two, get to know others at family parties, develop new relationships of *compadrazgo*, and as their children begin catechism at the parish, meet new families. One story illustrates countless others. A family of five arrived in Chicago on a bitterly cold Sunday in January 1995; they came directly to the 4:30 p.m. Mass after a long, harrowing drive from Denver. Their car lacked license plates and insurance, and the driver, the father,

61

had no driver's license. The parents had been selling mangoes and cucumbers on the streets for more than a month when police attempted to extort payment for allowing them to continue selling. A choir member at St. Pius V took them in, and soon with the help of parish staff were settled in their own apartment, with food and furniture from the parish, and a helping hand from parishioners in finding a job.

Inner-city parishes differ substantially from suburban parishes because people come to the former for every kind of need. Whether to find a lawyer, buy a house, locate a doctor, reconcile a spouse, deal with a gang, locate a loved one, or find a job, the church is their haven. A Mexican immigrant parish gets involved in all facets of people's lives not only because people have limited resources to solve their problems and little knowledge of the American system but because they generally trust the church and respect it for its service to the poor and needy.

Unfortunately, rather than offering the safe haven Hispanics expect, some priests resist incorporating them into their parishes. In 1999, a national study reported Hispanics are twice as likely as other Catholics to worship in "separate and unequal settings."[1] Unwilling to learn Spanish, some clergy defend themselves, declaring, "Let them learn English." They not only do not understand the difficulty of learning English for newly arrived immigrants but, they also fail to appreciate the relationship between language and faith and, consequently, miss the importance of celebrating liturgies and offering religious education in Spanish. For most Mexicans, Spanish is their mother tongue, the language in which they learned to pray, relate to family, and now wish to worship and celebrate family. For this reason, the Catholic bishops of the United States have recognized Spanish as an official liturgical language, declaring that for the Catholic Church, Spanish is not a foreign language.[2]

Priests offer many excuses for not ministering to Hispanics. Some deny many live in their area; others claim they cannot add a Sunday liturgy in Spanish because their schedule of Masses is already full or no Spanish-speaking priest is available to preside at one. Some priests learn to read the Mass prayers in Spanish, but because they do not speak the language, provide little or no pastoral ministry for their Spanish-speaking parishioners. Some claim they do not deny social services to Hispanics, but because they have no one to speak Spanish at the parish door, few Hispanics ever ring the bell. Some priests, skeptical of Hispanics' financial commitment to the church, limit their services to those who have registered at the parish and made weekly donations in envelopes for six months.

When Mexicans are not welcomed with open arms by the church they love, they are scandalized. When priests tell them, "You should go to your own parish," meaning one where services are provided in Spanish, they are deeply offended. Although they understand racism in society at large, they cannot fathom their own church discriminating against them. Many Mexican Catholics, suffering this rejection with a heavy heart, are forced to travel outside their neighborhood to find a parish willing to baptize their children, celebrate the fifteenth birthday of their daughter, or arrange a wedding.

But Mexicans have their limits. On Easter 1997, at a parish on Chicago's far west side, Mexicans exploded at the noon Mass when the pastor refused to open the balcony to accommodate the large crowd. Outraged by what they considered one more insult in a long history of discrimination, some Mexicans took over the pulpit, interrupting the Mass, to demand the balcony be opened. The pastor refused, claiming the balcony would not withstand the crowd. After considerable shouting back and forth, the priest left the altar, turned off the lights, and went home.[3] Eventually the pastor was removed, and Spanish-speaking priests from the Salesian Order replaced him.

While this protest was exceptional, the abuse against which it was directed is unfortunately far too common. Since the 1980s, many Hispanic immigrants have arrived in Chicago's suburbs, creating pockets of poor people within parishes of affluent suburbanites. As a result, churches like Mission Juan Diego sprout up, attracting Hispanics who prefer to travel great distances to welcoming churches rather than suffer rejection at their local parish. Ezéquiel Sánchez, archdiocesan director of Hispanic ministry, commented in 2000, "A lot of people are not very welcoming toward Hispanics, and, consequently, Mission Juan Diego ends up being an island of refuge for them. It's their own place."[4]

Mexicans also feel alienated in churches that lack the decoration and adornment found in churches in Mexico. They look for the image of Our Lady of Guadalupe, statues of their favorite saints, rows of candles, and Hispanic music. Churches that welcome Mexicans by incorporating their culture are quickly rewarded. For years, the pastor of one Chicago parish refused to permit a Mass in Spanish. Although claiming to be ideologically opposed to learning Spanish, he finally succumbed to pressure from the growing number of Mexican parishioners to allow a Mass in Spanish on the feast of Our Lady of Guadalupe in 1997. When more than 1,000 people attended, the pastor felt pressured to inaugurate a regular Sunday Mass in Spanish, which from the beginning exceeded the combined attendance of the three other Masses in English.[5] Within a year, he agreed to schedule a second Sunday Mass in Spanish that added even more parishioners to his membership and increased his revenues. Once a parish welcomes Hispanics, it may be overwhelmed by their response and be transformed into a vibrant community of faith.

Mexican Immigrants and Community

Mexican immigrants' predisposition to community stems from a number of sources. Many are from small villages, or *ranchos*, with a population under 5,000, where they experienced community among family and friends, living closely together and participating in the same parish. Nearly everyone is baptized and belongs to the Catholic Church even though some participate only occasionally in church activities. Many, though not blood relatives, are members of one another's extended families. Many communities also retain vestiges of indigenous community life, upholding communal ownership of land, local dialects, and native songs, dance, and dress.

Immigrants from urban areas in Mexico have different experiences of community and church. In larger towns, called *pueblos*, Catholic churches tend to be clustered downtown. Unlike in the

United States, participation in a Mexican urban parish is usually not based on the geographical proximity of one's residence to a church. On Sundays, people often attend different churches, depending on the feast day or their interest in shopping at a local market, eating at a nearby restaurant, or visiting a family member in the neighborhood. Consequently, many Mexican immigrants do not readily identify with a particular parish. Few comprehend the notion of "belonging to" or being a "member" of a parish. One frequently hears: "As a baptized Catholic, I belong to every Catholic church." Moreover, they frequently fear that "joining a parish" will subject them to financial demands or, if they are undocumented, to scrutiny of their immigration status.

Despite differences in small-town and urban living, Mexican culture fosters a sense of and a desire for community. Above all else, Mexicans want to live in equality and harmony with others. When Mexican immigrants are asked what needs to be improved at St. Pius V, they invariably respond "greater unity" (*más unidad*). To them, unity means cooperation, equality, and mutual respect. They recognize that differences will occur, but they want them aired openly and honestly so that unity is preserved. They are incensed when parish groups criticize one another or fail to support one another's activities. For events involving the whole parish, there is a high expectation that all groups participate amicably and enthusiastically.

Mexicans' sense of community is reflected in the strong tradition of *compadrazgo*, a social system that expands the nuclear family to an extended family. *Compadrazgo* not only strengthens the family but reinforces the community by extending the nuclear family through a broad network of godparents (*padrinos* and *madrinas*), with whom parents commit to form a lifelong relationship of mutual support. The most common and important way to form *compadrazgo* relationships is by inviting others to be godparents of children at baptism. Ada María Isasi-Díaz notes:

> To engage with us (Mexicans), Americans belonging to the dominant group...must reach beyond the liberal insistence on individualism, now bordering on recalcitrant self-centeredness. This is all the more urgent

65

given the importance of community and family in Hispanic culture. Community for us is so central that we understand personhood as necessarily including relationship with some form of community. Family has to do not only with those to whom we are immediately related or related only by blood; it is a multilayered structure constituted by all those who care, all those to whom we feel close, who share our interests, commitments, understandings, and to whom we will always remain faithful.[6]

Gary Riebe-Estrella, SVD, notes that the concept of *el pueblo* (the people) reflects a fundamental category in Hispanic self-identity—a sociocentric culture in which the basic unit of society is the group, primarily the family. Individiual identity emerges from membership in the group, whereas in egocentric cultures, such as the United States, the fundamental unit of society is the individual. Riebe-Estrella also notes that Hispanic sociocentric culture is organic, constantly evolving as the family grows through marriage and *compadrazgo*. Even friends may be included as family members because family is the primary paradigm for all relationships. In egocentric cultures, relationships tend to be based primarily on contractual agreements among individuals, as peoplehood is created through the voluntary association of free individuals who bind together for mutual benefit and reserve the right to dissociate when they choose.

The English language lacks an adequate word to translate *el pueblo*. While in Spanish it refers only to the collective, both people and town and usually to the masses of the lower classes, in English, "people" refers to individuals as well as to a group. Mexicans take pride in belonging to *el pueblo* because the collective, no matter how poor or uneducated, possesses a dignity worthy of respect. Since *el pueblo* takes on this mystique, people often speak as though *el pueblo* thinks and acts with one mind and heart, reflecting their desire for unity among all. Mexican immigrants are commonly scandalized when one of their own exploits or mistreats another, for this lack of solidarity amounts to a sin against *el pueblo*.

El pueblo is also used for a town or small city. Mexicans are proud not only of their country but of their town and state. Language, customs, music, dress, and food vary from region to region and help people identify among themselves. A common ritual at community events involves people cheering in friendly competition as the names of their respective states are shouted out. They are proud if someone from their region succeeds, and are more likely to talk to or reach out to someone from their home state, like finding distant family relations. Since small towns in Latin America are often coincident with the geographical boundaries of a parish, it is no surprise that Hispanics also use *el pueblo* to designate their identity as church, similar to Vatican II's usage of the "People of God."[7]

Another indication revealing the importance of community in Mexican culture is the people's love of large crowds—the larger, the better. On certain feast days—Passion (Palm) Sunday, Ash Wednesday, Easter, and Our Lady of Guadalupe—St. Pius V church is filled far beyond capacity as people stand along the walls and fill the aisles. Most Americans would complain about the inconvenience of "mobs," but Mexicans are exhilarated by the experience. Children in Pilsen frequently cite the annual summer street festival, *Fiesta del Sol*, which draws hundreds of thousands of visitors to the area, as a source of pride in their neighborhood. A crowd helps everyone feel one with *el pueblo*.

Mexican immigrants also band together to live more comfortably among their own and to deal more effectively with challenges in their strange new world. In their own neighborhoods, they experience their culture, freely speak their language, savor their ethnic foods, are recognized on the street, and greet neighbors along the way. They feel at home. When he retired to a new suburban home Humberto bemoaned, "I can watch out my window nearly all day and not see anyone walk by my home, whereas in Pilsen, I saw most of my neighbors and many friends pass by my house every day."

As previously noted, another force that brings Mexican immigrants together in homogeneous neighborhoods is the discrimination and rejection they experience from the non-Hispanic world. One year, during the novena of Our Lady of Guadalupe, oppression was selected as the theme for discussion. People reflected on oppression during three historical periods: biblical times, the colonial era of the Virgin of Guadalupe, and contemporary society. When asked if they had experienced discrimination and oppression, most participants had plenty to say about the injustices they encounter in the United States. They recounted the demeaning conditions under which they work, abusive treatment by landlords, and racial discrimination in stores, banks, and governmental offices. These experiences help forge among them a common identity and solidarity, which are foundational pillars of community.

Forging Unity Amid Diversity

The Christian faith envisions a communal life. Christ calls people to a life of sharing and caring in community, and the church exists to facilitate this process. Creating community in a large urban parish, however, is a challenge. First, it is difficult to create a sense of community among a large number of people. Most parishioners are interested in and capable of knowing only a limited number of people in a parish. Second, today's urban environment, plagued by high rates of mobility, violence, and crime, hardly foster open communication and mutual trust among neighbors. Since building community requires that people develop and maintain relationships, St. Pius V developed an organizational structure to facilitate lay participation and thus strengthen community. This chapter focuses on (1) building ministerial organizations, (2) developing a broad-based parish council, (3) celebrating festivals on the street and at parish dances, (4) sponsoring and celebrating meals, and (5) organizing parish days of reflection. It then examines the way in which the parish finances its ministries.

Building Ministerial Organization

Over the years, St. Pius V developed various committees and parish organizations to facilitate ministries so that people can serve and be served in an atmosphere of loving care. While joining their efforts in ministry, participants form community among themselves. In addition to Christian Base Communities, discussed in the next chapter, parish organizations and ministerial groups include the Charismatic Renewal, Guadalupe Group, St. Jude Thaddeus Group, social service workers, liturgical ministers, catechists, choirs, pre-Cana and family ministers, youth ministers and parents' council, members of women's groups, visitors of the sick, leadership trainers, the finance committee, and parish council. Each group carries out specific ministries in coordination with others and the parish staff and participates in fund-raising to help support its respective activities and the parish as a whole.

Since 1983, the Charismatic Renewal, a strong organization within the parish, is part of a lay movement officially recognized by and integrally connected to the church hierarchy. It provides a form of prayer different from that traditionally celebrated at parish liturgies and offers many opportunities for lay involvement. About twenty *servidores*, or active ministers, of the group meet each Friday night for their "vigil," consisting of prayer and planning of the group's activities, particularly the following night's "circle of prayer," an open prayer session attended by approximately a hundred people. At these sessions, the *servidores* read the scriptures, preach, listen to testimonies of God's work in their lives, and pray for healing. Occasionally a priest presides at a eucharistic liturgy for the participants. The *servidores* annually elect their leaders after a morning of evaluation of the previous year's activities, conducted with the pastor's participation. In many ways, the group functions like a small Christian Base Community. They share their faith and support one another by visiting one another's homes, celebrating birthdays, counseling and assisting one another in times of trial, and working together on parish projects. Many people suffering from depression, serious illness, addictions, and emotional stress seek out the *servidores* to find healing through prayer, and later many find professional assistance from parish counselors and integrate into the parish community. Thus, the group effectively fulfills an evangelizing or outreach function for the parish.

Like other lay movements in the Catholic Church, the Charismatic Renewal has a strong diocesan organization that commands allegiance from its members, at times appearing to supersede their commitment to the local parish. Problems occur in some parishes where members of the Renewal separate from the rest of the parish, at times operating autonomously from the pastor. Sometimes members create division within the parish because they interpret their experience of a second conversion or encounter with Christ as the only true experience of the Lord. They unwittingly create the impression they are closer to God than other parishioners. The parish council works to prevent these separatist and elitist tendencies by involving the Charismatic Renewal in common parish activities. They cook and serve food at the parish street festivals, take their turn serving *menudo* (hot tripe soup) on Sunday mornings in the church basement, take up biweekly collections for the parish, serve in most liturgical ministries, organize four weekend parish retreats, and offer a basic course on evangelization for newcomers interested in their style of formation. Moreover, the pastor stays involved with the group's activities, guiding them theologically and organizationally.

To advance lay involvement in the ministry of social service, a group of volunteers *(servidores sociales)* was formed in 1987. The group chooses its own officers each year and raises funds to assist its clients. They visit homes of needy families, staff the parish food pantry, organize the annual Christmas giving program, and distribute funds to families facing financial crises, such as evictions or shutoffs of gas and light. To assist them in their ministry, they received training in home visiting and case management. They organize two annual rummage sales and dances, and at both summer street fairs manage the raffles. Like the Charismatic Renewal, the *servidores sociales* share much more than just their ministries: they gather for celebrations and mutual support, forming community among themselves.

As social ministries expanded in the parish, another group formed, consisting of volunteers working in the parish soup kitchen and secondhand store. These volunteers, often including needy people who offer service in exchange for some parish assistance, develop a strong attachment to one another as they serve other needy families. Some of them join other parish groups while continuing to serve as social service volunteers.

Several years after the formation of the *servidores sociales*, a number of parishioners formed the Guadalupe Group to promote devotion to Our Lady of Guadalupe. A Guadalupe group is usually the first group organized by Mexicans entering a parish. At St. Pius V, this group not only helped to develop ministry but to promote a small community within the larger community. The members organized a weekly rosary and prayer vigil on the twelfth day of each month to honor Our Lady of Guadalupe and the annual celebration of the Guadalupe novena. They raise funds for the novena expenses by organizing dances and selling *menudo* in the church basement. On Fridays in May, they organize a traditional devotion in which young children dressed in white present a flower to the Virgin and pray the rosary. Under the direction of dedicated leaders, the group grew in numbers as well as in fundraising ability and thus began supporting other parish projects, such as the installation of a new baptismal font, new tables and chairs for the church hall, and a new sound system for the church.

Other groups of ministers formed during the years covered by this book are discussed in later chapters, but it is important to note them here. From parenting classes, a group called *Esperanza Familiar* (Family Hope) was formed to promote sound parenting and family activities within the parish. A large number of liturgical ministers, numbering more than 125 people, were trained and organized according to their specific ministries and the Sunday Mass they serve. In response to an initiative among communion ministers, a group of visitors of the sick was organized. The youth program expanded greatly in the mid-1990s and made its presence felt in the parish in a variety of ways. In response to an archdiocesan initiative, interested parishioners formed a group to work on issues related to racism. Parents of children in the parish school work together on the Parish School Board to assist the principal in designing policy and raising funds. Women seeking help for domestic violence formed support groups. Because some of them wanted to give something back to the parish as well as do something for themselves, they formed a group to decorate the church for weddings and *quinceañeras* and the church hall for special parish events. Catechists who teach the faith to children and those who prepare parents and godparents for baptism also formed ministerial groups. Parishioners who felt they had benefited so much from different parish programs formed a team to offer leadership training to other parishioners. In 2000, a pre-Cana group was established among couples trained in parish parenting classes in order to prepare engaged couples for marriage, and parents of children involved in the parish youth center formed a parents' council to guide the center's activities and support their children. The coordinators of small Christian Base Communities formed another ministerial group to support one another and plan activities in their respective small communities. All these ministerial groups provide an organizational structure that fosters lay participation and offers parishioners multiple opportunities to form relationships and build community.

The Parish Council

A parish council, a product of Vatican II's emphasis on collegiality, provides parishioners with the opportunity to participate in the overall direction of the parish's ministry and administration. In 1986, an advisory group of parishioners planned a new parish council to coordinate parish activities and strengthen community. The advisers designed a parish council composed of approximately twenty-five representatives of parish groups. Only people representing a parish constituency officially sit on the council, although it is always open to observers. Each group elects its own representatives, and the pastor appoints no one. The council, which meets bimonthly, best reflects the vision of a parish as a community of communities because representatives of all the small communities and organizations are involved.

The parish council members show little interest in dealing with traditional administrative matters affecting the parish, such as hiring new staff, approving the budget, or installing a new roof. Because council members feel they have access to the pastor and his staff, who respect their opinions and suggestions, there is no power struggle at council meetings. Perhaps Mexicans' traditional deference to clergy motivates them to leave administrative affairs to the pastor and concern themselves with matters such as improving parish services and raising funds for parish operations. The parish council has pursued the following parish goals it developed with the staff:

1. Increase parishioners' ownership of and participation in parish life.
2. Raise sufficient funds to support parish activities.
3. Develop more trained leaders to take responsibility for activities and programs.
4. Reach out to the unchurched or barely active, for example, English-speaking Hispanics.
5. Promote greater parish involvement in social justice.
6. Strengthen family life.
7. Work collaboratively with other parishes and organizations in the area.
8. Promote Christian Base Communities as the fundamental structure of the parish.
9. Strengthen the role of women in the parish.[8]

Celebrating Community through Festivals and Dances

Community emerges not only from the celebration of eucharistic liturgies and participation in committees but also from festivals and meals. The spirit of fiesta is integral to the Mexican soul, and central to the culture. They hardly need an excuse to organize a fiesta, which is more than a party. Roberto Goizueta, a noted Cuban-American theologian, writing about the Christian theological anthropology of fiesta, observes that the fiesta is a communal act of commemoration of the past that is experienced in the celebrated present and anticipates the promised future. More than simple merriment, the fiesta is ultimately an act of thanksgiving for the gift of life, a human response for a gift received. Because it normally has a certain structure, requiring significant preparation, it is both play and work, and because it

73

does not produce a product or accomplish something beyond the celebration itself, it is prophetic, subverting the modern idea of the human person as an active historical agent. Fiestas celebrate "being" rather than "doing." "What lies at the heart of the Latino affinity for festive celebration is not necessarily a happier, warmer, or more easygoing *temperament*, but a fundamentally different *understanding* of the human and, specifically, of the nature of human activity in the world."[9] Furthermore, the fiesta celebrates people's shared life in community, a quasi-liturgical act, whether a religious or civil celebration, performed in public, usually according to a prescribed ritual. Not only is everyone welcome, but all participants are recognized as equals, thereby making fiestas additionally subversive, countering the capitalist notion of a utilitarian community born of competitive individualism.

Octavio Paz, a Nobel laureate and renowned Mexican poet and essayist, wrote in his *Labyrinth of Solitude* that many fiestas, whether social, political, or religious, also reflect the deep Mexican need to compensate for loneliness. Two decades earlier, Samuel Ramos, a Mexican philosopher, noted that Mexicans compensate for their lack of economic or political power by organizing the noisiest fiesta possible, as though reaffirming their existence, generating a sensation of power and a feeling of exhilaration at least for a day. Undoubtedly, celebrating fiestas in a foreign land is doubly important for a people who daily experience discrimination.[10] St. Pius V rejoices and revels in the fiesta spirit.

In 1989, the parish council organized the first summer street fair, patterned on the Mexican *kermess*, which gathers the community for a fiesta in the street, including food of every variety, games for children, and music and dancing. The annual event soon took on an importance greater than anyone ever dreamed, and its fund-raising goal became secondary. The council decided that all parish groups and small communities should work on the *kermess* as a symbol of parish unity and cooperation and reach out to the broader, unchurched community. The youth group runs games for teenagers; the catechists organize activities for small children; the Charismatic Renewal manages the *lotería* (a Mexican bingo-like game) and prepares and serves hot soups (*menudo* and *posole*) and tamales; different Christian Base Communities and the women's groups staff other food booths; volunteers are added to the regular crew in the parish soup kitchen to prepare food; the *servidores sociales* run the raffles, while the choir serves beverages. People donate prizes for the games, food to sell, and money to help support the event. On the weekend of the *kermess*, people come from far and wide to savor the food and dance to live music played by Mexican bands blasting familiar rhythms from giant loudspeakers down the sultry summer night streets.[11] The *kermess* in June became so successful that within a few years the parish council added a second *kermess* in August. Throughout the year, people refer to the *kermess* as the grand parish event where everyone is present, working together to build community.

Other social events also bring people together in community. The *servidores sociales* was the first group interested in organizing a parish dance to raise funds for their programs aiding the poor. The Guadalupe Group then sponsored dances to support the celebration of the novena of Our Lady of Guadalupe. Families have little opportunity for entertainment together outside the home, as most local dance halls are for adults only. Parish dances attract the entire family, including small children, babies in portable cribs, teenagers, adults, and seniors; small children dart among couples on the dance floor as moms and dads teach their little ones how to dance. In time, other parish groups, such as the youth, catechists, and school parents, began sponsoring dances as fund-raisers and community-builders. Thus, parish dances now number seven per year, with parishioners supporting one another by selling tickets for one another's events.

Teenagers attend parish dances in droves. Because the Pilsen neighborhood can be dangerous at night, some parents do not allow their children to go out except to attend a dance at St. Pius V. In the late 1980s and early 1990s, the youth preferred disco music played by a DJ during the breaks between live Mexican music. At times, a quiet generational struggle was waged over which kind of music should be played until a new dance craze arrived in 1994. At that time, Mexican youth latched on to the latest dance fad from Los Angeles and Mexico, the *quebradita*. This popular Mexican dance is most enjoyed when presented by a *banda*, a group of ten musicians playing wind, brass, and drums, replicating the "down-home" sound from *ranchos* in Mexico. Men don western-style clothing, including leather vests and bandannas, usually tightly tied on the head underneath black cowboy hats. The girls wear miniskirts, vests, and shirts with leather fringe. With the arrival of *quebradita* music, parents and teens began enthusiastically enjoying the same music. As people gyrate to the music, a sense of Mexican pride fills the hall.

Sharing Meals in the Parish Community

Celebrating community is incomplete without sharing food, an effective symbol of and creative force for community. Three meals institutionalized at St. Pius V are the Sunday breakfast, the Passover seder meal, and the annual picnic. After Sunday Masses, many worshipers visit the church basement for a typical Mexican breakfast of *menudo*, a "morning-after" soup made from beef stomach and ox feet, seasoned with garlic, *guajillo* and *ancho* chilis, and thickened with hominy. Since most Mexicans prefer a *picante* (spicy) dish, raw, chopped jalapeno peppers and onions are usually added, as well as fresh lime to cut the greasy texture and soften the harshness of the chilis. Oregano is sprinkled on top for additional flavor. Preparing a bowl of *menudo* becomes a ritual itself.[12] Although the Guadalupe Group began serving *menudo* in October to raise funds for the annual Guadalupe novena, parishioners soon asked for the service to continue year round. When the *Guadalupanos* needed a rest, the parish Charismatic Renewal generously agreed to prepare and serve the *menudo*, and later a new organization, the St. Jude Thaddeus Group, formed specifically to share the work.[13] Gradually, other dishes, such as *gorditas, tostadas*, and tamales, were added to the menu. Soon other parish groups, such as the youth, social service volunteers, and catechists, requested the opportunity to serve *menudo* to raise funds for their activities. Thus, the *menudo* breakfast became an institutional part of parish community life on Sunday mornings.

In the mid-1980s, a Jewish woman on staff emphasized the importance of the seder meal during Passover, and soon the parish instituted the meal on Tuesday of Holy Week. Parish

ministers and their families as well as candidates to receive the
sacraments at the Easter Vigil are invited to a formal candlelit
meal, partly to thank them for their service and partly to celebrate and educate them in sacred history. The first seder, a relatively small affair involving only twenty people, expanded over
the years into the church basement, where now more than 225
guests participate. The staff of the soup kitchen prepares the
seder meal while different ministry groups set the tables and
serve the meal. The evening begins with everyone dancing a
Jewish line dance in a huge circle. One family from the parish
serves as the hosts, reading official texts and leading prayers
that recall the liberation of the Jews from slavery. Each table is
set with the proper ritual foods, a candle, wine, and grape juice.
The parish choir leads the singing of traditional Jewish songs.
During the meal, a child opens an outside door, symbolizing the
community's open invitation to the poor. One year a homeless
man was standing outside just as the door opened. To everyone's amazement, the child returned with a real, live poor person, who, of course, was warmly welcomed to the table.
Following the meal, the children search for the traditional
afrikomen (small pieces of matza) hidden throughout the hall,
and the lucky finders receive prizes. As the evening ends, everyone joins in to clean the hall.

The summer picnic, organized in the 1970s by a handful of
parishioners, is another parish event involving food that builds
community. When the Christian Base Communities formed in
1987, they shared the responsibility for organizing the day with
the parish youth group. Parishioners with little opportunity to
get out of the neighborhood took advantage of this parish out-
ing to enjoy a day with their families and expand their acquaintances in the parish. The picnic became more and more popular
as years progressed. In recent times, in addition to private cars
and vans, the parish orders six buses to accommodate hundreds
of picnickers. Upon arriving at the picnic, all gather to celebrate
the Eucharist. For the Liturgy of the Word, people reflect in
small groups on the scripture readings of the day and then share
their conclusions in the assembly. Organizers emphasize the
need to share what everyone brings by creating a common area

to barbeque and a community table for food. Families still gather among themselves, but they also share the food they have prepared. The afternoon is spent playing volleyball and soccer and swimming in the lake.

For Mexicans, sharing food helps create and celebrate community. Indeed, to guarantee the success of any parish event, it is always best to include food. People enjoy sweet rolls and coffee at evening meetings. Days of reflection for liturgical ministries conclude with sharing of food. Retreats organized by the Charismatic Renewal always provide a delicious hot meal for lunch. Food is a necessity at parish dances, and first communion Sunday services conclude with a reception where cake, cookies, and hot chocolate are abundant. By providing food for every kind of gathering, the parish imitates what Mexican families do at home: share food with family and friends and any unexpected visitor.

Parish Days of Reflection

To strengthen community among pastoral ministers, the staff organizes one or two annual days of recollection at which participants focus on common efforts and renew their commitments to work together in the parish. A key to success involves a simple process of sharing something that helps participants know one another at a deeper level. In small groups, people share a bit of their personal history or views on things in the parish, their family, or the community. The dimension of faith is always central to the day's reflection. Reports from small groups are gathered, shared with the entire assembly, and included in the closing liturgy. Of course, there is always a hearty meal of Mexican food at noon, as well as time for singing and joke-telling, which lift the spirits and forge unity amidst laughter. The dynamics of the days of recollection build solidarity among people in diverse ministries, as well as rekindle enthusiasm for their respective ministries. Most important, people learn to appreciate one another more for who they are than for what they do in the community.

A Rich Church of the Poor

A parish community, although called to live the poverty of Jesus, needs money to operate. Some inner-city pastors are hesitant to ask their parishioners for financial assistance, believing they are too poor to support their church. Consequently, their parishes barely function. But the poor are the church, as much as the wealthy, and they are capable of building strong communities, albeit in their own ways.

Most St. Pius V parishioners understand the importance of supporting their community. Their experience in Mexico taught them how to be responsible for their local parish. They often erected or remodeled their churches by contributing labor or organizing fund-raising activities. Even in Chicago, many Mexicans work hard to raise money to maintain their parishes back home.

Clergy who discourage Hispanics from joining their parishes, fearing they will not contribute financially, make a big mistake. Mexican immigrants are very generous. Study after study has demonstrated that the poor, including Hispanics, are more generous than the rich, giving a substantially higher proportion of their income to charity. However, many Mexicans need to see the specific needs of their church and experience it as theirs before sharing their limited funds. Allan Figueroa Deck, a Mexican American theologian, comments:

> Hispanics give generously to the church *when they know that the church is with them.* The key to fund-raising is developing a healthy personal relationship with the people. Anyone familiar with funding and development in Hispanic countries knows that their standards are much different from ours in the United States. Works begin well *before* the money is in hand. They develop slowly....*Seeing* the work actually moving forward is very important to Hispanics. Neat projections, drawings, and plans leave them cold. They want to see the action....A fundamental impasse occurs, then, when pastoral projects and decisions are predicated on "having the money."[14]

79

St. Pius V successfully employed this strategy when tuck-pointing its church building. Stretching out the project over a month allowed parishioners to observe its progress, to see the scaffolding go up, and to note how different the walls looked before and after tuck-pointing. The extended process gave parishioners more time to appreciate the work and to find the disposable income to contribute to the project.

Providing financial support to the church has not been a major part of Mexican tradition, however. Since the Spanish Conquest, Latin Americans have experienced the Catholic Church as a wealthy institution, staffed largely by foreign missionaries who live more affluently than their congregants. To the extent that Mexicans view the church as foreign and rich, they find it difficult to understand why it needs their paltry contributions for salaries, utilities, and maintenance. Moreover, because Latin American Catholics in larger cities generally do not "register" or "belong" to a specific parish, many often do not see maintaining the church as their responsibility. Making regular contributions by using Sunday envelopes is something totally new because they are accustomed to making offerings for specific services—for prayers offered, a home visit, a funeral, or the blessing of a car.

On the other hand, upon seeing a specific human need, Mexicans are eager to help. When Santiago, a Mexican baby, came to Chicago for brain surgery, St. Pius V parishioners contributed generously for his medical expenses. When religious sisters from Mexico come seeking financial assistance to restore a church destroyed by an earthquake or to support their work among the poor, parishioners dig deeply into their pockets, often contributing more than in the regular collection. This spirit of generosity also surfaces whenever the poor come with special needs, for example, a destitute family trying to bury the body of a deceased relative. Because it is important for Mexicans to know how their donations will be used and because of their compassion and generosity toward the poor, St. Pius V began announcing before each Sunday collection that 10 percent of the donations were for a specific need, such as the soup kitchen, the legal aid clinic, the men's shelter, or counseling for victims of domestic violence. The increased specificity and human interest of these announcements resulted in larger Sunday collections.

Mexicans genuinely want to make an offering when they receive services. They do not consider their contribution a payment but an offering to God for a blessing, a vigil light, or the celebration of a Mass. For example, men visiting a priest to make a *juramento* (pledge) not to drink alcohol for a certain period often leave a donation as part of their commitment. To refuse that offering offends them.

Mexicans have a history of tithing. In Mexico many of their parents gave the church a portion of their income, called the *diezmo*, meaning one tenth of one's income, or harvest, as outlined in the biblical text of Leviticus. Many rural families contribute livestock, produce, and/or money at harvest time to fulfill their *diezmo*. In some places, people bring the local priest the first egg laid in a week.

Consequently, on a Sunday in fall, St. Pius V celebrates the *diezmo* with everyone walking in procession to the front of church to deposit their weekly contribution. The ceremony, preceded by a brief homily about the meaning of *diezmo*, helps people understand and celebrate their responsibility to return something to God and support the parish. On several subsequent Sundays, different parishioners speak about their experience at St. Pius V and encourage others to actively participate in and financially support parish ministries. They urge the use of Sunday envelopes for a minimum donation of one hour's earnings per week. Each year, the number of regular envelope users increases as parishioners learn the importance of regular giving.

Because of their low-paying jobs and unstable employment and because many lack savings accounts, parishioners are frequently reluctant to pledge a specific amount for the future. Smaller, more frequent efforts to raise money reap greater benefits than occasional requests for larger amounts. Poor people have little disposable income at any one time and, consequently, are more willing and able to donate smaller amounts more frequently. Thus, the parish conducts raffles, sells *menudo*, organizes *kermesses*, and sponsors periodic dances, all generating considerable revenue for the parish.

In a poor parish, there is not much money to be invested or managed by the staff, nor do parishioners have much experience in handling finances beyond their household. Still, it is important to involve parishioners in financial matters to the extent they are able and interested. The parish finance committee reviews the annual financial report and budget, which are sent to the archdiocese and to parishioners. Because the parish has never faced a financial crisis, the committee is generally supportive of the pastor's financial plans and reports. However, because committee members are interested in increasing income, they work to develop ways to increase financial support among parishioners.

In the inner city, pastors respond differently to demands to serve the poor. Some fear beginning services such as a food pantry, because the demand may grow out of hand. For them, it is better not to raise unrealistic expectations. Other pastors think that providing many services will overtax their overextended staff. One pastor restricts community activities in the church hall because they increase his maintenance costs. Offering services, however, creates opportunities to touch people in their moment of need. At St. Pius V this spirit inspired the opening of a soup kitchen, a secondhand clothing store, a legal aid office, a religious goods gift shop, an overnight shelter, a youth center, a family counseling program, and a program for victims of domestic violence. People in need remember the assistance extended to them and return the kindness with faithful commitment to the parish. Although serving the poor stimulates even more demands for services, it also attracts additional funding from those who want to help the poor. Because a principal source of funds for St. Pius V is people living outside the parish who are interested in supporting its work, the staff developed a mailing list and four times a year sends them information about the parish and a request for financial support. News about the parish's efforts, particularly feeding the hungry, clothing the naked, welcoming the stranger, and sheltering the homeless, have encouraged generous donations, enabling the parish to establish three endowment funds to support scholarships at the parish school and salaries for youth ministers and pastoral counselors. In 2003, the parish hired a part-time fund-raiser to assist the staff in writing proposals for grants to private foundations.

The structures and activities described above helped create and celebrate community at St. Pius V. Some developed later than others, some with more initiative from the staff than the community; some changed over time, taking on new dimensions as people matured in their faith and experience. As time passes, these structures, programs, and activities need to be evaluated, renewed, and perhaps replaced. Communities of people are vibrant, living bodies that will die if left stagnant. As immigrants assimilate into the United States and first-generation Mexican Americans become the majority, many changes will inevitably occur. If the community is actively reflecting on its needs and experience, it will determine the time for change and the shape of new activities and structures it needs to create.

Notes

1. The National Conference of Catholic Bishops (NCCB) concluded in 1999 that Hispanics are often segregated from other Roman Catholics in United States parishes. "Catholic Study Decries Hispanic 'Segregation,'" *Chicago Tribune* (March 12, 1999), Sec. 1, 14.
2. Rosa María Icaza, CCVI, "Hispanics in Our Midst: A Problem or a Blessing?" *Liturgy 90* (November–December 1998), 5.
3. "Church's Easter Standoff Uncovers Deeper Wounds," *Chicago Tribune* (April 7, 1997), Sec. 1, 1. Parishioners accused the pastor of refusing to allow Spanish catechism classes in parish schoolrooms, of dismissing the Hispanic deacon from his position at the parish, and of refusing to allow the Spanish choir to sing for certain services.
4. Dan Mihalopoulos, "It's Mission Accomplished at Unique Palatine Church," *Chicago Tribune* (February 23, 2000), Sec. 1, 3.
5. Subsequently, the pastor wrote to his local bishop, acknowledging his mistake and recognizing the contribution that St. Pius V and St. Agnes parishes had made in training the lay people who develop ministry to Mexicans in his parish.
6. Ada María Isasi-Díaz, "Pluralism," in Deck et al., *Perspectives*, 25.
7. Gary Riebe-Estrella, SVD, "*Pueblo* and Church," in Orlando O. Espín and Miguel H. Díaz, eds., *From the Heart of Our People* (Maryknoll, NY: Orbis Press, 1999), 172–88. Riebe-Estrella provides an illuminating reflection on the role and importance of *el pueblo* for Hispanics. See also Roberto S. Goizueta, "The Symbolic World of Mexican American

Religion," in Timothy Matovina and Gary Riebe-Estrella, SVD, eds., *Horizons of the Sacred: Mexican Traditions in U.S. Catholicism* (Ithaca, NY: Cornell University Press, 2002), 119–39. Goizueta analyzes how Mexican culture subverts major dichotomies, such as individual/community, material/spiritual, public/private, and life/death.

8. "St. Pius V Parish Goals," February 1991.

9. Roberto S. Goizueta, "Fiesta: Life in the Subjunctive," in Espin and Díaz, *op. cit.*, 90.

10. Pablo Helguera, "Twice as Exciting: For Mexicans Here, the 'Fiesta' Is a Complex Ritual," *Exito* (July 30, 1998), 11–12. Helguera offers some of the ideas in this paragraph while reflecting on the annual celebration of the Pilsen street fair, *Fiesta del Sol*.

11. Parishioners organize two activities common in *kermesses* in Mexico. In the first, men are charged a dollar for the privilege of dancing during the night. In the second, a few people indiscriminately and playfully arrest young men on the dance floor and put them in jail, a fenced-off area to the side. In order to get out, the men must pay a fine (another dollar) and "marry" a young girl selected by them or those staffing the jail. The "marriage" takes place in front of someone acting as judge. For a fee, a photographer takes a picture of the couple dressed up as bride and groom.

12. Some claim that *menudo* has a medicinal effect. They believe that the boiled hooves in the soup create a natural gelatin that coats the stomach and prevents headaches caused by a hangover *(la cruda)*.

13. Washing the meat clean, removing the fat, cutting the stomach wall into bite-size squares, and then deseeding, deveining, and cooking the chilis require many hours of work for a team of cooks.

14. Allan Figueroa Deck, "Multiculturalism as an Ideology," in Deck et al., *Perspectives*, 30.

4.

Developing Christian Base Communities

Because many Catholics attend Sunday liturgies with hundreds of people they do not know, it is difficult for them to experience church as community. The church may seem more like an assembly of individuals connected by faith than by personal relationships. To address this situation of the "anonymous" Catholic, some large parishes organize small communities dispersed throughout the congregation. These communities not only strengthen interpersonal relationships among participants but create a sense of community within the larger parish. This chapter examines the development and impact of small Christian communities at St. Pius V.[1]

The Emergence of *Comunidades de Base* in the Catholic Church

Christian Base Communities (CBCs), *Comunidades Eclesiales de Base*, were first developed in Latin America, evolving in part from the Catholic Action Movement brought by European missionaries to the Americas after World War I.[2] This movement promoted lay involvement in the world. Within each sector of society, be it education, industry, labor, commerce, health, or agriculture, participants organized small groups, or "cells," where they prayed and reflected together to garner the strength to live as apostles in their daily work. Focusing attention primarily on their personal experiences rather than on church doctrine, they committed themselves to effect change in their respective sectors of society.

85

Unlike Catholic Action cells, which were organized principally according to economic sectors, CBCs developed along geographic lines. Whereas Catholic Action cells tended to appeal more to professional people, CBCs have overwhelmingly attracted the working-class poor. The word *base* in Spanish means "grassroots," indicating that *Comunidades de Base* consist of common people, which in Latin America means the poor. In 1956, Dom Agnello Rossi, bishop of Rio de Janeiro, launched a catechetical movement from which small communities first developed, eventually involving several million Brazilians in an estimated 200,000 small communities. CBCs then spread to Chile, Honduras, Panama, and soon to all Latin America and eventually to Africa, Asia, and the United States.

CBCs are not bible study or prayer groups, nor are they block clubs or cells of a political movement; they are not just another parish committee or program or even a church-wide movement focused on rejuvenating the parish. Various movements and programs, such as Marriage Encounter, *Cursillos de Cristiandad,* and most especially RENEW and Christ Renews His Parish, have promoted small faith-sharing groups. CBCs are more comprehensive, encompassing a form of community life espoused by the early Christians. Although CBCs are intended for all parishioners, many choose not to participate. Because people often prefer anonymity in a parish, as well as the freedom from commitments stemming from a more intimate involvement in a small community, parishes generally allow people to select their own desired level of participation in parish life, with CBCs as an option.

CBCs are Christian communities, or small churches, often called "a new way of being church." Latin American bishops have referred to them as the church in miniature. Both Pope Paul VI and Pope John Paul II insisted that CBCs are organic cells of the church because they encompass the essential characteristics of the universal church and make available, or incarnate, the saving will of God in history. In 1975, Paul VI devoted an entire section of his encyclical *The Evangelization of Peoples* to small communities, recognizing them as a sign of hope for the Church.[3] In 1968, Latin American bishops wrote that the CBC is "the first and fundamental ecclesiastical nucleus."[4] Pope John Paul II added his clear support in 1989:

So that all parishes...may be truly communities of Christians, local ecclesial authorities ought to foster the...small basic or so-called "living" communities, where the faithful can communicate the Word of God and express it in service and love to one another. These communities are true expressions of ecclesial communion and centers of evangelization, in communion with their pastors.[5]

CBCs should manifest all the characteristics of the church. Bishop John J. Fitzpatrick explained in his letter outlining the significance of CBCs for the Diocese of Brownsville, Texas: "Base communities are not a replacement for traditional parishes, nor mere subdivisions of them. Rather, they are a fresh way of being church within the structured parish."[6] They are inclusive, egalitarian communities of faith where people experience God's life and manifest it to those around them. Their members grow in faith as they face common challenges together, studying the scriptures and reflecting and praying together as they develop ministries of social service, education, mutual support, and prophetic confrontation. They are missionaries by bringing the church and its ministry into every corner of the neighborhood. The only ecclesial dimension they lack is the sacramental power of ordained clergy. However, by virtue of their faith and community, they realize the presence of Christ and are, therefore, a sacrament of Christ. Although most CBCs exist without a priest member or even frequent visits from local clergy, CBC promoters insist they are not simply a response to the shortage of priests.

Some Catholic Church authorities in Latin America have expressed concern over CBCs, accusing them of creating a "popular" or "parallel" church, that is, a church unconnected to the "official" or "hierarchical" church. Their concern stems from the power struggle between the hierarchical model of organization promoted by clergy and a more communitarian model embraced by most lay people. Because of their reflective and democratic methodology, CBCs teach people not only about their faith but about a less authoritarian model of church that emphasizes equality in membership and shared decision-making. Although theologians recognize that the church arises in part from "an initiative from above," namely, from the Spirit working through the pope, bishops, and priests, they emphasize that the church also emerges from the Spirit working from below, from the faith of the people. Some bishops and pastors fear that because CBC leaders are laypeople, they will not be able to control them, either doctrinally or pastorally, as easily as the clergy. Because CBCs are often intimately involved in local community affairs, they sometimes support social or political positions or groups not approved by the bishops.

The development of leadership in CBCs also differs from the clerical model. In CBCs, leaders emerge within the community rather than from above or outside it. Furthermore, in CBCs, the community selects and empowers its leaders, whether male or female, not once and forever, but through ongoing evaluation and confirmation. Accountability is informal but constant and is achieved in face-to-face contact between leaders and their communities. Throughout most of history, however, church leadership has been restricted to ordained, celibate men, selected, trained, and ordained by other clergy and then assigned to an ecclesial community, whether a parish or a diocese, usually without any consultation with the local community. These leaders, once ordained, need not share authority with the faithful or subject themselves to their review.

Although the worlds of Latin America and the United States are very different, Hispanic Catholic leaders across the United States have repeatedly supported the development of CBCs.[7] After organizing two national *encuentros* (meetings) of Hispanic leaders in the 1970s, the National Conference of Catholic Bishops (NCCB) issued a pastoral letter in 1983, that supported the conclusions of the *encuentros* on CBCs:

> Hispanics in the Americas have made few contributions to the (American) church more significant than the *comunidades eclesiales de base*. The small community has appeared on the scene as a ray of hope in dealing with dehumanizing situations that can destroy people and weaken faith....Since these communities are of

proven benefit to the church, we highly encourage their development....The *comunidad eclesial de base* should be an expression of a church that liberates from personal and structural sin; it should be a small community with personal relationships; it should form part of a process of integral evangelization; and it should be in communion with other levels of the church. The role of the parish in particular is to facilitate, coordinate and multiply the *comunidades eclesiales de base* within its boundaries and territories. The parish should be a community of communities.[8]

After organizing the *III Encuentro Nacional* in August 1985, which again supported CBCs,[9] the NCCB issued "The National Pastoral Plan for Hispanic Ministry" in November 1987, which clearly designated the formation of CBCs as a major priority.

The Hispanic community recognizes that the parish is, ecclesiastically and historically speaking, the basic organizational unit of the Church in the United States, and it will continue to be so; at the same time it is affirmed that conversion and a sense of being Church are often best lived out in smaller communities within the parish which are more personal and offer a greater sense of belonging.

These small ecclesial communities and other groups within the parish framework promote experiences of faith and conversion, prayer life, missionary outreach and evangelization, interpersonal relations and fraternal love, prophetic questioning and actions for justice. They are a prophetic challenge for the renewal of our Church and humanization of our society.[10]

Comunidades de Base in the Parish

The goal of parish ministry is to build a strong Christian community, a goal that transcends increasing attendance at Sunday

Mass. Community implies that people feel a certain closeness, that they know and are known by others. How to create this community in a large inner-city parish? How to reach the thousands of unchurched Catholics on the neighborhood streets of Pilsen? Nearly 50,000 people live in Pilsen, 90 percent of whom are Hispanic. Although the vast majority are Catholic, in 1988 only 10 to 15 percent attended church on a given Sunday at one of ten Catholic churches. Consequently, St. Pius V decided to reach out to the neighborhood by providing CBCs as foci of evangelization.[11] These communities, or at least people aspiring to be communities, celebrate the life of Christ and bring the good news of God's love to the neighborhood in practical ways. They are the church on the neighborhood blocks. They began in the following manner.

In 1985, before becoming pastor, I celebrated the 10:00 a.m. Sunday Mass, after which I taught a Bible class for approximately twenty to thirty adults. The class was conducted in a dialogic fashion, allowing plenty of opportunity for questions. When the semester ended, the people asked me to hold similar discussions in their homes because many of their family members seldom attended Mass. I agreed and began visiting a different house each week. Each meeting attracted new people, usually family and friends of the hosts. Although some people did not continue with the group, the traveling participants grew in number as word spread that a priest was visiting homes, explaining the Bible, and talking with people about their problems. People crowded into tiny apartments, some standing in doorways and corridors, with children sitting on the floor in an inner circle. People's enthusiastic response confirmed that they enjoyed the opportunity to gather, pray, reflect on, and learn more about their faith. Many were too timid to talk in public, unsure of themselves, and fearful that their opinions would sound foolish. However, when prompted to explain their personal experiences, how they lived and celebrated their faith in their hometown, they seemed comfortable, even proud, recounting stories about their families and former communities. As more people asked me to visit their homes, I initiated a second night of meetings. Within six months, these groups were institutionalized into two CBCs, each with its respective coordinator. In time, other CBCs were added.

CBC meetings were successful in no small part because of the presence of a priest. The sad truth is that few priests actually visit homes other than to respond to a crisis, to bring communion, or to socialize. People constantly commented that they had never heard of a priest taking time to talk to them about their faith in their home. Mexicans very much want a priest to visit their homes and discuss their faith with them; his visit is a blessing.

A second factor contributing to the success of the meetings was that they consisted principally of monolingual Mexican immigrants who are largely poor, from rural areas, with little or no education. More than first- and second-generation Mexicans, these people thirst for guidance in their new society, are more tied to the church and its clergy for nearly every kind of assistance, are more explicitly religious in their personal and family life, and are more at home associating with other Hispanics.

A third factor explaining people's enthusiasm was their interest in the Bible, which served as a resource in all discussions. Mexicans love and revere the Bible, even though many have little knowledge of it. Few can find the New Testament in the book; many have never heard of David and Goliath or are unable to distinguish Abraham from Moses. Barbara E. Reid, OP, a biblical scholar, explains why the Bible has not played a prominent role for Hispanic women.

First, the type of Christianity that was brought to the Americas by the Spanish *conquistadores* was not a biblically based Christianity. Rather, it was one in which doctrines, commandments, and Church practices were emphasized. A second factor is the centrality of the saints in Hispanic devotional piety. The saints are more readily seen as intercessors and models to be emulated than is the Jesus of the Gospels. Women, in particular, find that Mary understands their lot and offers consolation much more readily than could her male son. A third reason for the marginal role of the Bible is that it is perceived to be difficult to understand and its interpretation belongs to the domain of the official Church. Devotions to the saints, by contrast, allow for a greater degree of control and creativity on the part of the faithful.[12]

91

While Reid notes that this attitude was not uncommon in the pre-Vatican II church in other cultures, including the United States, an important additional reason for Mexicans' ignorance of the Bible is their low level of literacy and the fact that their culture is primarily oral, not written.

Because every CBC meeting includes a reflection on a biblical passage, many people purchase Bibles. In fact, over a seventeen-year period, the parish sold more than 3,000 Bibles to families. This CBC reflection on the Bible is not a Bible study such as the Little Rock Bible Study Program. Carlos Mesters, a Brazilian theologian famous for his development of materials for CBC reflections, has stated that the principal objective of reading the Bible in community is not to interpret it but to interpret life with its help.[13] Reid notes:

> Liberation theology regards the Bible not as a deposit of timeless truths formulated in a bygone day that can be mined and applied equally in every time and place. Nor is biblical interpretation an attempt to arrive at "the correct meaning" of the text. Rather, it is a way of understanding the living Word by which God speaks in our midst today, revealing new possibilities of meaning.[14]

The Bible is integrated into a reflective methodology called "see, judge, act," developed earlier by Catholic Action. Participants "see" by identifying significant conditions in their world, often presented as an event or story from their daily lives. Discussion during this stage tends to be lively, for people have a lot to share about their lives. To "judge," or decide, involves bringing the wisdom of the sacred scriptures to bear on the event or situation just described. God's Word provides the criteria according to which one's world is evaluated and decisions for action are taken. To "act" consists in participants committing to a concrete action, however small, in order to put into practice the wisdom gathered from reflection on their experiences in the light of faith. At the next meeting, participants evaluate their action and its impact. The starting point for this kind of reflection is the people's experience of life, emanating from questions or concerns raised by them; it does not begin with the Bible or doctrine. Reid highlights the importance of this step:

> This first crucial component of the method is that it relies on the faithful reflection of ordinary people of faith, not solely or primarily on that of biblical scholars. What is required to engage in the process is a willingness to reflect on experience in light of faith and the biblical tradition in solidarity with other believers. One need not have a degree in theology or be trained in biblical exegesis to do this. Telling one's own story, the joint story of the community, and relating that to the biblical story is essential. Narrative mode is particularly important: parables and stories of lived experience are the stuff of both real life and the biblical text.[15]

This theological perspective views the world and the scriptures from the point of view of the poor because the God of the scriptures demonstrates a loving preference for the poor, defending them, choosing them as leaders of the people, messengers of the divine, and the first to hear and accept the good news of God's love. The Bible encourages the poor as the principal heirs of the Kingdom of God to struggle together for the transformation of the world. Participants in CBCs are asked to connect their experience, the liberating message of the Bible, and its challenge to take appropriate action today. Since poverty is the experience of the majority of Hispanics in the United States, this perspective is enlightening and encouraging.

A fourth factor contributing to the success of CBC meetings was their openness. An atmosphere of cordiality and sharing encouraged everyone to speak. A lot of laughter filled the air as people told stories and discovered humorous coincidences among themselves. After several years of participation, Jovita Calderon, an elderly, illiterate woman, testified that when she began participating in the *pláticas* ("the talks"), she did not speak for fear of embarrassing herself. She felt she knew nothing. "Now I feel I too can contribute and I can say whatever is on my mind."

Although the staff named the groups "small Christian base communities," the people did not fully understand this terminology. For most, these gatherings involved talks presented by the priest. Only years later when the number of groups had multiplied and it was impossible for a priest to attend every meeting did participants begin to understand that they were indeed part of a community that gathered to share life and faith together.

Over the course of several years, CBC meetings developed a certain rhythm. Generally, they begin in late September and continue until Thanksgiving (usually eight weekly sessions). During the first week of December, people celebrate the novena to Our Lady of Guadalupe, which is followed by the Christmas novena of *posadas*. Both these celebrations involve the CBCs. Because January is the slowest period of the year in the parish, the staff conducts educational sessions for all CBC members during this time. CBC meetings in homes begin again just before Lent, recess during Holy Week and Easter week, and resume with another four- to five-week series until Pentecost. Instead of holding home meetings during the summer months, the CBCs decided to organize Masses on the street. Each CBC organizes a Mass on its block.

To guide the discussions in the communities, the parish staff consults CBC coordinators about topics of interest to their communities and works with a few of them to design reflection sheets for each season (fall, Lent, and Eastertide), each with a specific theme. Themes cover the gamut of people's life experiences, ranging from the Christian response to violence to the plight of immigrants to the problem of addictions to the role of women in the family. Inevitably the best discussions occur when themes include people's sharing of their personal experiences and stories. During one season, when the theme was housing, people reflected on their experience in their home countries as well as in Chicago. They examined the housing on their block, who owned what property, and the relative advantages and disadvantages of being an owner or a renter. These topics were educational, exemplifying the pedagogical model developed by Paulo Freire, which involves people learning by reflecting together on their own experience.[16] While it is difficult to conduct participatory discussions about doctrinal themes without turning them into classroom-style sessions, people request informative reflections, particularly on the sacraments and the Bible. In response, one entire season was dedicated to the Eucharist.

The humble surroundings in which CBC meetings are held, the generous response of participants, and the simple but profound level of their discussion inspire not only participants but the parish staff. One evening when I arrived, the woman hosting the session was out borrowing chairs and cups from neighbors to use later to serve participants piping hot *canela* (cinnamon tea) and cookies. She and her children, darling twin girls and a hyperactive five-year-old boy she called *el tremendo* (the terrible), lived in an apartment furnished with a few spartan chairs, a table, and a threadbare sofa surrounded by barren walls. At the meeting's end, after discussing how to help the host family, the guests each decided to bring a donation (a can of vegetables, an onion or tomato, some fruit or bread) to the next meeting.

On another occasion, the week before the feast of the Transfiguration, CBCs discussed experiences of transformation in their neighborhood. In one community, ten adults shared their enthusiasm for positive changes, such as the new library and laundromat, the new fieldhouse in the park, the new homes being built, better trash pickup, and people coming together around common needs. They identified their own gathering together to share their faith, develop trust, and learn more about the Word of God as a sign of personal and communal transformation. Perhaps the best discussions occur in meetings held in homes of new participants as CBC members are touched by the stories and living conditions of the new families, and the latter are pleased and encouraged to have found new friends to support them in their struggles.

Each CBC meeting finishes with prayer, usually spontaneous prayer. People stand in a circle and hold hands. At first, many people are hesitant to mention anything, preferring to recite an "Our Father" or a "Hail Mary." Coordinators assure participants that everyone, including children, has some prayer to offer. Often children help reticent adults gain confidence to pray openly as they ask God to help their parents and grandparents. These spontaneous prayers help people articulate in front of others what they want to say to God, creating a bond of solidarity in the faith and often motivating them to do something about that for which they are praying. Before concluding, coordinators seek a volunteer to host the next session. This request presents a serious challenge because some people resist. In some cases, the husband does not want anyone in his house. In others, the people have no room or are simply embarrassed to have visitors see the poverty in which they live. Still others, fearful of robberies, do not want people to see their apartments. Of course, it is much easier to obtain a volunteer if a priest promises to be present. His presence calms concerns and adds a sense of prestige to the meeting.

After several semesters of meetings, people began to ask for two things: more education and opportunities to meet the participants in other CBCs. People gradually expressed their desire to learn more—more about their faith, more about their neighborhood, more about parenting and family, and about one another. They also wanted to get to know people in other CBCs and learn about their experience, a sentiment reflecting Mexicans' strong desire for unity and inclusiveness as well as a healthy ecclesiology that seeks the communion of communities. Thus, the parish began scheduling assemblies for all CBC participants as the first and last session each season. All CBC members gather in the parish hall for some teaching and sharing in mixed small groups, followed by a short social with refreshments. These assemblies help people sense they are participating in something much larger than their own small community and offer opportunities for coordinators to develop leadership skills by facilitating different parts of the meeting.

Leadership and Ministries

Through their participation in CBCs, Mexican immigrants learn a model of leadership different from what most may have observed in their homeland. Some Mexicans, rather than demanding that their leaders act democratically or collegially, expect them to make decisions and tell them what to do. Because the term "leader" in Spanish connotes an authoritarian style of leadership, CBC leaders are called "coordinators." Since people generally resist being CBC coordinators because they feel unprepared, after choosing their coordinators, the communities must encourage them to accept the responsibility. John Linnan states: "The essence of the basic church community as a form of ecclesial life is that (leadership) emerges from the community in which it lives and develops by discovering and energizing the talents and abilities latent in the members of the community itself."[17] Since most people have never coordinated a group, the staff trains coordinators, using role-playing to teach them how to listen, affirm, challenge, and facilitate dialogue. Staff also instructs them to arrange a room for good communication, welcome new people, distribute tasks and responsibilities, stay on the topic, involve everyone in the discussion, attend to body language, avoid lecturing or preaching, guarantee acceptance of diverse opinions, resolve conflicts, play games, respond to unexpected matters, and refer to one another by name. The staff also offers classes on the Bible to help coordinators understand its basic structure and fundamental elements of biblical theology. The formation of coordinators is an ongoing process designed to instill self-confidence, and as adults with little educational background, they learn best by "on-the-job training." While pastoral staffs may be impatient with their gradual progress, coordinators themselves feel they are growing by leaps and bounds.

A major task for coordinators, as well as for other CBC members, is to invite new people to join their community. While this responsibility is key to accomplishing the evangelizing mission of their communities, it can be intimidating. People feel uncomfortable knocking on doors of strangers and inviting them to their meetings, primarily because they fear rejection. To encourage them, the staff suggests they first visit St. Pius V parishioners from whom they can expect a friendly welcome. To assist them, they receive a computerized listing of the parishioners living on their blocks. In fact, CBC members are generally surprised to discover that most people receive them warmly. Of course, not everyone invited accepts the invitation; some people agree to attend but later fail to appear. Nevertheless, people appreciate being invited and taken into consideration, and visits to their homes establish some minimal relationship between them and a CBC. The staff prepares CBC coordinators for this frustration and encourages them to re-invite people periodically.

Coordinators have an important pastoral role that many do not grasp at first. Most begin by considering their ministry as a task they have been asked to perform. Only with time do they recognize their role as animators of a community of people. Although coordinators need not be well educated, they must be pastoral, caring people who communicate love and concern for their members and enthusiasm about getting people together to share their lives and faith. They must not be pessimists, focusing on the negative, or incommunicative or unavailable for anything beyond the weekly meeting. Three of the most successful coordinators were illiterate women, very skilled at gathering people. They acted like shepherds with a flock, and people responded to them warmly as their pastors. Some people, on the other hand, do not work well as coordinators because they are domineering or overly rigid, talk incessantly, or run their meetings like a classroom. While finding able coordinators is a challenge, once found, they are extremely valuable for further extending the pastoral work of the parish into the community.

After the CBCs had been meeting for a number of years, the parish staff formed a steering committee comprised of CBC coordinators. Their tasks included developing and promoting different activities among the CBCs, setting a calendar, and identifying and responding to special issues arising among the CBCs. This committee helps coordinators develop a wider vision of the role of CBCs in the parish and provides an opportunity for them to support one another in the various challenges they face in their respective communities.

Leadership in CBCs is not limited to coordinators but shared as much as possible among all members. Each CBC selects someone as an assistant to accompany coordinators to nearly every CBC function, including training sessions. In this way, assistants are gradually prepared to substitute for coordinators and eventually assume their ministry of coordination. Only a few men are active in CBCs, and rarely do they become coordinators. Although men are almost as equally represented as women in

Sunday liturgies, in matters of church leadership and participation in CBCs, they are a minority. Linnan comments on the experience of Brownsville and Omaha.[18]

> There is something to the idea…that women have a special talent for community leadership. "Being a mother is the best training for leadership," said one regional coordinator. It may be that there are social and cultural factors at work here: (1) the special role of women in a family-oriented culture; (2) the role of women as the protector and transmitter of familial and, therefore, communal values; (3) the need for men to work often at several jobs, when and where they can be found; (4) the social, political, economic, and educational barriers that restrict the immigrant women in the exercise of their abilities and talents to the home, the family, the neighborhood; (5) the capacity of women to network more effectively than men, precisely because men must function in a more competitive arena in order to secure a minimum of financial security for their families; (6) the role of *machismo* in the culture; and (7) the impact of a hostile and dominant culture, most directly experienced by immigrant men in their struggle to wring a livelihood from an unfriendly workplace.[19]

At various times the staff and the coordinators have addressed this situation. Women want their spouses to be involved in CBCs, convinced their participation would strengthen and enliven their communities. When a CBC meeting is held in their own homes, some men attend, but few leave their home to meet elsewhere. Many women think men do not join because they do not want to be the first or only man in the group. Perhaps men, whether Hispanics or not, are also less interested in reflecting on life, discussing faith, or sharing experiences. James O'Halloran suggests it should not be surprising that men participate less than women:

> Who traveled with Jesus ministering to him during his public life? Who came forth willingly and wiped his

face on the road to Calvary? Who wept over him on that same road? Who stood by the cross when all the apostles save John had fled? And who were the first witnesses to the Resurrection?...So what's new?[20]

The prevalence of women in CBC meetings can be beneficial, however, facilitating open discussions about problems women share in common. Women gain self-confidence in the midst of other women, as well as a heightened consciousness of themselves as responsible adults with rights and obligations. Esther Rivera commented, "I never saw myself as a sheltered person or an underdeveloped woman, but when I began sharing with other women in our CBC, I realized that I had a lot of energy and interest in working for the community and growing as a person."

Arthur Baranowski, author of many books about CBCs, notes that not only are the selection and formation of coordinators important for the development of CBCs but so is accompanying the people. At St. Pius V, the pastor and staff try to attend as many CBC meetings as possible not only to communicate their support for the coordinators but also to underscore the importance of the mission of CBCs within the parish. When coordinators and other CBC members see the commitment of the staff, they are more likely to make their involvement in CBCs a high priority. Many priests claim they lack the time for CBC meetings, and, admittedly, they do take time. But their importance for developing community and extending pastoral ministry deeper into the community justify making CBCs one of the parish's highest priorities.

A Response to Non-Catholic Proselytizing

CBCs are an important response to the aggressive proselytizing of evangelical and pentecostal religious sects, as well as Jehovah's Witnesses, Mormons, and Seven Day Adventists, among Mexican Catholics in Pilsen. Each Saturday morning and often on Sundays, cleanly scrubbed and impeccably dressed missionaries walk the neighborhood streets, stopping people on the sidewalk and knocking on doors in the hope of finding a tepid or alienated Catholic to recruit. Frequently, the people, not wanting to appear inhospitable, succumb to their insistent requests to enter their home for a well-planned and skillfully prepared presentation of half-truths. Most Mexican immigrant families have suffered the painful experience of losing a member to these *sectas*. Converts become true believers and virulent evangelizers, threatening the family with certain condemnation if all do not leave the Catholic Church. Family gatherings, usually occasions for celebrating unity and family customs, often turn into painful religious discussions, dividing the family and undermining trust among its members.

Approximately twenty-two small non-Catholic churches, often housed in refurbished storefronts or former funeral parlors, operate in the neighborhood. Many come and go, unable to gain or sustain a viable congregation. A large proportion of their membership lives outside the neighborhood, drawing predominantly from Puerto Rican communities. Although these churches are small, averaging between twenty and fifty families, they cause significant confusion and division among Catholic Mexican immigrants with their attacks against the Catholic Church. At CBC meetings, their criticisms are a frequent topic of conversation: Mary was not a Virgin because she had other children; Catholics are idolatrous because they pray before statues; Catholics sin by praying to saints because Jesus alone is Savior and mediator; Catholics blaspheme by calling priests "father" because Jesus said, "call no one 'father'" but God; Catholics fail to recognize Jehovah as God's true name and promote infant baptism, ignoring that only by knowing Jesus through adult conversion and baptism are people saved.

It is difficult to calculate how many Mexican immigrants leave the Catholic Church permanently for these non-Catholic groups. In 1988, Archbishop Pio Laghi, apostolic *pronuncio* to the United States, told the bishops: "The annual loss of Spanish-speaking Catholics to non-Catholic sects is significantly—I would say disturbingly—high."[22] Andrew Greeley calculates that since

1972, one of seven Hispanics left Catholicism to join another church or no church at all.[23]

A number of factors contribute to the success of non-Catholic churches in the Hispanic community, notably the failure of the Catholic Church to warmly welcome Hispanics. Too few Catholic pastors speak Spanish and embrace Hispanic cultures, while almost all clergy of non-Catholic Hispanic churches are Hispanic. Furthermore, their preaching is delivered in good Spanish and with effusive emotion. Since their congregations are small, people know and support one another in a familial atmosphere. Also, their belief system and religious discipline are fundamentalist, based on literal interpretations of the Bible, providing a simple, clear, and authoritative approach to the scriptures. Although their rules and regulations are strict—tithing 10 percent of one's income to the church and abstaining from alcohol, cigarettes, gambling, and dancing—members believe that compliance with the church's code guarantees them salvation.[24]

Many Catholics, after having participated for a time in these churches, return to the Catholic Church, largely because they found them religiously alienating, failing to recognize the role of saints, and especially of Our Lady of Guadalupe. Others confess that the financial assistance they received was an important reason for joining the sects, but once participating in their new church, they became disillusioned, discovering it had no social services for the needy beyond their own membership. To stem the outflow of Hispanics from the Catholic Church, Archbishop Laghi recommended a "concerted effort" to welcome them, embrace their culture, and center Catholic preaching on the person of Jesus Christ.[25] While implementing these recommendations, St. Pius V helps people defend themselves against the proselytizing efforts of these churches by providing educational materials for CBCs and by preaching on Sundays about their distorted attacks upon Catholic faith and practice.

A Community in Action Leads to Ministry

Responding to local needs, small communities facilitate the development of ministries. For example, certain individuals develop a facility for leading prayer; others, sensitive to the needs of the sick, assume responsibility for coordinating visits to the sick and include them in the prayer at CBC meetings; others become excellent organizers of community celebrations. Some bring to the attention of the community or parish staff people needing special assistance, such as a family where the breadwinner has lost a job, the children are sleeping on the floor, or where some members need counseling. These ministries are often not officially recognized or organized at the parish level, and yet the parish affirms and promotes them. Because it is difficult to find someone in each community for each specific ministry, ministries tend to develop where individuals have the interest, time, and talent for them. At one time, for example, when neighborhood security was a high priority, some CBCs selected representatives to work as liaisons with the community policing program.

Although CBC members tend to refer people in need to the parish staff, the latter frequently encourages them to handle the situations on their own. Moreover, the staff often refers people coming to the parish for sacraments or social service to CBC coordinators. Because Noemi, a monolingual Mexican mother of two children, suffered a mental disability, she had difficulty with homemaking. When she came to the parish office for help, the staff assisted her as well as it could and then contacted the base community on her block, which invited her to its meetings and soon assisted her in all sorts of ways. Most dramatically, when the State of Illinois took away her children, the community helped to clean her apartment and obtain furniture to provide a more suitable living environment so that she could recover them. Noemi will always be a dependent person, but now she has a community to share her life and support her.

Some CBCs are excellent at celebration. Juanita's community, for example, celebrates its members' birthdays at the first meeting of each month. Each week, members contribute a nominal amount to a kitty that covers the expenses of their fiestas. They organize a potluck dinner followed by sharing of a cake and gifts. Juanita has a special talent for motivating people to celebrate life even in the midst of poverty and hardship, and her example has inspired other CBCs to celebrate the lives of their members in a similar fashion.

For several years, CBC meetings made no special provisions for children. Youngsters simply sat among the adults or on the floor in the middle of the room. Many parents felt reluctant to attend the meetings because they would have difficulty disciplining their children during the meetings. As a result, the staff developed the ministry of the teenage catechist, one or two teens from the CBC families who work directly with the smaller children. On a weekday afternoon the teens gather with a staff member to receive instructions and materials for the weekly activity with the children in their CBC. This arrangement works extremely well. The teens develop a sense of pride and responsibility and learn the skills of teaching and relating to younger children, while offering them an important role model. At the end of each CBC meeting, the children are called into the living room from the kitchen or hallway where they have been meeting to present the results of their activity—a drawing, song, or game. Parents listen and applaud, and then all join in the final prayer.

Divide and Multiply

When a CBC becomes too large to fit into an apartment (more than fifteen people), it must consider dividing into two. CBCs at St. Pius V multiplied to seventeen groups, a sometimes painful process for people who have grown attached to one another. To avoid separating into two groups, some large CBCs ask to hold their meetings in the church basement. The staff resists these requests because meeting in homes is an essential component of CBCs, providing a new way of understanding church. In January 1995, one CBC faced this predicament when the community had grown to nineteen adults and thirty children.

The coordinator called a special meeting to discuss alternatives. While some people thought it better to leave the children at home, a few mothers volunteered to attend with their children only occasionally. Neither proposal was accepted. In the end, the members decided to divide their community in order to keep everyone involved, including children.

Community and Door-to-Door Evangelization

In 1993, as CBCs reflected on various aspects of the church, they analyzed how their parish and small communities were missionary. To be missionary, they believed they should visit everyone on their block. When they presented the idea of an evangelization campaign to visit as many homes as possible to the parish council, it was accepted enthusiastically. Because St. Pius V parishioners are interspersed with those of other neighborhood parishes, the staff invited and included other parishes in the program. St. Pius V developed the campaign objectives, planned the schedule, and trained people to overcome their hesitancy to visit total strangers. The staff formed sixty teams of two people each to visit fifty blocks, with an average of thirty homes or apartments on each side of the street. The goals of the campaign were:

1. Invite the unchurched to participate in the parish and invite parishioners to become more active in their respective parishes.
2. Gather and organize information about Catholics in the neighborhood.
3. Heighten awareness among the general population about the work of the Catholic Church in the neighborhood.
4. Train and involve new leaders to reach out to every home in the neighborhood.
5. Strengthen Christian Base Communities where they exist.

6. Assist active parishioners in getting to know more people and seeing themselves as builders of church and community.

Visiting apartments in a crowded inner-city neighborhood is not an easy task. Entryways may be in the back or on the side of the house, difficult to find. Apartments are generally unmarked and stairwells often unlit and frightening. Doorbells generally do not function, and people often do not readily answer a knock at the door. Because some residents fear police and immigration officials, they are not helpful in guiding visitors through this maze. Since visitors feared being mistaken for Jehovah's Witnesses or being asked difficult theological questions, the staff helped them carefully define their role. The visits were not to be proselytizing or argumentative. Their purpose was primarily to visit Catholic families and invite them into greater participation in their church. The visitors would encourage non-Catholics to participate actively in their own churches. If residents wanted to enter into theological or religious discussions, people would answer if they felt comfortable doing so; otherwise, they would refer questioners to a parish priest. In addition to a computer list of names and addresses of registered parishioners living on their block, visitors received a page from the "reverse" phone book listing the names and phone numbers of people in the numerical order of their house on the block.

At the training sessions, the visitors reflected on St. Luke's account of Jesus sending the seventy-two disciples to surrounding towns and villages to preach the Kingdom of God.[26] This reflection generated enthusiasm and energy for the task ahead. Because Hispanics love participating in dramas, role-plays were used to teach possible responses to the various scenarios that might occur during the visits. These preparations generated a lot of laughter, helping visitors forge a bond as a band of missionaries. Although each team received a supply of parish brochures to leave with each household, the staff emphasized that the visitors' own experience with the parish was more important than any memorized script or list of parish services. Thus, they practiced explaining how they personally had benefited from their involvement in parish activities.

They took brochures from the surrounding parishes in case they encountered families belonging to other parishes. The visitors also collected information about the sacramental status of members of each household, inviting the unbaptized or uncatechized into fuller participation in the church. In fact, they discovered many people lacking the sacraments of baptism, Eucharist, confirmation, or matrimony, which troubled and motivated them to return to those families in the future.

In order to emphasize the presence of Christ in people and the community, a campaign slogan was developed: "Christ lives here." A colored picture of the Sacred Heart was offered to every family to hang in their window so that as the campaign progressed more people would become aware of it. Interestingly enough, some Jehovah's Witnesses and evangelicals, most likely former Catholics, also asked for copies of the pictures for their homes.

Twice during the campaign, the staff held evaluations of the visitors to assess their progress. Many told stories of visits that involved humor, pathos, and creativity. Juanita commented that she and her partner always prayed before knocking on a door, fearing what awaited them on the other side and seeking enlightenment about what to say. Some had negative experiences, such as people not at home, residents confusing them with sects, and just plain rudeness. Others were surprised at the poverty they found and commented on how they felt empowered because they were able to refer these families to the parish for assistance. Most visitors gained confidence and enthusiasm as they talked with pride about their parish and their role as missionaries. As a result of their work, additional people began coming to church regularly, and the religious education program experienced a substantial increase in enrollment.

To conclude the campaign, the parishes organized a bilingual Mass in the local park at which Joseph Cardinal Bernardin, then Archbishop of Chicago, presided. Approximately 1,500 people attended. Many brought their picture of the Sacred Heart and held it high over their heads at the end of Mass for the cardinal to bless. CBC members felt proud and thrilled with the attendance of so many people, the unity reflected among the parishes represented, the presence of the cardinal, and the public witness given by holding the event in the park.

In subsequent years, the CBCs conducted other activities. In 1997, for example, they organized to visit people on their block or in their own CBC community. Each member visited a different person each week for six weeks, spending approximately an hour in getting to know them better. This project evolved from a formation program designed to help CBC members learn to listen to others and draw out their deeper beliefs, values, and concerns. These efforts aimed to help them build power among residents by developing mutual trust and commitment to remedy problems affecting the local community. Mirna, for example, related how each Friday she observed an African American mother washing her clothes and trying to control her children in the laundromat. After the two talked, the woman invited Mirna to her apartment in a public-housing project just north of Pilsen. Mirna discovered a beautiful woman who cared not only for her children but also for her disabled father. The woman thanked Mirna for her initiative because, as an African American, the woman had always felt strange coming into a Hispanic neighborhood to wash her clothes where she knew no one. Now she had a friend.

The parish and the participants benefited greatly from these outreach efforts. Their self-confidence rose, as did their sense of participating in a missionary church. They got to know more people in their immediate neighborhood and of course became known to more people, expanding and strengthening personal relationships, the foundation of any community.

Taking Religion to the Streets

Every summer, each CBC organizes a Mass in its street, an experience that gathers the community and evangelizes the churched and unchurched alike. CBC coordinators first obtain signatures of local residents on a petition requesting a city permit to close the street. They then distribute fliers to every home, inviting families to participate in the celebration. CBC members set up a table in the street and decorate it as an altar, including tablecloth, candles, crucifix, and flowers. They remove cars in the immediate area, parking some at the street's entrance to block traffic, sweep gutters around the altar, and set up chairs brought from their homes. They select and prepare people to proclaim the scripture readings and prayers of the faithful, take up a collection, present the gifts of bread and wine, and serve as ministers of communion. The parish musician arrives early to play lively Mexican music over loudspeakers to alert local residents to gather for the celebration.

Mass begins as people follow the priest in procession up and down the block, singing while he blesses homes and cars, as well as the street and sidewalk. Children swarm around trying to catch a spray of holy water to cool their backs, already damp with sweat from the summer heat. Some families arrange small altars in front of their homes, complete with tablecloth, candles, religious pictures, statues, crucifixes, flowers, and a pitcher or empty milk carton filled with water to be blessed for later use in the home. Monolingual English speakers are less inclined to participate actively in the Mass, but they still like to have their homes blessed. Even people of other religions look for the priest's blessing. The procession up and down the block serves to call people to the Mass and increases the crowd to nearly a hundred people. Some people sit on their front steps and watch the Mass from a distance; others bring their chairs to sit in the street in front of the altar, but most sit on a curb or lean against a building or a parked car. Children often ride their bikes and play in the street during Mass, since they rarely have occasion to play in the street safe from traffic. Gang members occasionally parade through the assembled worshipers to make their presence known and strut their colors.

The Mass presents an excellent opportunity for preaching. The poignant message of community, forgiveness, commitment, and the presence of Jesus inherent in eucharistic theology provide ample material for a call to renewed Christian life among residents. One Saturday night during Mass, a group of men grilling steaks and drinking beer in a nearby front yard appeared to be paying little attention. They could easily hear the music but continued their festivities during Mass. When Mass finished, one of them came over to thank the priest for organizing the Mass. "This is what we need here. I heard everything you said, and I agree that we all need to watch over our children more carefully." That said, he gave the priest a twenty-dollar donation for the church.

Sometimes the street Mass is celebrated in front of gang hangouts, taverns, or sites where someone was killed, recalling the similar desire of the early Christians to celebrate Mass in the catacombs, grave sites of early martyrs. On such occasions, it is important that the preaching address the evils of gang life, particularly for attending gang members. The Mass provides a unique opportunity to address the meaning of being Catholic and Mexican. Do they stand for unity and life or division and death, for brotherhood or fratricide? One Mass, celebrated in front of the home of a five-year-old girl paralyzed by a stray bullet in a gang shootout, was reported in the archdiocesan newspaper. It reached Thomas Muñoz, a twenty-six-year-old former gang member from the community who was in jail at the time. He was so moved by the tragic story and the photo of the community gathered around the altar in the street that he wrote the parish about how he had changed his life in prison. When released, he wanted to be a deacon in order to work with Hispanic youth and warn them of the danger of gangs. "In your picture I can see the grief of the people looking out the windows. It's so sad. There is a war out there....A lot of these guys don't realize what it's like to have to identify a loved one at a morgue or end up in prison for twenty years." Efforts such as these not only strengthen the role of the CBC but serve to evangelize those distant from Christ and the church. Parishioners believe the Masses have an uncontrolled and unplanned impact far beyond what is immediately evident.

Base Communities and Parish Structures

A parish should be a communion of smaller communities. CBCs, even with a small number of parishioners, differ from other parish organizations like the Charismatic Renewal, social service committee, and liturgy committee which are functional or ministerial, because they are communities. In order to give CBCs the importance they deserve, St. Pius V structures their involvement in the parish in key ways. First, all coordinators and their assistants sit on the parish council. Second, the parish program for catechetical preparation for first communion for children is structurally linked to the CBCs. Parents of children making their first communion participate in CBC meetings in their area to experience a new kind of church. Third, the CBCs each commit to serve in two *kermesses*, either staffing a food booth, collecting food, or donating money or items for a raffle. Fourth, CBCs take turns sharing the ministries at the novena of Our Lady of Guadalupe, assuming responsibilities for ushering, reading, commentating, providing servers, taking up the collection, baking bread for the Eucharist, greeting people at the door, preparing hot chocolate, and serving the ever-present *pan dulce* (sweet rolls) after the service. Similarly, during Lent the CBCs have taken turns organizing the Friday night Way of the Cross.

Even though a relatively small number of people participate in CBCs, these communities have an impact on the larger parish beyond their size and numbers. Their presence and spirit operate much like a myth, projecting a vision and energy much greater than their actual size. Although CBCs struggle to be true communities and some dissolve, their efforts create a communitarian mystique that inspires and enlivens the whole parish. People visiting the parish often comment about feeling the community spirit in the congregation, a spirit developed largely by the CBCs. People recognize one another, greet one another, and engage in conversations before and after Mass. New CBC members testify that although they have seen most people before at the laundromat, the grocery store, or even in church, they never said hello until they met at the CBC. CBC members often comment that years ago they lived next door to one another without exchanging a greeting. Now they are friends and interested in extending their friendship to other neighbors. Once involved in a CBC, they feel more at home in the community.

The communitarian spirit fostered by CBCs is the mortar that cements a healthy and vibrant parish community. Contrary to some pastors' fears that CBCs would further burden their already busy schedule, St. Pius V staff has found that CBCs energize their ministry. The staff is inspired by the people's faith and commitment and enriched by listening to their experiences. CBCs also help stabilize a neighborhood, because their members develop relationships in the community they do not easily abandon. People want to stay in the area precisely because of their involvement in their CBC. As Baranowski notes:

> Calling people together to be church for each other is hard work and demands a steady effort over many years. There is no magic or immediate results. But the process is worth our best efforts, for through it parishioners revitalize each other, the staff, and the parish in an ongoing way.[27]

Notes

1. This chapter does not pretend to be a complete explanation of the nature of Christian Base Communities or their methodology. Abundant literature exists about CBCs for those interested. Some interesting resources include Marcello deC. Azevedo, SJ, *Basic Ecclesial Communities in Brazil: The Challenge of a New Way of Being Church* (Washington, DC: Georgetown University Press, 1980); Arthur Baranowski, *Creating Small Faith Communities: A Plan for Restructuring the Parish and Renewing Catholic Life* (Cincinnati, OH: St. Anthony Messenger Press, 1988); Patrick J. Brennan, *Re-Imagining the Parish* (New York: Crossroad, 1990); Stephen B. Clark, *Building Christian Communities: Strategy for Renewing the Church* (Notre Dame, IN: Ave Maria Press, 1985); Gregorio Iriarte, *¿Qué Es una Comunidad Eclesial de Base?: Guía Didáctica para Animadores de las CEB* (Bogota, Colombia: Ediciones Paulinas, 1991); Bernard J. Lee and Michael A. Cowan, *Dangerous Memories: House Churches and Our American Society* (Kansas City, MO: Sheed & Ward, 1986); Bernard J. Lee, SM, *The Catholic Experience of Small Christian Communities* (New York: Paulist, 2000); Jose Marins, *The Church from the Roots* (London: Catholics for Overseas Development, 1987); National Secretariat and Hispanic Communities, *Guidelines for Establishing Basic Church Communities in the United States* (Liguori, MO: Liguori Publications, 1981); James O'Halloran, *Signs of Hope: Developing Small Christian Communites* (Maryknoll, NY: Orbis, 1991); James O'Halloran, *Small Christian Communities: A Pastoral Companion* (Maryknoll, NY: Orbis, 1996). U.S.

Bishops' Committee on Hispanic Affairs, *Communion and Mission: A Guide for Bishops and Pastoral Leaders on Small Church Communities* (Washington, DC: United States Catholic Conference, 1995), 1–3.

2. Different translations of *Comunidades Eclesiales de Base* are used, such as small Christian communities. The important factors are that the groups are church and belong to the church, consist of lay people, and involve relatively few people (8–25) to insure face-to-face interaction.

3. Pope Paul VI, *Evangelii Nuntiandi, On Evangelization in the Modern World* (Washington, DC: United States Catholic Conference, 1976), no. 58.

4. *Conferencias Generales del Episcopado Latinoamericano, Medellein Conclusiones: La Iglesia en la Actual Transformación de América Latina a la Luz del Concilio*, 15 (nos. 10–12), in *Conferencias Generales del Epsicopado Latinoamericano, Rio de Janeiro, Medellein, Puebla, Santo Domingo* (Bogota, Colombia: *Consejo Episcopal Latinamericano, CELAM*, 1994). See also the Latin American Bishops' statement at their conference in Puebla, Mexico: *Puebla: La Evangelización en el Presente y en el Futuro de América Latina*, nos. 641–643, *loc. cit.* See also John E. Linnan, CSV, "Basic Church Communities in the Mexican American and Mexican Community and Their Ecclesiological Significance," in Ana Maria Pineda and Robert Schreiter, eds., *Dialogue Rejoined: Theology and Ministry in the United States Hispanic Reality* (Collegeville, MN: The Liturgical Press, 1995), 118–21.

5. John Paul II, *Apostolic Exhortation on the Mission of the Lay Faithful in the Church and in the World*, written to implement the recommendations of the October 1987 World Synod of the Bishops on the Laity, cited in Pelton, *op. cit.*, 70.

6. Linnan, *op. cit.*, 122.

7. For a recent study of the broad spectrum, extent, and continued growth of small Christian communities in the United States, see Lee, *Catholic Experience of Small Christian Communities.*

8. NCCB, "The Hispanic Presence: Challenge and Commitment," in *Origins* 13, no. 32 (January 19, 1984): 538.

9. "Prophetic Voices, Document on the Process of the *III Encuentro Nacional Hispano de Pastoral*," IV, 10, in NCCB, *Hispanic Ministry: Three Major Documents* (Washington, DC: USCC, 1995), 35.

10. NCCB, "National Pastoral Plan for Hispanic Ministry," VI, B, 1, 37, in *Hispanic Ministry*, 76–77. During the 1970s, 1980s, and 1990s, the Archdiocese of Chicago held three diocesan Hispanic *encuentros*, each of which emphasized the importance of CBCs.

11. Although most parishes organize a variety of activities and services, such as Catholic informational classes, Bible study, social service, and

auxiliaries, most attract relatively few participants. Studies show that adult education programs generally reach a small portion of parishioners, with class size averaging only twenty-five people. Small staffs, supported by limited funding, make it impossible for parishes to create enough programs to involve many members.

12. Reid, *op. cit.*, 75–76. She relies on Ada María Isasi-Díaz, "The Bible and *Mujerista* Theology," in Susan Brooks Thistlethwaite and Mary Potter Engel, eds., *Lift Every Voice: Constructing Christian Theologies from the Underside* (San Francisco: Harper, 1990), 262–65.

13. Carlos Mesters, "Como Se Faz Teologia Hoje no Brasil?" *Estudos Biblicos* 1 (1985), 10, cited in Reid, *op.cit.*, 76.

14. Reid, *op.cit.*, 78.

15. Barbara E. Reid, OP, "Biblical Exegesis from a Hispanic Perspective," in Pineda and Schreiter, *op. cit.*, 77.

16. See Chapter 9 for a brief description of Paulo Freire's educational principles.

17. Linnan, *op. cit.*, 112.

18. *Ibid.*, 116–17.

19. *Ibid.*

20. O'Halloran, *op. cit.*, 111.

21. Interview, March 15, 1999.

22. Archbishop Pio Laghi, "Stemming the Outflow of Hispanic Catholics," *Origins*, 18: 387.

23. Andrew M. Greeley, "Defection Among Hispanics (Updated)," *America* (September 27, 1997), 12–13.

24. Greeley notes that many ambitious Hispanics also perceive Protestantism as a path of upward mobility, a position supported by his 1998 research that found those changing religion to be better educated, wealthier, older, and more likely to be married. Greeley, *op. cit.*

25. Laghi, *op. cit.*, 388.

26. Luke 9:1–11.

27. Baranowski, *op. cit.*, 21.

5.

Celebrating Community in the Sacraments

Community involves celebration, and the church calls the community's celebration of its life and its relationship to God *liturgy*. Liturgy involves words, actions, and gestures that celebrate and call forth God's presence. Movement, sound, color, and fragrance convey meanings that transcend the material. Hispanics love rhythm and music, crowds and drama, and consequently, they appreciate Catholic liturgy. They are a sacramental people; they believe God is present and acting in their lives through these visible realities and rituals. For them, liturgy is the community at worship and at play; it is fiesta.

The seven sacraments are seven public rituals of the Catholic Church through which Jesus Christ bestows a special life called grace on the church and its faithful. They are acts of the church through which Christ empowers its members with faith and love.[1] The sacraments celebrate pivotal moments in people's life of faith and the church's development as community. Through these signs and symbols, Christ's Spirit guides the church and sanctifies humanity. This chapter describes the celebration of Eucharist, baptism, reconciliation, matrimony, and funerals.

Celebrating the Eucharist

The Eucharist is the center of the Christian community, the principal liturgical ritual passed down through centuries. In gathering around the Lord's table, people acknowledge their relationship to God and to one another; at the Eucharist, they see each other as brothers and sisters, created by God and loved by Jesus, who, through his Body and Blood, unites himself more intimately with them and strengthens them for everyday living. The meal also inspires them to live his commandment of love. During the Last Supper, Jesus washed the feet of his apostles and instructed them to do the same for one another, teaching them that the greatest in the Kingdom of God is the person who serves others.

Who Comes to Mass

All weekend liturgies at St. Pius V are celebrated on Sunday, for most Mexicans immigrants do not consider a Saturday evening vigil Mass adequate to fulfill the biblical mandate to worship on the Lord's day. About 3,000 people regularly attend six Masses, two in English and four in Spanish. Approximately half the parishioners at Sunday Mass attend every week, while another 25 percent may attend monthly, and the remaining 25 percent participate occasionally. As in most churches, attendance is highest in the fall and spring, especially during Lent and Eastertide. Then the two Spanish Masses, at 9:15 a.m. and 1:15 p.m., are filled beyond capacity with nearly 1,000 people attending each service, many standing in the aisles or sitting on the floor around the altar. The English Masses, which serve predominantly Mexicans and Mexican Americans, average 200 people. Many first- and second-generation Mexicans whose first language is English still prefer to worship in Spanish.

Sunday liturgical celebrations are family events, often with entire families attending together. Since Mexican families are young and large, the assembly is filled with children who not only raise the noise level but at times wander down the aisles exploring unfamiliar terrain, looking for ways to entertain themselves. While some Mexicans are annoyed by rambunctious children, most are tolerant. Some people claim that in Mexico children behave better because parents discipline them more closely. Some liturgists believe worship should be a carefully choreographed ritual in a peaceful environment where sunlight plays against stained-glass windows as a celebrant leads a synchronized congregation through tranquil prayers and rites. Such an environment is foreign to Mexican family life and, consequently, to their sense of liturgy. Most Hispanics are horrified at the idea of a crying room, the soundproof, glass-enclosed area in contemporary churches that isolates crying children. Children are part of family, and their presence brings joy to the Mexican heart. Maria, a single mother of two young boys, frequently struggles to control her children during Mass but is often relieved when someone unknown to her offers to help with one of the boys while she gets in line for communion, a clear demonstration of community and the community's love of children.

Many men attend Sunday Mass, comprising nearly half the assembly. This surprises many non-Hispanics, who commonly, though mistakenly, think Hispanic men do not practice their religion. While fewer men than women assume active leadership and ministerial roles in the parish, they do attend Sunday Mass and frequent the church for private devotions. In typical teenage fashion, many Mexican youth resist accompanying their family to Sunday Mass, even though they are more likely to be present than teenagers in non-Mexican parishes. The following sections address some aspects of Hispanic liturgical celebrations.

To Be at Mass Is to Participate

Liturgy implies participation, and singing is a major way for everyone to participate. A successful Hispanic liturgy has lively, rhythmic music that expresses the Hispanic spirit. Hispanic music transforms the Mass into a joyful experience, and even non-Hispanics embrace it enthusiastically. Through music, they come to understand and accept Hispanics as their brothers and sisters in Christ.[2] Although St. Pius V has promoted Hispanic music since its first Mass in Spanish in 1963, it faces the odd situation of being a community populated with many musicians, few of whom are willing or able to play on Sundays. Although for several years, two young musicians played at the Spanish Masses, most Mexican musicians are more interested in playing at weekend celebrations of baptisms, weddings, and *quinceañeras* and, consequently, are generally unavailable for Sunday liturgies. Moreover, since most Mexican musicians play by ear and do not read music, to be incorporated into a group, they need to practice extensively together to learn the group's musical style.

Even though Hispanic musical groups play lively music for Mass, a dynamic cantor is needed to encourage the congregation to sing. Occasionally, a Mexican *mariachi* group plays, and the congregation's reaction is electric. But people listen rather than join in the singing. *Mariachis* themselves do not encourage community singing and generally pitch their music beyond the people's range. For many years, St. Pius V benefited from a cantor who insisted on everyone singing. Before every Mass, he taught new hymns and rehearsed familiar songs. The result was an enthusiastic, singing community.

Until the 1990s, most Hispanic parishes sang a very limited repertoire, usually songs in one of the missalettes commonly used in Catholic Churches. Many of these songs were overly pious and theologically shallow, lacking a biblical perspective and failing to reflect the people's struggle for building church and the Kingdom of God. Many songs originating in charismatic renewal groups emphasized praise and intercession and were played to simplistic and monotonous rhythms. St. Pius V was determined to add music reflecting indigenous rhythms, with lyrics expressing people's struggle to live the Gospel. Since missalette companies were slow to publish books of Hispanic liturgical music, the parish searched for interesting and theologically appropriate songs in Latin America and arranged its own song sheets. At first, some Mexican parishioners reacted negatively, criticizing the music as not Mexican, unaware that most songs they had been singing were from Spain. Others were grateful for the new, more uplifting and substantive hymns. Octavio Ponce and his family travel all the way from Chicago's north side to St. Pius V's liturgies because "the music keeps us coming." The lyrics, reflecting working-class struggles, particularly appeal to Octavio, who works long hours in an upholstery factory.

The Eucharist Is a Meal

Full participation in the Eucharist means receiving communion. Eating and drinking the Body and Blood of Jesus are principal parts of the Mass, and in some sense, the Mass is not fully complete for those not receiving communion. Many Latin Americans, however, have not benefited from the Catholic Church's twentieth century effort to promote frequent communion. They appear stuck in a Jansenism of the past. Until recently, many clergy in Mexico emphasized the unworthiness of laity to receive communion, stressing the need to confess to a priest each time before receiving it, regardless of the gravity of their faults. Instead of announcing the Good News of salvation, the Church instilled an exaggerated sense of sinfulness, discouraging people from frequent communion. In 1986, only about 10 percent of those attending Sunday Mass at St. Pius V received communion. They had not been taught the power of the penitential rite at the beginning of each liturgy during which the assembled people recognize their sinfulness, ask for God's forgiveness, and receive the priest's absolution. Jesus invites everyone to his table, and people do not have to be perfect to accept his invitation. After years of preaching this hope-filled message, the number of communicants increased to more than two-thirds of those attending Mass.

A person's sense of worth is further enhanced by receiving communion in the hand, receiving under both forms, bread and wine, and baking bread for sharing at Mass. Since insisting that laity receive the consecrated bread on the tongue implies they are unworthy to touch it, the priests, staff, and liturgy committee encourage reception in the hand. After all, Jesus did not put his Body and Blood into the apostles' mouths at the Last Supper. While these arguments are compelling for many, some cannot bring themselves to change a lifelong devotional practice of receiving communion on the tongue. In the end, parishioners are free to choose the form they prefer.

To enhance the symbols in the eucharistic celebration and to bring the liturgy closer to its original form, the liturgy committee introduced unleavened bread, baked each Sunday by parishioners. To the delight of many, the bread generally arrives still warm from the oven. Although communion under the form of bread alone was the accepted norm for centuries, it is symbolically inadequate because it omits drinking the Blood of Christ.

Even though few churches in Mexico offer consecrated wine, Mexicans readily adapt to drinking from the chalice. They understand it as an integral part of eucharistic participation, and most lack the excessive hygienic concerns of many Americans who refuse the cup for sanitary reasons.

Because parishioners may resist certain liturgical changes, the priests provide orientation during homilies on the occasions of first communion and the feast of Corpus Christi. Homilists explain the church's earlier abandonment of traditions from the primitive church and current efforts to restore them, helping them understand their prior exclusion from full participation in the Mass and their current opportunity to participate more fully.

Ministers at Mass

The development of trained and plentiful liturgical ministers is key to creating lively and spiritually moving Sunday celebrations. The common practice of relying on a few stalwarts who serve for years in the same ministries overlooks the importance of constantly incorporating new people into ministries in order to create among the faithful a sense of ownership of the celebration. A few faithful ministers are consoling to pastors, but they can appear as functionaries and preserve passivity among the laity at large, who may not recognize their responsibility for assuming a more active role in the Eucharist.

Although there is a high level of illiteracy in the parish, good lectors and commentators can be found and trained. Most readers take their ministerial responsibility seriously; some even memorize their reading, much in the Hispanic tradition of *declamadores* (persons who dramatically read poetry). Some of the parish's best readers are youngsters between ten and fourteen years of age, who easily memorize their readings and learn pacing and phrasing. They mesmerize the congregation as their crystal-clear voices sing out the readings in the assembly.

Like most parishes, St. Pius V struggles with a group of longtime ushers who resist changing their traditional role of just collecting money to that of being official greeters. When the liturgy committee invited parishioners to serve as greeters at the front door and assist people in finding a seat, women responded more positively than men. Maintaining a solid group of ushers/greeters for six Masses on Sunday remains a challenge. The parish also struggles with recruitment, training, and constancy of altar servers. Some children interested in serving, girls and boys alike, live outside the neighborhood and find it difficult to attend practices during the week because no one is available to bring them to church. The committees of ministers for each Sunday Mass eventually organized their own groups to train and schedule their servers. Allowing children to serve at Mass provides a great opportunity to educate them not only in the meaning of the sacrament but in many dimensions of life, such as mutual respect, responsibility, cooperation, and punctuality.

Most laity view the position of communion minister as one of great prestige. Some consider themselves unworthy to distribute the Body and Blood of Christ and even criticize those who do.[3] Others want to be communion ministers for the wrong reasons, for example, to be seen by the congregation as closer to Christ. The incorporation of new ministers helps avoid creating a quasi-clerical caste of eucharistic ministers and promotes a sense of wider community participation. Since participation in church life involves more than serving at Mass, the parish asks communion ministers to serve in another parish ministry.

A common complaint is that women are communion ministers. While no one seems to have a problem with girl altar servers, criticism of women on the altar, a reflection of *machismo*, is widespread and perhaps even more common among women than men. The ancient idea that women are somehow unclean, and thus less worthy than men to touch the Body of Christ plays a role here. However, Jesus himself, while respectful of certain laws of religious purity, sharply criticized them insofar as they oppressed innocent people. Because the church helped create a false notion about women's impurity, it now needs to assist in freeing women and others from this distorted idea. Incorporating women into service at the altar is a good place to begin. Rather than succumb to criticism, St. Pius V uses it as an opportunity to teach the fundamental equality of men and women and how Jesus defended and promoted women. Women have been the traditional transmitters of faith in the Hispanic community. Their example, teaching, and devotional practices have transmitted faith and practice from generation to generation. Yolanda Tarango, a Latin American theologian, writes:

> I feel I entered the church at my grandmother's side through the stories she would tell me of her childhood. These were usually narratives of family and communal events framed in liturgical celebrations, such as parish patronal feasts and holy days. When she described encounters with the official church, the men of my family were usually the principal actors. Many stories included accounts of my great-grandfather and uncles and their confrontations with the foreign priests in an effort to preserve cultural rituals. In these episodes women appear to have been merely passive observers. Yet, in their accounts of religious rituals and celebrations in the home, the women of the family always emerged as the central characters. My grandmother and the women of her generation exercised their religious leadership in the Hispanic community as healers, prayer leaders, and dispensers of blessings. They were also the main persons responsible for passing on the traditions. They did so in a uniquely female manner, teaching through stories, rituals, and example.[4]

Aided by the postconciliar promotion of lay ministry and a more feminist culture in the United States, Hispanic women are now serving more visibly in pastoral ministry and leadership in the church, as well as assuming a central role in Hispanic communities. Arturo Pérez Rodríguez notes:

> Where previously they (women) were catechists, they are now directors of religious education; where previously they were sacristans, they are now lectors and ministers of communion; where previously they were helpful neighbors, they are now ministers to the sick

and shut-ins. Hispanic women are the ones who know the "right ways" of praying for the dead, for celebrating *posadas*, and for organizing feast days. They are the newly found pastoral associates, leaders of liturgy teams, and directors of social ministry. And it is their link with tradition and vision for the future which is enabling new ways of faith to grow.[5]

After many years, the St. Pius V staff began organizing an annual day of formation and celebration for all ministers participating in the Eucharist. The day involves a reflection on the important role ministries play within the parish community and the need for them to perform their responsibilities with dignity and respect. They share their personal reasons for serving and the benefits they receive from it, and as the day concludes, they renew their commitments to serve, leaving energized to improve their service and encourage others to join in their ministries.

Liturgy of the Word at the Eucharist

Preaching is of utmost importance for Mexicans, as it is for most Catholics. Some people attend Mass at a particular parish solely because the preaching there inspires and challenges them. Good preaching helps people experience the eucharistic celebration as connected to their lives. Because it enhances their Christian life, providing spiritual nourishment and direction, it also instills a sense of personal and community involvement in the celebration of the sacred mysteries.

Every year, at a course on preaching for Hispanic candidates for the diaconate, students describe what constitutes a good homily. Their responses are always similar: it should be clear, orderly, scripturally based, passionate, and related to people's lives. The preacher must communicate Christian commitment and convey personal conviction about the message. The homily should challenge people to change, while helping them experience the Good News of God's love. In the Hispanic community, the homilist's message should frequently be doctrinal, connected to the Bible as well as to the teaching of Vatican II, because many Hispanics have had little education in the faith. For most Hispanic adults, catechetical preparation occurred years ago and probably involved little more than basic instructions in the faith and the memorization of traditional prayers. Pastoral work, whether through Christian Base Community, counseling, or home visits, generally helps preachers not only understand people's struggles but also articulate their hopes and fears. They can hold up a mirror for people to see themselves honestly, the good and the bad; thus, the Word of God illuminates God's grace as well as the reality of sin.

Each Sunday the homily should address a question or problem in people's lives. Because the Word of God is alive and must touch the contemporary world, parish preaching must include not only personal challenges like forgiveness, anger, and resentment but also current events and social issues. Frequently preachers are afraid to treat the hard issues. While teaching preachers, I discovered few participants had ever given, or even heard, a sermon about child sexual abuse or domestic violence, problems so common in the Hispanic community they should be addressed every year. Other concerns include the possession of guns, school dropouts, racial discrimination, lack of communication among spouses, alcohol abuse, and division within families. To express the Good News, preachers should also replace a traditional Hispanic notion of God as a severe judge punishing people for their sins with Jesus' teaching about a loving and merciful Father.

Sometimes preachers at St. Pius V involve people in a dialogue homily, using questions to bring the people, their concerns, and understanding into the liturgy. Stepping down from the pulpit and walking among the people helps bridge an often perceived gap between preacher and people. Questions are generally aimed at soliciting people's thoughts and experiences rather than quizzing their knowledge. The best questions are simple, clear, and easy to answer. Questions asking about the ways people celebrated life and faith in Mexico bring people's traditions into the

Mass and spark lively reflections on what to preserve and celebrate in their communities in the United States. These dialogues
sometimes reveal surprises. When asked about how many had
learned about sex from their parents, only six of seven hundred
people raised their hands. In January 1994, when the Zapatista
rebels launched their uprising against the injustices suffered by
peasants in Chiapas, Mexico, the vast majority, although questioning the rebels' use of violence, sympathized with them and the
indigenous people. Most wanted the parish to express its solidarity with the Zapatistas, and all wanted to support the church of
Chiapas in its efforts to bring justice and peace to the region.

At times, the liturgy committee plans homilies that include
simple dramatizations, usually prepared by several people before-
hand and sometimes with volunteers spontaneously drawn from the
assembly. Dramas not only hold people's attention, they also tend
to speak clearly about people's lives. Once the committee selected a
group of people at each Mass to dramatize different aspects of
domestic violence. The priests and staff followed the drama with a
dialogue among the people, analyzing what they had witnessed.

Although preaching includes a personal dimension, challenging individual conscience and encouraging deeper personal spirituality, homilies at St. Pius V have a social, or community, orientation
as well, because Mexican immigrants believe and want to feel they
are *el pueblo*. Feeling isolated and alone, many need to be part of a
Hispanic community of faith. Thus, the homilies frequently touch
the dialectics of unity and division, service and *egoismo*, hope and
despair, justice and discrimination, commitment and passivity.
Preaching about community issues, events, tragedies, and celebrations helps to create a sense of participation in people, as well as foster relevancy in the liturgy. Identifying, graphically describing, and
analyzing real-life issues must be done sensitively, always communicating a basic appreciation of the people and their culture while raising the challenge of the Word of God to the status quo. The tough
topics of *machismo*, racism, alcoholism, and sexual, physical, and
emotional abuse, and other family problems, as well as people's passivity in the face of injustice and community problems, are addressed
firmly and repeatedly, and it is this frank, honest, and direct
approach that draws people to the liturgies.

Hispanics are not greatly concerned about the length of sermons. Although conventional wisdom maintains that Sunday homilies should run eight to twelve minutes, Hispanics are more concerned about the quality of sermons. In Hispanic churches, parishioners do not race to the parking lot after communion and before the final blessing. They are hungry for formation in their faith and, consequently, willing to listen for fifteen or even twenty minutes to homilies that offer them instruction, inspiration, and guidance. Mexicans are very tolerant of preachers speaking Spanish as a second language, sometimes complimenting them with unwarranted praise for their *mocho* (massacred) Spanish. Their flattery is meant to show appreciation for the preacher's efforts. In fact, the preacher's need to speak slowly and clearly in simple Spanish helps, rather than hinders, the people's ability to understand the homily's message. Mexicans like "fire and brimstone" sermons. Often the tougher the preacher, the more they like it. Unlike Euro-Americans, some prefer priests who scold them for their sinfulness. But preachers must be careful not to reinforce an unhealthy negative self-concept among Hispanics, and thus alienate them from the church. Rather, Mexican immigrants need to appreciate the many ways God has favored them and their culture.

Lay people occasionally preach at Sunday Mass. On Catechetical Sunday, catechists preach; on Mother's and Father's Days, mothers and fathers offer reflections on their vocations; on the Sunday dedicated to retired religious, a religious sister preaches; and on Labor Day weekend, workers give testimonies of their experiences and the need for Hispanics to organize. On days when there is a special topic, such as child abuse or domestic violence, women preach. Lay and clerical visitors from Central America and Mexico also share their experiences from the pulpit. Exposing the people to other preachers enriches their experience and highlights the participatory nature of the parish community. After a guest homilist finishes preaching, the community always shows its approval with a spontaneous round of applause.

The parish staff has tried to connect Sunday preaching with people's lives by encouraging and assisting families to reflect in their homes on themes presented in the Sunday homilies. These reflections are designed to support popular religiosity in the home, assisting families in talking and praying together, thus deepening their mutual communication and spiritual life. The best example involved a Lenten theme focusing on violence: "Break Down the Barriers, Work for Peace." Because violence separates people from Christ and from one another, people were invited to identify and root out violence in their lives. Preachers challenged people to be peacemakers by respecting, affirming, and forgiving one another, expressing anger more appropriately, doing good works, and improving communication. People were asked to eliminate all insults, calumnies, offensive language, slapping and hitting, threats, viewing of TV violence, and playing with toy guns. Each family member, including children, was asked to do something extra for someone in the family each week, a simple but intentional act of kindness. To help families pray together once a week, the staff distributed a sheet that included the peace prayer of St. Francis of Assisi, a reflection on the dimensions of violence discussed in the Sunday sermons, and a ritual for family reconciliation and spontaneous prayer. These family reflections helped preachers focus their homilies more directly on people's lives and helped people integrate the Sunday preaching into their daily experience.

Ways of Participating at the Eucharist

How can hundreds of people attending Mass become involved in the liturgical action and experience it as their own? Presenting babies, passing a crucifix from family to family, joining hands during the Lord's Prayer, introducing visitors, gathering children around the altar, helping to decorate the church's environment, and hearing announcements about activities in the parish and community, all create a greater sense of participation and ownership among the laity, as well as a feeling that the worshiping assembly is a true Christian community.

Presenting Babies

Mexicans have a beautiful tradition of presenting their babies in church, a practice based on an ancient Jewish tradition that Mary fulfilled by presenting herself and her son in the temple. Within days or weeks of birth, parents bring their babies to church wrapped in blankets, even in the dead of winter. A two-day-old child holds the record for the youngest ever presented. By presenting their babies, Mexicans thank God for their children, ask God's blessing on them, and announce the birth of their child to the larger community.[6] Another Mexican tradition dictates that parents bring their already baptized children to church on their third birthday to present them again. Presenting babies is so popular that families unable to obtain the service in their own parish bring their babies to St. Pius V for a blessing. After the presentation of bread and wine in the offertory procession, parents, or special *padrinos* and *madrinas*, present the babies to the priest, who carries each baby to the top of the stairs, elevates the child toward the altar and large crucifix behind it, praying silently for the baby, and then turns around to present the baby to the assembly.[7] At times, the presentation is quite emotional, as when brand-new twins or an obviously sick baby are presented. Although people are singing the offertory song at the time, most raise their heads to get a glimpse of the newborn. Smiles ripple through the congregation, and after an audible gasp of delight, the assembly erupts with a round of applause. Clearly, incorporating the presentation of babies into the eucharistic celebration encourages family participation and enlivens the liturgy.

Passing the Crucifix and Praying for Vocations

In 1994, the Hispanic auxiliary bishop in Chicago asked Hispanic parishes to pray for lay, religious, and priestly ministers. To involve people, the bishop gave participating parishes a beautifully hand-carved crucifix that a different family takes home each week for its daily prayer for vocations. People responded so enthusiastically at St. Pius V that the practice was institutionalized at different Masses. Each Sunday, the family having the crucifix during the previous week carries it to the altar during the offertory procession and in front of the presiding priest and congregation passes it to another family. Early enthusiasts purchased silver trays, made crimson pillows on which to lay the crucifixes, and decorated them with colorful, handmade silk flowers. Some families invite friends and family to pray with them, and some take up a collection to present to the church when returning the crucifixes. This custom brings many into closer relationship with the Sunday liturgy. At the same time, it helps the assembly appreciate the connection between home ritual and public liturgy, as well as the need for ministerial vocations.

Praying the Our Father, Celebrating Birthdays, and Gathering Children at the Altar

Singing the Lord's Prayer is an emotional moment in the Sunday liturgy. To begin, people join hands, even across aisles, so that a sea of people united in prayer extends into every corner of the church and around the altar. Hispanics not only do not resist holding hands, they love to touch, and the symbolism of unity-in-community is powerful as people sing their hearts out. Mexicans also make much to-do about birthdays, and recognizing them in church pleases everyone. Although singing *"Las Mananitas,"* the Mexican birthday song, takes several minutes, people thoroughly enjoy it. The community sings it monthly after communion to celebrate the birthdays of the month. Those being celebrated stand for the song and a round of applause. This brief ceremony energizes the community while integrating its culture into the liturgy.

At St. Pius V, the sacramental preparation of children occurs principally on Sundays. After gathering in the church hall for the Liturgy of the Word, children enter the church in procession and join the rest of the community during the presentation of the gifts. Most children sit on the floor behind and around the altar, creating a sense of community involvement in the Mass. Parents and the community as a whole appreciate seeing the children enjoying a place of honor during the Mass. In fact, the prominent place given to children often has an evangelizing effect, motivating other families to enroll their children in the religious education program.

Decorating the Church

Parish staffs commonly look for ideas to enhance participation of the faithful in liturgical celebrations. During Lent, the liturgy committee developed an effort, including beautiful decorations, that resonated with people.[8] The theme, "If anyone wishes to follow me, let them deny themselves, take up their cross and follow me," was chosen because it appeals to Mexicans who have a strong devotion to the cross and Jesus crucified. While the preaching focused on people's different experiences of the cross, the committee invited families to participate by sewing a cross on small pieces of cloth. Packets prepared for families contained four pieces of material in Lenten colors, as well as simple directions, sample designs of crosses, and a prayer to use as they made their crosses. People designed and sewed their cross on the square and added their family name. The parish deacon and his wife, Miguél and Soledad Pérez, sewed all one hundred squares into banners, which were hung around the church to create a cultural icon of Christ and his cross. The gorgeous banners stirred parishioners to admire the artistic contributions of their friends while experiencing a new sense of personal and communal participation in the mystery of Christ.

Including Mass Intentions, Announcements, and Visitors

During Sunday liturgy, attention to matters such as including people's intentions in the Mass, introducing visitors, reading announcements, and publishing an informative bulletin help nourish community life. Many people want a Mass offered for their intentions, often for the eternal rest of a deceased relative or the recovery of someone sick. Most people want to attend the Mass offered for their intentions, which usually necessitates a Mass on Sunday. But if only one intention is accepted for each Mass, many others cannot be included. Mexicans accept that a Mass offered for their intentions includes others; they easily understand that the value of the Mass is not diminished by sharing its merit with others. Thus, at Sunday Masses people are encouraged to add their intentions, which are mentioned during the Prayer of the Faithful. If people wish, they make a goodwill offering for the Mass.

The liturgy committee prepared a Mass intention book, so that people can write their intentions for Mass upon entering church. The book is carried in the entrance procession to a table near the altar, and the written intentions are included in a summary fashion in the Prayer of the Faithful, further enhancing the sense of the community's involvement in the Mass.

Each Sunday after reading the announcements, the commentator invites people attending Mass for the first time to stand to be recognized. As people rise, the assembly enthusiastically applauds, and many crane their necks to see the new people. Visitors are impressed to be received so warmly, usually smiling and appearing somewhat embarrassed as they receive their welcome. But this simple act of recognition may please parishioners more; they feel proud and honored that new people are constantly coming to their parish.

In a culture that is more oral than literate, reading announcements becomes a necessity. The announcement of activities in the community at the end of Mass helps create the sense of a lively parish. People like hearing about what is happening in their community and are proud to learn about their parish's involvement. The parish bulletin provides more detailed information, especially about job opportunities. Its main feature is a commentary relating the scriptures of the day to people's lives and communicating the vision of the parish as a community of faith, building the Kingdom of God here and now. In order to avoid a commercial flavor, the bulletin contains no commercial advertising. By producing it in the parish office, the staff can include late-breaking parish and community news.

The Sacrament of New Life: Baptism

Baptism is the first, and for Mexicans, the primordial sacrament, a rite of initiation into the people of God and union with Jesus Christ. Supported by the national culture in Mexico, baptism is nearly automatic for Mexicans; it is part of being Mexican. Virgil Elizondo explains that:

> Baptism is never thought of as simply the entry of another individual into the institutional church. In baptism the child is accepted and welcomed…into the life and memory of the entire family—parents, siblings, grandparents, relatives, and in-laws. The newly baptized becomes *uno de los nuestros* (one of ours).[9]

Popular beliefs about baptism among Mexicans reflect a mixture of theologies from different times in church history. For many, it is the washing away of original sin and, therefore, necessary to save a child from eternal damnation. For others, it is receiving God's blessing, or becoming a follower of Jesus, or fulfilling a family tradition. Whatever the response, parents and grandparents generally believe they have a grave responsibility under pain of sin to baptize their children and grandchildren. Some grandparents are concerned about their own standing with God as long as their grandchildren remain unbaptized.

Extending Family Through Compadrazgo

Baptism is a religious and family celebration, strengthening and extending the family beyond the boundaries of blood. Parents look for godparents or sponsors, who are called *padrino* and *madrina* in relationship to the child, and are called *compadre* and *comadre* in relationship to the parents. Godparents usually form a strong spiritual relationship with their godchildren *(ahijados)* and their entire family. Out of respect for their relationship, both parents and *padrinos* rarely call one another other by their first names but by the formal titles *"comadre"* and *"compadre."* Asking people to be *padrinos* implies establishing a relationship of trust and commitment; *compadres* promise to include one another in their respective family affairs and to support one another their whole lives. In fact, some immigrants do not baptize their babies soon after birth as in Mexico because they cannot find suitable or willing *padrinos* here. Because Mexicans do not easily accept the alternative of a proxy standing in for a real godparent unable to attend, they often wait until godparents arrive from Mexico. Although a priest or deacon actually baptizes the child, the importance of baptismal godparents is underscored in the expression *"padrinos bautizan al nino"* ("the godparents baptize the child"). Sometimes their responsibility entitles godparents to select their own church for the baptism instead of the parents' parish, a practice that may cause misunderstandings when pastors refuse to baptize a child whose parents are not registered at their parish. During the baptismal ceremony, parents usually hand their children to the godparents to hold at the moment of baptism *(llevan el nino al bautizo)*. To conclude the ceremony, godparents pass the children back to the parents in a gesture known as the *entrega,* or handing over, a celebration of the special bond of *compadrazgo* just established.[10] Additional relations of *compadrazgo* are created through the celebration of other sacraments, such as Eucharist, confirmation, and marriage, but the strongest ties are formed at baptism.

A major responsibility for godparents is financial. They may pay expenses that include invitations, a baptismal garment, candle, prayer book, rosary, medal of Our Lady of Guadalupe, donation to the church, photographs, hall rental, food and drinks at the fiesta, and musical entertainment. The godparents also provide a bag of coins, usually dimes and quarters, called the *bolo,* which at an appropriate moment are thrown into the air for children to gather up. The joyful *bolo* is a symbol of the godparents' sharing and generosity. Since the costs can be substantial, some parents ask others to share them with the godparents.

While the Catholic Church requires only one baptized person to be a godparent, Mexicans have a strong tradition of choosing a married couple. Non-Catholics and persons not in good standing with the Catholic Church (for example, unmarried couples living together or persons married by civil law but not by the church) are excluded by church law. This regulation creates a problem because many Mexican immigrant couples are not married sacramentally, either because it is not a priority for them or because their immigration status motivates them to postpone their wedding. While some pastors refuse to baptize the children of such couples, others assess the commitment of couples on an individual basis and encourage but do not require both parents and *padrinos* to be married in the church. This inconsistency in pastoral practice motivates families to shop among parishes for one willing to baptize their children.

The new relationship established through baptism with Christ, community, and family is evident in the enthusiastic celebration Mexicans plan for the occasion. Because local apartments are too small to accommodate a large number of friends, families often rent halls or organize activities in backyards, garages, basements, and back rooms of taverns. To respond to people's needs, St. Pius V installed a soundproof curtain to divide the church hall into two sections for such celebrations. Beginning in mid-afternoon, the party usually extends late into the evening, with plenty of food, drink, music, and dancing. People come and go during the day to pay their respects, bringing presents and participating in the festivities. To economize on costly celebrations, couples may combine their wedding with a baptism, whether of their own child or of another for whom they are *padrinos*. After the exchange of vows, parents and *padrinos* move to the font for the baptism. Joining two sacraments in one ceremony helps reduce expenses and enhances the celebration.

After a baptismal pool was constructed in the church, parents were presented with the option of fully immersing their children in warm water or simply bathing their foreheads. Many think immersion, the more ancient tradition, is a recent innovation. While immersion was quickly accepted by half of the parents, some resisted. Many parents change their minds at the last minute, however, after witnessing other babies immersed naked in the water. One difference between Hispanics and Euro-Americans is evident. While many non-Hispanics ask for a "private" baptism, that is, a special ceremony celebrated only for their child, Hispanics tend to prefer a celebration with the whole congregation. They want everyone to witness and enjoy the baptism of their children.

Although baptisms are celebrated every Saturday, the parish also celebrates baptism at Sunday Masses once a month. Even though the abbreviated ceremony may slightly lengthen the Mass, the immersion of children into water and their spontaneous reactions, varying from smiles of delight to screams of terror, thrill the congregation—which expresses its approval with spontaneous and jubilant applause.

Catechesis for Baptism

In 1987, six parishes in Pilsen decided to work together on a pre-baptismal catechesis. Since the parishes were experiencing a brisk demand for the sacrament and since many parents were shopping from parish to parish to find the program asking the smallest donation and the least requirements, pastors adopted a uniform preparation program. Because baptism is so important to the community and because most Mexican immigrants have received little formal preparation in the faith, the parishes use the celebration as an opportunity for broader catechetical formation instead of simply a teaching about baptism. Parish leaders and staffs designed a formation program of two classes, each of three hours, offered on two Friday evenings or two Saturday mornings to accommodate people's different schedules. Although some worried that increasing the hours of classes would discourage families from baptizing in local parishes, the result was just the opposite. In fact, some participants are so enthusiastic about the classes they return to serve as catechists themselves. Rosa María Icaza correctly notes that pastoral ministers should not view sacramental preparations simply as legal requirements: "Among Mexicans there is always the element of sacrifice, of doing without, of learning, of practicing. Along with that comes a sense of expectation for a big day, for a new relationship, a new commitment."[11]

The parish staffs trained teams of baptismal catechists in each parish to use a lively and participatory pedagogy and coordinate the program's administrative details. An opening dynamic facilitates people meeting one another and clarifies their purpose for seeking baptism. Then participants gather in small groups to read the Bible, respond to questions, and later share conclusions. When they discover they can understand the Bible and are learning more about their faith, they feel proud of themselves and grateful to the church. Dramas, used in Mexico to teach as well as entertain, help the time pass quickly because everyone participates with laughter or pathos. Catechists act out the different reasons for selecting *padrinos*, for example, wealth, prestige, friendship, or faith; participants then share their own motivations. Another drama presents a family, first as conflictual and disrespectful and then as harmonious and cooperative; participants comment on the different impact the two families have on the formation of children. In the two classes, the catechists develop four key theological points directed at correcting misunderstandings priests helped create among Mexicans.

1. The first segment treats God as acting in history to save the human family, rather than as an angry and severe God punishing his children. Salvation for the Jews meant liberation from oppression and the establishment of peace, justice, and freedom. This section emphasizes the distinction between God the Creator and Jesus the Son, because some Mexicans, owing to their limited catechetical formation, confuse the two persons of the Holy Trinity, evident in the expression *Jesus, mi padre Dios* (Jesus, my father God). Because the Catholic Church has at times emphasized the kingdom of God in the next life, omitting or minimizing the significance of building the kingdom on earth, the class also emphasizes its presence in the world.

2. The second segment teaches that Jesus is the Son of God, sent to continue God's plan of salvation. Because he cured the sick, welcomed the foreigner, challenged the rich, uplifted the poor, defended women, and challenged the

powerful, the authorities resisted, criticized, and finally eliminated him. It is important for Mexicans to see Jesus' suffering as a direct consequence of his struggle for the kingdom of God, because some tend to interpret his passion and death only as obedience to God's will, a view that tends to eviscerate Christianity of its radical call to denounce injustice and creates a church of passive, uninvolved believers. In addition, Mexicans tend to emphasize the expiatory effect of Jesus' sufferings. Asked, "Why did Jesus die?" they often answer "for our sins." Although partially correct, their response spiritualizes Jesus' suffering and death, lifting it from its historical context and ignoring the socio-political reasons for his crucifixion.

3. In the third segment, participants reflect on their need for conversion in order to participate in the kingdom of God. Participants examine the example of Zacchaeus, the repentant tax collector, to help them understand the dynamics of conversion and their own need for it.

4. In the final segment, participants reflect on Jesus' call for people to live in community, the church, where they are to serve and share their lives with one another. By studying how the first Christians lived in communities, participants are challenged to change the way they live their faith in their local parishes.

In summary, everyone is called to believe in a compassionate and liberating God, actively saving people in the world today, and to unite themselves with Jesus to build his kingdom of peace, justice, and love. To accomplish this task, people must be personally converted and join together in communities of faith, love, and service, namely, the church. Through baptism, they introduce their children into this church and the life, death, and resurrection of the Lord. The four catechetical sessions conclude with a brief teaching on the sacrament of baptism.

After a few years, the baptismal catechists accommodated parents and godparents returning to classes to prepare for another baptism by developing new material. After reflecting on the enormous economic and social pressures disintegrating many immigrant

137

families, they focused on family and parenting while maintaining some of the same elements in the first curriculum.

The Rite of Christian Initiation of Adults (RCIA)

The Rite of Christian Initiation of Adults (RCIA) is the liturgical and formation process through which adults are initiated into full participation in the church. People involved grow in the knowledge of the Christian faith, as well as spiritually through catechetical formation, liturgical celebrations, and service projects. Sponsors accompany them through the process, providing encouragement and example. Once they have studied the basic teachings and participated in church activities, candidates receive the sacraments of initiation, namely, baptism, confirmation, and Eucharist. This communal, experiential process leads to both the conversion of the individual and the renewal of the parish community.

Because few Mexican immigrants have not been baptized, most candidates in RCIA seek confirmation. Because they have not been fully introduced into the Catholic faith, the RCIA rite asks participants to leave the worshiping assembly during the Eucharist. This restriction appears strange and even offensive to most Mexican candidates because they have participated in the Catholic Church, however irregularly, most of their lives or have received some Christian formation by living in a predominantly Catholic culture. Most are not newcomers to the church, but only to the formal reception of a sacrament. Indeed, the embarrassment of being a Mexican who has not received all the sacraments deters many adults from asking to receive them.

St. Pius V offers the RCIA program on Sunday mornings, integrating it into the Sunday worship and helping the candidates feel part of the church. After the liturgy, the candidates and their sponsors gather with catechists for a reflection on the biblical readings of the day and specific church teachings. Specific rituals at Mass during Lent help both the candidates and the community prepare for the joyous celebration of the Easter Vigil, at which they are fully initiated. Because participants enjoy sharing their faith with others and form friendships with other participants and catechists during the program, some continue their formation when the program concludes.

The Sacrament of Reconciliation

Since Vatican II, the Catholic Church has experienced a decline in participation in the sacrament of reconciliation, commonly known as confession or penance. Most people began believing that if they had committed no serious sin, it was unnecessary to confess privately to a priest. Some understand that the ritual confession and absolution at the beginning of each Mass forgives small sins. Nevertheless, St. Pius V schedules individual confessions weekly and hears about twenty to thirty each Saturday afternoon. While providing inner peace, private confession attracts people with serious difficulties, whom confessors refer to the parish pastoral counselors.

Children learn about the sacrament in the parish and school religious education programs and then make their first confession in a communal reconciliation service. This celebration, new to most Hispanic immigrants, has gained popularity over the years. On a Saturday night before Advent and Holy Week, the parish celebrates this ritual for approximately six hundred people. Parents of children making their first confession and communion, who might not otherwise attend a reconciliation service, accompany their children, who in turn expect them to confess just as they do. Because so many families are present, the preaching generally focuses on the need for reconciliation within the family. After confessing some sin to one of many priests stationed around the church, people receive absolution. Some cry with relief after confessing their sins for the first time in years, while all rejoice in their children's initiation into reconciliation. For a penance, people circulate in church asking one another for forgiveness and offering a sign of peace. The priest concludes by leading the congregation in an enthusiastic cheer: *"Viva nuestro Dios misericordioso."* As the service ends, all burst into applause.

The Sacrament of Marriage

In recent decades, marriage and marital life in the United States have undergone major changes. The percentage of marriages ending in divorce has steadily risen during the latter third of the twentieth century, reaching approximately fifty percent today. In addition, an increasing number of couples are living together without marriage and for increasing lengths of time.

Civil and Sacramental Marriages

When people come to baptize their children, the parish discovers many unmarried couples living together. Some argue they want to test their relationship before sealing it with the indissoluble bond of the sacrament, while others no longer believe in the church's teaching about marriage. Some Mexican couples also believe that if their marriage is working smoothly, it is bad luck to disrupt it with a church wedding. Others live in this *union libre* (free union) because the man resists a marital commitment, or because the couple plans to marry later in Mexico where they can celebrate with their families, or simply because they lack the money for a wedding. Others ask to marry in the church but not by civil law because they are waiting for the lengthy process of legalization begun when they were dependents of legal residents. Since civil marriage would disqualify them as dependents, they want to be married "in the eyes of God" but not according to civil law. On the other hand, approximately one-third of the seventy-five weddings at St. Pius V each year involve couples already married by civil law or living together.

Others come for the sacrament at a young age. High rates of school dropouts and overcrowded apartments push teenagers out of the nest and into marriage long before they are ready. Many teens seeking marriage come primarily because their parents pressure them "to do what the church requires" and "to show respect for God." The high divorce rate among teenagers, however, has convinced most dioceses not to sanction weddings involving young people under eighteen years old.

140

In marriage preparation, a number of issues require thorough discussion. Some couples, living far from their parents in Mexico, know little of one another's family and their traditions. Often couples have different expectations about visiting or sending money to family in Mexico. Many couples are unaware of the influence of *machismo;* for some, it is the only way of relating between the genders they have known. Often women minimize their fiancé's controlling behavior, benignly labeling it jealousy. Alcohol consumption and the use of violence are also major points of discussion, since they are so prevalent among Hispanic men. Most Hispanic engaged couples respond positively to marriage preparation or pre-Cana classes as an opportunity to reflect on the challenges awaiting them in marriage and to feel part of the larger church. Because these workshops are hardly adequate preparation for many young people with little schooling, low self-esteem, and limited communication skills, St. Pius V developed a ministry to serve them, staffed by mature married couples who offer a series of workshops and a retreat.

Mexican traditions surrounding engagements flourish in many families. Some ask a priest to accompany the young man to his fiancé's home while he asks her parents for permission to marry. The priest's presence adds credibility to the young man's request and demonstrates his seriousness, responsibility, and respect for tradition. More often, however, the young man and his parents visit her home. Traditional parents sometimes refuse to meet their daughter's suitor or allow him in the house until he has performed this ritual. Until then, their courtship is conducted semi-clandestinely, with him picking her up in front of the house or down the block. While this custom keeps parents ignorant of their daughter's boyfriend, some parents prefer it because they do not want their daughters bringing one young man after another for them to meet, or introducing young men into their home who might cause problems with younger daughters.

Wedding Liturgies and Receptions

Culture and liturgy come together as Mexicans celebrate weddings. If the bride lives close by, tradition dictates she walks in procession to church, accompanied by family and friends and perhaps a musical group. During the Mass at church, sacramental objects are particularly important: designated *padrinos* bring coins *(arras)* for the couple to exchange as they pledge to care for one another; other *padrinos* provide a rosary and prayer book and sometimes a Bible and/or a crucifix for their bedroom, symbols of their faith and devotion. Most important is the *lazo*, an ornate cord donated by other *padrinos*, who place it over the couple's shoulders, symbolizing their bonding together. Traditionally, *padrinos* tuck the bride's veil under the *lazo* over the groom's shoulders, strengthening the symbolism of spousal unity. As couples assimilate into American ways, some add the unity candle, which the newly married husband and wife light together. The *padrinos de velacion* (godparents of the candles) play the most important role, ordinarily receiving a place of honor near the bride and groom at the altar, replacing the maid of honor and best man. In Mexico, they traditionally supply the candles for the altar and pay for the church ceremony. An abundance of flowers decorate a few arches and the pews in the main aisle, but because natural flowers are so expensive, Mexicans usually use artificial ones—all paid for by other *padrinos*.

Weddings reflect the cultural transition of immigrant families. Women generally dress formally, while men wear almost anything; some dress in tuxedos, others in cowboy shirts and boots. A groomsman might wear new black and white Air Jordan gym shoes or a shirt open to the chest, revealing an array of gold chains. Brides almost always dress in magnificently embroidered, long, flowing dresses that show off the community's sewing artistry. Martha and Juan (already married by civil law) saved money for years to marry in the church and host a lavish fiesta. She spent a year sewing her wedding gown, and it was spectacular. Her husband wore a freshly pressed pair of blue jeans, accented by an ornate, oversize metal buckle, cowboy boots, and a shirt with a western-style bolo tie.[12] Music by a *mariachi* band, which is sometimes a surprise for the couple, was a special treat.

Receptions for Mexican weddings have their own structure. Frequently they are held in small neighborhood halls, where family and friends crowd in for a night of eating, drinking, and dancing. The usual fare includes rice and beans, chicken *mole*, and tortillas served from aluminum trays onto paper plates. More assimilated families often rent banquet halls, where the menu remains the traditional Polish fare—kielbasa sausage, baked chicken, boiled beef, succotash, and mashed potatoes. In time, these halls will offer a Mexican menu, complete with jalapeño peppers. Frequently the crowd swells well beyond expectations. Although Eva and Eleazar invited two hundred guests, four hundred came because like many couples they did not request an RSVP or limit the number of guests per invitation. Although the hall was packed and food ran out, the couple was thrilled so many people came to their wedding.

Festivities begin after the meal with the formal presentation of the *padrinos*. Whereas in the United States, the bride's family generally pays the wedding expenses, among Mexicans, costs are distributed among many others. Often weddings have as many as thirty pairs of *padrinos*, including those who pay for the church, hall, music, food, limousine, dress, cake, flowers, rings, coins, and even the knife to cut the cake. In the future, the newly married couple will be expected to reciprocate when fiestas are held in the families of their new *padrinos*.

The *baile del dolar* (dollar dance) follows. As men dance with the bride and women with the groom, they pin money to the bride and groom's clothing while the band plays the same waltz over and over.

Next comes the *baile de vibora* (snake dance) in which the male attendants and guests, and later the women, join hands and run through the hall at breakneck speed. As the bride and groom stand on chairs, holding up her veil to form a bridge between them, the snake dancers skip underneath to rapid traveling music. The maid of honor and best man stand guard to protect the bride and groom from being knocked over. The snake symbolizes the evil that may attack their marriage, while the attendants are the couple's protectors against harm.

143

Mexicans also include the ritual of the bride throwing her bouquet to single women and the groom removing her garter and throwing it to unmarried men. The groomsmen then grab the groom, remove his shoes, and proceed to throw him into the air.

All these ceremonies take nearly two hours, after which the guests are invited to dance the night away. Near the end of the evening the bride and groom cut the cake, and children in the family commonly distribute pieces to guests. Nearly half the cake is left over, a symbol of the largesse of the fiesta, and it is packaged in small sandwich bags for guests to take home. Since weddings are premier social functions, gathering people from the same family and towns in Mexico, they are opportunities for great celebration, as well as for young single men and women to meet.

Divorce and Annulment

Women's new sense of self and personal dignity, as well as people's increasing unwillingness to make permanent commitments, have greatly affected the shape and stability of marriages. Although their traditions help Mexican immigrants face these challenges, they, too, are developing new understandings and practices of marriage.

Even though Mexicans respect the Catholic Church's teaching on the indissolubility of marriage, for some, marriage ends in divorce or separation. In Mexico, many women, marrying at a young age and frequently to older men, are ill-prepared for married life and often suffer devastating physical and emotional abuse. If they were raised in a home torn by violence, they often accept it as normal. Only after many years of abuse do some wives look for assistance in freeing themselves from their alcoholic, violent, *machista*, or just plain absent husbands.

Some husbands travel to *El Norte* to earn money, leaving their wives alone in Mexico to raise their children and visiting them every year or two. Since being alone in the United States is difficult, some resort to living with another woman. In

144

Mexico, the culture tends to condone the promiscuity of men while condemning the infidelity of women. For example, when Leticia discovered her husband had another woman, her mother counseled her to be understanding and patient; her husband was weak, and this fling would certainly pass—common advice from Mexican mothers. Because young girls are often taught by their mothers and grandmothers that men have stronger sexual needs than women, some women tolerate their husbands' frequenting prostitutes "to satisfy their desires."

Many couples married only by civil law live good Christian lives. Through their participation in the church, they develop a strong sense of morality but are unable to receive the sacrament of matrimony because of a previous marriage and divorce. While many might qualify for annulments, they are unaware of the opportunity or hesitant to avail themselves of it, believing their first marriage was for life. This difficult situation means that many divorced and remarried Mexican Catholics do not receive Holy Communion and feel alienated from the church.

Sacramental Death

Although a funeral ceremony is not an official sacrament, it is an important moment for people to celebrate their faith and experience God's presence. Those who grieve draw strength from the church's rituals: anointing during the final sickness, prayers and accompaniment at the wake, viewing of the body, celebration of Mass, procession to the cemetery, solemn committal to the tomb, and *novenario* (a novena of prayers) after the funeral.

Approximately half of Mexican immigrants who die in Chicago are buried in Mexico, usually with no Mass celebrated here. However, because of financial limitations or the lack of legal documentation, usually few family members accompany bodies to Mexico for the funeral Mass and burial. Thus, the wake service is an important opportunity to gather family and friends for support and prayer and for a reflection on the life of the deceased, as well as on the teaching of the Catholic faith about death. The services are directed not only to mourning family members but to all attendees, preaching a basic catechesis on the meaning of being baptized into Christ's life, death, and resurrection. The preacher invites family and friends to share their memories of the deceased, to offer a prayer for them, and to express their gratitude for their life. Invariably, testimonies emerge that inspire participants to draw closer as family and community, and to put their faith into action. If the deceased was a grandparent, it is safe to assume that one of his or her dying requests was greater unity among the children and grandchildren. They are encouraged to maintain a spiritual relationship with their beloved dead, to still include them in some way within their family, whether with photos, an altar, or occasionally special mentions and prayers. Whether in Mexico or Chicago, the family almost always requests a grave-site burial; they want to see the body being lowered into the grave and fully covered with dirt, partly to add finality to burial and partly for fear someone might tamper with the body.

Pastoring in an inner-city immigrant community almost certainly involves officiating at funerals for young men killed in gang violence. Some priests react so strongly against gangs they deny church funerals for active gang members because they are public sinners, unworthy of the church's service, unless, of course, they repent before death. The opposite view maintains that funerals of gang members provide a unique pastoral opportunity.

At a wake or funeral of gang members, the assembly is diverse. The family of the deceased is stricken with grief. Friends and classmates are in shock over the loss of someone so close to them. They gather around and hug one another, sobbing deeply. Surviving gang members grieve as well, but are often consumed with rage and itching for vengeance. They stand stone-faced, arms folded defiantly across their chests, jaws set in determination to avenge their homeboy's death. Some, however, are stricken with fear, terrified that more violence will consume them. Many in the community who have seen it all before are sadly resigned to the tragedy of yet another senseless death. The preacher must respond to this diverse congregation with a focused but varied message. It is important to speak directly to the different emotions present in the assembly, articulating them so that people can recognize them and respond themselves.

The true response, of course, is found in Jesus, the total and complete answer to violence. Thus, funerals for gang members inevitably involve four points:

1. *Community support for victims.* Unity among family and friends helps heal the wounds of violence and restore life to mourners. Parents suffer the permanent loss of their murdered children, and friends suffer lifelong emotional wounds. Survivors need community support and solidarity. On the cross, Jesus said to Mary, "Woman, behold your son," and to the Apostle John, "Behold your mother." He asked each to care for the other. Thus, the whole community must gather around those affected by violence to support them.

2. *Forgiveness.* Jesus' answer to hatred and revenge is forgiveness. Often surviving gang members serving as pallbearers for deceased friends sit in the front pews decked out in gang colors with hatred firing their hardened stares. They seem to be meditating on revenge. Family members are hardly thinking of forgiving the person who killed their brother or son. But Jesus has a message for them. When seized in the Garden of Olives, he reprimanded a disciple who drew his sword: "He who lives by the sword, will die by the sword." By pardoning those who put him to death ("Father, forgive them for they know not what they do"), he taught forgiveness and even love for his enemies.

3. *Courage to confront violence.* Although people need courage in the face of violence, they are often afraid to confront it, whether with spouses, parents, neighbors, or gang members. To escape it, some move from their communities or close their eyes to it, while others refuse to call the police or report abuse because they fear violent retaliation. Jesus recognized the risks in challenging the violent, warning, "If anyone wishes to

be my disciple, let them take up their cross and follow me," and counseling, "Fear not those who kill the body, but those who kill the spirit."

4. *Commitment to peace.* Many people despair of a peaceful community. They have lost hope in working for change and sometimes withdraw from community involvement. But Jesus never tired of working for the reign of peace. He taught: "Blessed are the peacemakers, for they shall be called the children of God." People need to believe in the possibility of a peaceful world and the power of God's Spirit working within them to create it. They must remember how Mary, the mother of Jesus, stood valiantly at the foot of the cross, watching her son die. Although she mourned his death, she did not bury herself in sorrow or despair; rather, she gathered her strength and joined the apostles in responding to Jesus' call to create peace based on justice.

The celebration of death is a pastoral opportunity to assist people in expressing and renewing their faith. It is a solemn and holy moment when pastoral ministers can provide strength and support. The Gospels teach that the life, death, and resurrection of Jesus help people triumph over violence in their lives and bring new life to their communities.

Mexican spirituality recognizes the presence of God in and among them. Mexicans love ritual that celebrates the divine presence. Sunday liturgies celebrate their faith and life in Jesus Christ, incorporating their culture and tradition. They are joyful and participatory, resounding with their music, uplifting to their spirit, yet challenging to their lives. The sacraments of baptism, reconciliation, and matrimony, as well as funeral liturgies, touch their hearts and souls and enliven their faith. Each sacrament and liturgy in its own way serves to strengthen their bonds of family and community. In the following chapter the sacramental theme is explored further, beyond the official sacraments.

Notes

1. *Catechism of the Catholic Church* (Vatican: Libreria Editrice Vaticana, 1994), nos. 1113–18; Richard P. McBrien, *Catholicism* (San Francisco: Harper, 1994), 784.

2. Mary Frances Reza, "Crosscultural Music Making," in Kenneth G. Davis, *Misa, Mesa y Musa* (Schiller Park, IL: World Library Publications, 1997), 97. Reza observes, "Participating in the artistic creativity of another culture often brings an understanding of that culture on its own terms. Cross-cultural music can provide us with both an appreciation for racial and cultural diversity and also a commitment to the commonality that unites all of us in the Catholic Church."

3. Some Mexicans prefer that priests, and maybe religious sisters, be the only ones distributing communion. To discourage people from crossing the church to receive communion from a priest, coordinators occasionally move priests to different communion stations.

4. Yolanda Tarango, "Women," in Deck et al., *Perspectives*, 41.

5. Arturo Pérez-Rodríguez, *Popular Catholicism: A Hispanic Perspective* (Washington, DC: The Pastoral Press, 1988), 16.

6. Mark R. Francis, CSV, and Arturo Pérez-Rodríguez, *Primero Dios: Hispanic Liturgical Resource* (Chicago: Liturgical Training Publications, 1997), 23–24. The authors describe a related custom called *echar agua* (literally "to pour water"), which is practiced by Puerto Ricans. Although *echar agua* involves pouring water over a child, it is not the sacrament of baptism but has a direct relationship to it. The words spoken during the pouring are *"Me lo entregaste moro, y te lo devuelvo cristiano"* ("You gave him to me a Moor [that is, a 'Moslem'], and I give back to you a Christian").

7. Francis and Pérez-Rodríguez outline a rite used when the baptism is performed outside of Mass that includes signing the baby with the cross and anointing with the oil of catechumens, a pattern responding to suggestions of the Rite of Christian Initiation of Adults, where the rites of initiation take place in a progressive way over time. Francis and Pérez-Rodríguez, *Primero Dios*, 24–25.

8. Lilian Lewis, who served on the staff of St. Pius V, where she contributed exceptional creativity and innovation to the parish work, developed this idea.

9. Virgil Elizondo, *Galilean Journey*, 45.

10. Francis and Pérez-Rodríguez, *Primero Dios*, 33.

11. Rosa María Icaza, CCIV, "Prayer, Worship, and Liturgy in a U.S. Hispanic Key," in Allan Figueroa Deck, SJ, ed., *Frontiers of Hispanic Theology in the United States* (Maryknoll, NY: Orbis, 1995), 149.

12. Sometimes the contrast is rather humorous. One young man "gave away the bride" (his sister), who was dressed in an elaborately hand-embroidered gown, complete with a twelve-foot train, while he walked at her side with blue jeans, a denim shirt, and a cellular phone hanging from his belt. Once a father of a bride accompanied his daughter to the altar wearing his baseball cap.

6.

Liturgy and Culture: The Sacramental Dynamic

Liturgy connects the divine and the human, the spiritual and the material, and when the physical faithfully expresses the spiritual, it is sacramental. For Mexicans, life necessarily involves sacred ritual, celebrating the spiritual world active in the material, uniting the cosmic and the personal. A passing encounter with Mexican religious practices reveals the centrality of their personal relationship with God, the importance of multiple sacraments and sacramentals, their belief in a world filled with spirits, and their devotion to the Virgin of Guadalupe as their loving and influential mother and to the saints as their personal advocates before the Almighty. This chapter examines how Mexican people celebrate rituals and feasts proscribed by the official Catholic liturgical calendar as well as how they sanctify their personal, family, and community life through religious practices.

In Latin America, traditional religious beliefs and practices are commonly referred to as "popular religiosity." It is "popular" not because it is necessarily widespread but because it is born of the people, an expression of their culture. In 1979, Latin American bishops declared:

> By religion of the people, popular religiosity or popular piety, we mean the whole complex of underlying beliefs rooted in God, the basic attitudes that flow from these beliefs and the expressions that manifest them. It is the form of cultural life that religion takes on among a given people.[1]

Two Hispanic theologians in the United States, Orlando Espín and Sixto J. García, offer a technical description of popular religiosity:

> ...the set of experiences, beliefs, and rituals which more-or-less peripheral human groups create, assume and develop (within concrete socio-cultural and historical contexts and as a response to these contexts) and which to a greater or lesser degree distance themselves (superficially or substantively) from what is recognized as normative by church and society, striving (through rituals, experiences and beliefs) to find an access to God and salvation which they feel they cannot find in what the church and society represent as normative.[2]

Because Hispanic popular religiosity originates among people of faith, principally the poor, Espín believes it constitutes a true *locus theologicus* (theological source), the place where theological reflection should begin. As such, it assumes the authoritative role assigned by the church to the *sensus fidelium*, that is, the faith of the people.[3]

Attention to popular religiosity in recent decades stems primarily from the importance Vatican II gave to the local church. It has also been propelled by pastoral work in Latin America and is reflected in the current interest in inculturation, that is, the inclusion of cultural values and traditions of ethnic minorities in mainstream liturgical practice.[4] The "Constitution on the Sacred Liturgy" from Vatican II states:

> The Church has no wish to impose a rigid uniformity in matters which do not involve the faith or the good of the whole community. Rather she respects and fosters the spiritual adornments and gifts of the various races and peoples...[like] private prayer and popular piety, present in the soul of our people, [which] constitute evangelization values.[5]

Reminiscent of anti-Catholic apologetics prominent during the late nineteenth and twentieth centuries, some scholars and sectarian evangelists characterize the ritual and symbolic world of Hispanic Catholics as obscurantist, superstitious, and pre-modern.[6] For their part, Latin American bishops note positive and negative aspects of this religiosity. Positive aspects include

> a sense of the sacred and the transcendent, openness to the Word of God, marked by Marian devotion, an attitude of prayer, a sense of friendship, charity, and family unity, an ability to suffer and to atone, Christian resignation in irremediable situations, and detachment from the material world.[7]

They also add "abandonment to God's mercy, commitment in faith to the Gospel, strong family and community ties, deep thanksgiving for seemingly so little, unmediated experience of the Holy in every aspect of life."[8] Some negative aspects noted are the lack of a sense of belonging to the church, a divorce between faith and real life, a disinclination to receive the sacraments, an exaggerated devotion to the saints to the detriment of knowing Jesus Christ, a distorted idea of God, a utilitarian view of certain forms of piety, an inclination toward religious syncretism and spiritism.[9]

For Latin American bishops and theologians, popular religiosity is a means of symbolically expressing liberation from past oppression and a prophetic call for social justice in the present.[10] Most of these rites grew up alongside official rites of the church and reflect a worldview comprising elements from Spanish, Native American, and African cultures.[11] The bishops at Puebla recognize that popular religion also facilitates people's contact with the holy, to which the ecclesiastical power structure frequently limits their access. It is a source of unity and healing, offering hope for a better future and strength to those struggling on the fringe.[12]

In his study of popular religiosity, Roberto Goizueta recognizes its subversive socio-political role in challenging dominant values, as well as its aesthetic dimension in affirming the intrinsic value of human life. These celebrations help the poor and marginalized find their identities and self-worth and, thus, "resist the dominant culture's attempts to destroy that identity through assimilation."[13]

Pastoral ministers unfamiliar with Mexican culture may be confused, bewildered, and even irritated by its religious traditions. While some do not see the connection of these traditions to official liturgical celebrations, others consider them quaint or superstitious. Espín notes: "Today, the encounter between Euro-American and Hispanic Catholicism frequently produces conflict. Modern logic tells symbol it must yield to the claims of positive reason, while symbol tells logic that it has lost its poetic reason and perhaps its heart."[14] But, in the end, he believes that the clash has more to do with conflicts of power and powerlessness, that is, struggles between rich and poor, between dominant and minority cultures, than with differences in doctrine and theology. James L. Empereur, rector of the Cathedral in San Antonio, Texas, observes, "The main reason that co-existence of popular and official Catholicism often become confrontational is that the same definition of church does not underlie both."[15] One stems from a hierarchical, uniformly ordered church, while the other emphasizes community and diversity.

The Emergence of Popular Religiosity

Some authors emphasize that popular religiosity in Latin America developed from late medieval Christianity brought by Spanish missionaries in the sixteenth century. In fact, much of Latin American Catholicism stems from the following century, characterized by the baroque. While the sixteenth-century brand of Catholicism articulated at the Council of Trent in 1570, and reinforced later by the Enlightenment, moved away from an analogical and sacramental understanding of Christianity to one focused more on church doctrine, organization, and authority, often summarized in concise doctrinal catechisms, many Spanish missionaries to the New World promoted the baroque emphasis on symbol, ritual, and celebration, highlighting the exuberance and positive expanse of the Christian religion.[16] Less concerned with orthodoxy than the post-Tridentine church, many European missionaries evangelized through nonverbal activities, such as processions, statues, paintings, music, and drama. In contrast to the rationalist worldview of the Enlightenment, which originated amidst more urban, modern, and individualist environs, the worldview of Hispanics developed from rural, traditional, and family-oriented societies and thus preserved a more analogical and sacramental perspective of things. This worldview predates and has continued alongside the rationalist perspective.

Indigenous peoples were brutally massacred during the conquest, and survivors were subjected to centuries of servitude under a cruel colonial system. Virgil Elizondo notes that the most devastating violence was spiritual, destroying "the conquered's inner worldview, which gives cohesion and meaning to existence."[17] The conquerors imposed their own culture and religion, while rejecting and even outlawing indigenous customs and traditions, even though to some extent, according to Bartolomé de las Casas, writing in defense of indigenous peoples in the 1550s, the indigenous religious world was positively suited to receive the Gospel.[18]

Although the conquered gradually interiorized their oppressors' thinking and values, largely rejecting their own traditions as inferior, they nevertheless preserved some religious practices. In some instances, Spanish missionaries took the beliefs, rituals, and feasts of different indigenous peoples as the starting point for their evangelization, trying to co-opt them by substituting Christian symbols for pagan ones and bestowing on them a Christian interpretation, eventually producing a syncretic Christian faith and ritual. Because of a shortage of priests, largely resulting from Spanish policies limiting ordination to non-*mestizo* candidates (a *mestizo* is a person of mixed race), indigenous people, often unschooled and illiterate, lived relatively isolated from colonial clerical influence and, consequently, subversively maintained some of their own religious traditions. Thus, a form of *mestizaje* was created in religious belief and practice. This analysis helps explain Mexicans' traditionally casual attitude toward regular Sunday Mass attendance. Deck observes:

The standard norms for measuring the religious commitment of Catholics in post-Tridentine Catholicism—attendance at Sunday Mass, frequent communion, and involvement in the life of the parish—were not exactly relevant to the majority of Mexican Catholics for most of their history.[19]

The marginal status imposed on indigenous peoples in the church also helps explain their attitude toward frequent communion. While most Mexicans absorbed the viewpoint of European Jansenism that fostered a sense of the laity's unworthiness to receive communion and accepted that they must confess their sins to a priest each time before receiving it, they are not so troubled or guilt-ridden about "living in sin" because they have not confessed recently.

Indeed, Hispanic morality emerges less from a collection of laws than from an ongoing conversation with God. While important, law is subservient to community, people, and the need to survive. Perhaps Mexicans have a healthier, more balanced understanding of church because they view it as an institution governed by human-made rules and regulations. God's power and grace are not mediated solely through its bureaucracy. The spirit world is much greater, more extensive, and profoundly more intimate than any institutional church could be. *Curanderos* (healers) and *rezadores* (official leaders of prayer), who intercede with the divine and exercise influence in the world of spirits, also deserve religious respect.

Through conquest and colonization, a *mestizo* people were born from a mixture of ethnic groups, producing a new cultural identity that is still evolving. In the case of Mexican and Mexican American *mestizaje*, the first intermingling began in 1519 with the Spanish conquest, and the second started with the American invasion of northern Mexico in the 1830s. Elizondo, writing extensively on *mestizaje*, notes: "This new and more clearly defined self-image of who we are as Mexican Americans is presently beginning to take shape."[20]

Some authors observe that Hispanic popular religiosity differs from pre-Vatican II devotionalism. Mark Francis notes that

Hispanic religiosity is more oral than literate, more communal than individualistic, more lay-based than clerical. While Hispanic religiosity involves "cathartic experiences of collective memory,"[21] European-based devotionalism consists more of individual acts of piety, with little interest in relating people to community. In fact, pioneers of the liturgical movement encountered strong resistance to their community-oriented reforms when they attempted to wean churchgoers away from praying their rosary during Mass. Latin American religiosity, on the other hand, is more tied to family, community, and the earth.

Since many religious practices are celebrated in the home (*religión casera*) and the community, Catholic bishops regard the communal nature of Hispanic popular religion as of utmost importance. Richard Rodriguez, a noted Mexican American commentator, said it most concisely: "The central pronoun for Hispanics is the we, *nosotros*, while for Americans it is the I."[22]

Because popular religiosity reflects a spirituality so intricately interwoven with the culture, encompassing cosmic as well as personal dimensions, ever present but eluding facile definition, it is often referred to as a *mística*. The 1987 *National Pastoral Plan for Hispanic Ministry* described this mystique or spirituality as

> a sense of the presence of God, which serves as a stimulus for living out one's daily commitments. In this sense, the transcendent God is present in human affairs and human lives. Indeed, one might speak of God as a member of the family, with whom one has recourse, not only in moments of fervent prayer, but also in one's daily living.[23]

Hispanics believe that their human condition is not much different from that of Jesus and his mother, Mary. Like them, they are poor and persecuted. This identification helps them feel personally linked with the holy and the saints, and helps explain their tender, intimate language in prayers, hymns, and devotions.[24] Much is expected of God and the saints, as of other friends and family. Thus, when a favor is not granted, it is not uncommon to turn the statue of a saint to face the wall as an expression of dissatisfaction with their response.[25] This familial relationship is nurtured through religious devotions that recognize the holy in what others might consider mundane. Hispanic popular religion is embodied worship, using sacramentals engaging all five senses to connect it to the world of the spirit. Through sacramentals, the particular mediates the universal; the worldly incarnates the divine. Goizueta notes:

> When...an elderly Mexican woman approaches the Crucified Jesus to plant a gentle kiss on his feet, or reaches to touch Mary's veil during a procession, there is little doubt that for the elderly woman, Jesus and Mary are present *here*. These religious statues or figures are not mere representations of reality completely external to them, rather they are the concrete embodiment, in time and space, of Jesus and Mary. These are, in short, sacramental images: natural, particular entities that mediate, embody, and reveal a supernatural, universal and absolute reality.[26]

Within Hispanic communities, it is often women, mothers, and grandmothers who are the leaders of popular religion. They offer blessings, arrange home altars, say the prayers, provide children and grandchildren with religious instruction, and lead the family in religious song. Espín believes the strong Marian spirituality among Hispanics results from the dominant role of women in popular religion:

> Women are the center and pillars of the families, and Latino popular Catholicism is definitely woman-emphatic. It is no exaggeration to say that older women are our people's hermeneuts. They are the ministers and bearers of our identity. And so this explains, at least to me... the Latino inclination to image and explain the divine and religious through feminine symbols and categories, and through women-led rites.[27]

Although most Mexicans recognize that their experience of religion is different from that of most Americans, they are not always able to articulate the substance and meaning of this *mística*. It is too much like the air they breathe to notice, much less describe. Similarly, it is difficult for many pastors to appreciate the differences between Hispanic religiosity and that of mainstream American Catholicism. Understanding the differences requires much more than simply learning Spanish. Church officials need to listen carefully to Mexican expressions of faith and be open to accepting their religious practices and the spirituality underlying them.[28]

St. Pius V tries to respect people's traditions by incorporating popular religion into its parish liturgy. Because the staff believes that people's faith and religious practices are constantly evolving and, in particular, because the people are inserted into a hostile dominant culture, the parish adapts new practices as the *mestizo* congregation develops its religiosity. To respect people's traditions, St. Pius V has adopted the pastoral method outlined by Pérez-Rodríguez and Francis: 1) listening to the experience of the people; 2) entering into dialogue with the tradition; 3) developing a tentative new liturgy; 4) evaluating the rites in the light of the gospel in an ongoing fashion."[29]

The Cultural Cycle of Seasonal Liturgies

While popular religiosity is often unique, it is generally connected to the church's official liturgical calendar, albeit with adaptations and additions.[30] Francis notes:

> It would not be accurate to overly dichotomize the "official" liturgical year from its "popular" Hispanic version since, in a sense, we are dealing with two different but overlapping phenomena....The Hispanic liturgical calendar is not conceptually organized, nor can it be neatly reduced to a set of rubrical norms....Rather, it is the year of grace lived by people that serves to sacralize their existence and mark the passage of time in a cosmos filled with God's presence.[31]

This section reviews the official liturgical calendar and notes some contributions from Mexican popular religion to St. Pius V's liturgical celebrations. Because customs vary in different parts of Mexico, the parish liturgy committee sometimes debates about the "correct" or "authentic" Mexican way of doing things, but in the end, its members usually accommodate one another's traditions, blending their differences into something new.

Liturgy is important for immigrants because traditional songs, rituals, and customs help them experience continuity with their communities of origin and provide them with a sense of stability and identity. At times in Latin America, liturgical reforms failed to interest the faithful, partly because they were initially based more on the revision of texts than on actual liturgical practices and partly because they generally ignored popular religious practices.[32] Also, Latin Americans, including many First World missionaries there, are often too focused on economic survival or political conflict to be concerned with liturgical formalities. Rosa Maria Icaza notes the situation is quite different in the United States: "In Latin America, they (Hispanic people) use liturgical ways of celebrating perhaps more freely because they do not see such practices as part of their identity as a people as consciously as Hispanics living 'in exile' from the homeland."[33]

Since most Mexican immigrants generally lack basic liturgical and theological preparation, the liturgy committee faces the challenge of identifying traditional Mexican religious practices, understanding the liturgical reforms, and planning liturgical celebrations meaningful to the immigrant community.[34] Some people insist on rigidly preserving traditional (and often provincial) rituals, with little regard for liturgical reforms. They may not be able to explain the origin or meaning of their traditional rituals, except to say, "That's the way it was always done in my town." Most people, however, readily accept changes once they are explained to them. Others attend diocesan liturgical programs that help them apply sound liturgical principles as they struggle to preserve centuries-old rituals deeply rooted in people's hearts.

Advent

What to do during Advent? The Advent wreath, familiar to Euro-Americans and used in most churches, means relatively little to Latin Americans, even when explained. Likewise, the European tradition of self-denial practiced in preparation for Christmas is unknown among Latin Americans. In fact, it runs counter to Mexican tradition, for which Advent is a time of fiesta.

Advent includes two Marian celebrations, the novena of Our Lady of Guadalupe, followed by the novena of *posadas*, which, while highlighting Mary's experience in the final days of her pregnancy, prepares families for *la navidad* (Chirstmas). In addition, December is a time for weddings and family parties in Mexico, much as May and June are in the United States. Thus, because Mexicans are busy celebrating to prepare for Christmas, they have little time, interest, or tradition to celebrate Advent in the somber and penitential Euro-American way. Perhaps their way is more in tune with the universal church's specific directive:

> Advent has a twofold character: as a season to prepare for Christmas when Christ's first coming to us is remembered; as a season when that remembrance directs the mind and heart to await Christ's second coming at the end of time. Advent is thus a period for devout and joyful expectation.[35]

Feast of Our Lady of Guadalupe

The most popular saint for Mexicans is Our Lady of Guadalupe, a Spanish mispronunciation of the ancient Nahuatl term *Tecoatlaxope*, meaning "she will crush the serpent of stone." According to tradition, Mary, the mother of Jesus, appeared on several occasions to an indigenous man, Juan Diego, in 1531 on the outskirts of Mexico City. The Spanish, who had conquered the territory just ten years earlier, had enslaved the native inhabitants. By the end of the century, the vast majority of indigenous people had died either from forced labor or diseases imported by the conquerors. Mary requested Juan Diego to ask the archbishop of Mexico to erect a church dedicated to her in Tepeyac, a neighborhood of indigenous poor, where she could demonstrate her motherly love and compassion for the oppressed. Juan Diego thought himself unworthy and incapable of her request, but the Virgin insisted. When the archbishop demanded a sign to verify his story, the Virgin directed Juan Diego to pick roses, an unlikely harvest in December, to take to the prelate. When Juan Diego opened his cloak before the archbishop, the roses tumbled to the floor, leaving the Virgin's imprint on the cloth. From that moment on, the Virgin of Guadalupe became the patron saint of Mexico. Through Our Lady of Guadalupe's apparitions and message, indigenous Mexicans were introduced to Christianity and incorporated into the Catholic Church.

Although their religion was changed by their relationship to Mary, Mexicans feel privileged that she appeared to one of their own. She identified with Juan Diego's people, bearing symbols familiar to them, such as an emblem representing the reconciliation of opposites, and appearing like them, dark-skinned (and, consequently, often referred to as *la morenita*) and speaking Juan Diego's native language, Nahuatl. Her tunic and mantle, sprinkled with stars, and the moon, firmly planted under her feet, indicate her cosmic role. She appears in an environment filled with birds singing and flowers blooming, reflecting the indigenous cosmology where harmony reigns amidst flowers and song *(flor y canto)*. She replaced an important ancient feminine deity, Tonantzin, who according to tradition, resided on mountaintops, including Tepeyac, and was depicted either as pregnant or carrying a small child. Like Tonantzin, the Virgin appeared pregnant, symbolized by a dark sash around her waist and a flower over her womb. Unlike Tonantzin, who was married to the serpent-high god and cruelly castigated humans, Mary is pictured crushing a serpent with her foot, fulfilling an Old Testament prophecy that she would triumph over evil.[36]

Being a Mexican is closely interwoven with being a *Guadalupano*, a devotee of the Virgin. She is a national heroine and, as the founding mother of the nation, casts her religious aura over the country. Until the Revolution of 1910, her image graced the country's flag, and even today the flag's colors are taken from her mantle. On the Virgin's feast day, Mexicans feel extremely proud of their birthright and congratulate each other as if it were their own birthday.

Her appearance in Mexico conveys divine recognition for Mexicans as a people, especially the indigenous, and her message to Juan Diego encourages Mexicans to struggle for dignity and respect in the United States. In the 1970s and 1980s, Cesar Chávez used the standard of Our Lady of Guadalupe prominently in his marches to extend the United Farm Workers in the Southwest.

Not only is she a national figure, she is like a second mother to most Mexicans, specifically honored on Mother's Day as their heavenly mother who loves and protects them. It would be difficult to find a Mexican who does not display her image somewhere: a picture on a wall, a medal around the neck, a rosary dangling from the rearview mirror. Almost every baby receives a medal of Guadalupe, as she is commonly called, at baptism. Although she officially intercedes with God for her children, she often seems to stand in for God. A stanza in one of the most popular hymns to her reflects the personal tenderness Mexicans feel for her:

Desde que niño nombrar te supe,	I knew your name since I was little
Eres mi vida, eres mi vida,	You are my life, you are my life,
Mi solo amor.	My only love.[37]

One year members of the parish Guadalupe Group explained their devotion to the Virgin by sharing the wonders she had worked in their lives. Maria Soto spoke of her recent bout with cancer, which had disappeared after treatment. "I just put myself in the Virgin's hands and trusted she would work a miracle. She didn't let me down. She never does." Francisca Rodriguez told how she and her children had nothing to eat after having arrived in Chicago. "I asked the Virgin to find me work, and the very next day she found me a job." When Ana Moreno was about to cross the Rio Grande, like so many immigrants crossing the border, she knelt down to implore the Virgin's protection before entering the water. Thanks to Guadalupe, she says, she made it across. The stories go on and on. Although some people might think that Hispanics exaggerate her position, Vatican II clearly reaffirmed her preeminent role in the history of salvation and in the church.[38]

During the nine days before the feast day of Guadalupe, it is difficult to schedule community events because people's attention turns to the celebration. Each evening, the parish Guadalupe Group organizes novena prayers, rosary, and Mass.

Over the years, parishioners have preferred that a priest from Mexico preach the novena. Their desire for one of their own is understandable; this novena is a nostalgic time when people long for experiences from their home country. A priest from Mexico, speaking good Mexican Spanish peppered with local idioms, referring to events and places in Mexico and poking fun at Mexican idiosyncracies, helps people connect with their roots.

But bringing priests from Mexico is expensive. Moreover, because these priests are unfamiliar with the immigrants' new world, their homilies often miss the mark. Thus, St. Pius V looked for alternatives.

In recent years, a different parish group directs the celebration each night. They lead the rosary and make a presentation (dramas, testimonies, songs, poems) at the time of the homily, relating some aspect of the historical narrative to contemporary life. One year the Guadalupe Group dramatized the Virgin's efforts to counter the racism against indigenous peoples in the sixteenth century, and her contemporary call to parishioners to eliminate bigotry. The youth group dramatized how Guadalupe's appearance strengthened a young man tempted to enter a gang. The Women's Support Group presented testimonies of women who had found personal strength through their relationship with the Virgin.

Celebration of the feast itself begins at 3:00 a.m. on December 12 with a serenade to the Virgin organized by a radio station. Thirteen hundred people rapidly fill the church beyond capacity, standing in the aisles and sitting around the altar. For two hours, they listen to traditional songs about the Virgin. Occasionally people shout out *"Viva, la Virgen,"* evoking enthusiastic cheers and applause from the crowd. The birthday song, *Las Mañanitas*, begins the Mass at 5:00 a.m. In recent years the parish has scheduled an additional Mass at midnight to accommodate the thousands wanting to serenade the Virgin on her feast day.

Mariachi-style music has been adopted as the traditional music for the feast. Violins and guitars blend with blaring trumpets. No drums, electric guitars, or synthesizers are played, and musicians rarely use microphones. They rely on the *vihuela*, an instrument also called a *guitarrón*, for the bass. The snug-fitting vests worn by *mariachis* are borrowed from the world of bullfighting. The silver-laden trousers and wide *sombreros* come from Mexican cowboys, called *charros*.[39] The fact that a group of *mariachis*, six to ten men, charges approximately $500 per hour (with a two-hour minimum) does not deter contracting their services. *Mariachi* music sends shivers up the Mexican spine. Juan Díaz, community relations director at the Old Town School of Folk Music in Chicago, commented, "When a *mariachi* band starts playing, that's when something starts rising in your blood, and drives you to shout, '*Viva México!*'"[40]

After the early morning Mass, the Guadalupe Group invites everyone to the church hall for a complimentary breakfast of hot *menudo*, accompanied by the *mariachis*. Some people leave early for work, but hundreds, including schoolchildren and homeless people, stay to enjoy the community festivities. During the day, people bring hundreds of bouquets of fresh roses to adorn the specially arranged shrine to the Virgin. Buckets of water accommodate the cut flowers, and special tables are erected for the candles people place before their mother's image.

During the evening, Mexican parishes generally celebrate the "Mass of the Roses." Again a packed crowd gathers early, and everyone receives a fresh rose, the symbol authenticating the Virgin's appearance to Juan Diego. Some people pluck extra roses from the mountain of bouquets at the Virgin's shrine to take home for relatives unable to attend. Many parents dress their children specially for the occasion, little girls as the Virgin Mary, boys as Juan Diego. Volunteer musicians, some of whom have promised the Virgin to play on her day every year in return for a favor, swell the size of the parish choir as a trumpet or two, a violin, an accordion, drums, and extra guitars enhance the evening's pageantry. The entrance procession, barely passing through the pressing crowd, stops in the middle of the church and turns toward the side wall, site of the alcove shrine honoring the Virgin. Once again everyone sings *Las Mañanitas*, followed by the official entrance song, *Buenos Días, Paloma Blanca* ("Good Day, White Dove"), never mind that it is 7:30 at night. After the Gospel, the church is darkened and spotlights illumine a dramatization of the Virgin's apparitions presented by the parish youth. At the moment when Juan Diego opens his cloak before the bishop, roses fall to the floor, revealing Mary's image. The assembly gasps with renewed awe and breaks into spontaneous and sustained applause. It is an emotional moment.

The homily generally focuses on two points: (1) the dignity and value of Mexican people, primarily the poor and indigenous whom the Virgin chose to honor with her apparition, and (2) Mary's challenge to Juan Diego and to all Mexican people. Our Lady's request that a church be erected on the outskirts of the city and Juan Diego's reluctant but faithful response, including his confrontation of colonialist authorities, challenge contemporary Mexican immigrants to build her a renewed church that will struggle for justice in their new land.

During the offertory procession, dancers, dressed in brilliantly colored metallic Aztec costumes, dance down the aisles and around the altar amidst the fragrant smell of incense and the haunting rhythm of drums. In Mexico, indigenous people customarily dance long hours outside the church before Mass as an expression of their joy and prayer. After communion, as everyone holds up their rose high above their heads for the final blessing, the church appears as a shimmering sea of red roses. To conclude the Mass, at least two closing songs are sung in their entirety, *"Adios, O Madre Mia"* and *"Adios, O Virgen de Guadalupe."* No one leaves the church until all the verses of both songs are sung.

It is hardly possible to overestimate the power of the celebration of this feast for Mexican immigrants. It builds strength and solidarity among them, awakening a sense of ethnic pride and faith in God, and provides a beautiful introduction to the Christmas season when the faithful welcome the newborn Savior into their communities, families, and hearts.

Church authorities, however, do not always understand the feast's importance or manner of celebration. In the nineteenth century some clergy prohibited dancing as a vestige of pagan worship. In the 1960s, however, Archbishop Francis J. Furey of San Antonio invited people to dance in the church when he learned that dance for them was a form of prayer. On the other hand, in 1999, upon witnessing an Aztec-style dance, a bishop in Chicago asked the local pastor, "What god are these people worshiping?"

The National Conference of Catholic Bishops appeared insensitive to Mexican popular religiosity when it mandated in 1995 and 1999 that because December 12 fell on a Sunday, the readings for Mass had to be those of Sunday and not those of Our Lady of Guadalupe. They only provided that the Virgin be mentioned in the Prayer of the Faithful. If St. Pius V had followed this directive, parishioners would have been confused, if not furious.

Christmas

To celebrate the Christmas season, which lasts from Christmas Day until the second Sunday of January, the liturgy committee arranges a nativity scene at one side of the sanctuary. Mexicans have a custom of placing the crib and traditional nativity figures in the context of a full country landscape, complete with statues of chickens, cows, dogs, pigs, peasants farming, maids milking, and children playing. Every kind of figurine is welcome, no matter its size or artistic style. For years, the nativity scene was placed in the midst of a miniature replica of the Pilsen neighborhood, complete with three-flat buildings, schools, elevated commuter train, post office, church, and prominent stores. Figurines of people appear to walk down the snowy neighborhood streets, while traditional figures of farmers, blacksmiths, cowboys, and animals in the city's outskirts connect the nativity scene to parishioners' small hometowns. Families pray before the display as parents explain Jesus' birth to their wide-eyed children.

Mexicans have a special fondness for the infant Jesus, or *el niño Dios* (the Infant God). Many bring relatively large statues of the infant—usually life-size, unclothed, and often with blue eyes—from Mexico to adorn their nativity scenes at home. Before and after Christmas, many bring their doll-like images of the baby Jesus for the priest's blessing before placing them in the creche amidst other smaller images of Mary, Joseph, the shepherds, and the magi. On one occasion, during a dialog homily, three people brought their infants to the altar. As the priest held up each for everyone to see, the congregation beamed big smiles. When asked why the baby Jesus brought them such joy, people responded that he represented simplicity, vulnerability, innocence, love, and God's desire to be one with them. This response reflects what American bishops wrote: "Hispanic spirituality places strong emphasis on the humanity of Jesus, especially when he appears weak and suffering, as in the crib and in his passion and death."[41]

The Mass at midnight, *misa de gallo* (Mass of the rooster), is celebrated with a cultural flare, beginning with liturgical ministers gathered in the church entrance together with two youngsters dressed as Mary and Joseph. For the entrance procession, the assembly sings the traditional *posada* song antiphonally. After the procession, Mary and Joseph take their places of honor near the nativity scene. The Mass proceeds as usual until the offertory procession when a married couple *(padrino* and *madrina)* bring the infant Jesus—sometimes a real baby—to Mary and Joseph. A small *a capella* choir accompanies them, singing a haunting traditional lullaby while the *padrinos* rock the baby in a long white cloth. When they reach the nativity scene, Mary and Joseph lay the baby in the crib, and Mass continues. After the final blessing, the *padrinos* remove the baby from the crib and place it on a tray filled with pieces of wrapped hard candy. While the choir sings traditional *villoncicos* (Christmas carols), people press forward to kiss the infant Jesus and receive a piece of candy, symbol of the joyful celebration, God's munificence, and the sweetness of the baby Jesus. This closing ritual is repeated during the Masses on Christmas Day.

Feast of the Kings

Mexicans traditionally celebrate the feast of the Epiphany with more enthusiasm than Christmas. Although observed for centuries on January 6, it is currently celebrated in the United States on the first Sunday of the new year. On this day, known among Hispanics as *El Día de los Reyes* (The Day of the Kings), people exchange gifts. To celebrate this tradition, the parish organizes a Christmas party the preceding Saturday for children participating in religious education at which they receive small gifts and candy. The next day three men dressed as the kings enter the church during the offertory procession, while people sing a traditional song recalling their visit to the Christ Child. When Mass is finished, preselected sponsors again place the Christ Child on a tray filled with candy for all to reverence.

On this Sunday, when crowds of people attend Mass in the Mexican community, St. Pius V distributes its parish calendar. After the homily, the priest blesses the calendars, and a representative from each family comes forward to receive one. Calendars, particularly religious ones, are important to Mexicans. Frequently, more than one hangs in a Mexican home, accomplishing the multipurpose of scheduling the new year, providing artistic decoration, and asking for abundant blessings on the household. Religious calendars become sacramentals reminding people of the days of life God grants them and their desire for God's presence in them.

Ash Wednesday

More Hispanics attend church on Ash Wednesday, the first day of Lent, than any other day of the year. Many people, including those rarely attending Mass, do not miss receiving ashes on their foreheads. Approximately 6,000 people attend church at St. Pius V on Ash Wednesday. For many pastors, it is a day of dread because of the dogged determination of so many people to obtain their ashes. Some park their cars in the bus stop in front of church, hoping to run in and get ashes in seconds. Because of their employees' interest, some employers call for a priest to

169

distribute ashes at their work site. Once a scuffle broke out in the back of church when members from two rival gangs arrived for ashes and unexpectedly encountered one another. After separating the groups, the ushers kept an eye on them as each gang walked down different aisles, received their ashes, and quietly left the church, content to have fulfilled their annual sacramental ritual.

At St. Pius V, ashes are distributed in the context of a prayer service. These ceremonies, approximately twelve throughout the day, alternate every half hour in the late afternoon between the church and the parish hall in order to accommodate a constant flow of people. The liturgical service provides a moment of communal prayer, scriptural readings, and a homily with some instruction, inspiration, and challenge to conversion. Because almsgiving is central to Lenten spirituality, a collection is taken and, following a Mexican tradition, is donated to help the poor.

Why do Mexicans seek blessed ashes with such fervor? Although ashes are powerful sacramentals for Mexicans, most have difficulty explaining their significance. Nevertheless, each senses their meaning deep in their being, perhaps connecting them to their pre-Columbian roots. Elizondo points to three aspects:

> On Ash Wednesday, Mexican Americans renew their cultic communion with mother earth. For them the earth has always been sacred, and they retain a fundamental identity with it....Mexican Americans sense that the earth belongs to them and they to it—like mother and child....Through conquest and exploitation, much of their land has been taken away from them....like depriving children of their mother. They are called "foreigners" and are treated as illegal intruders by another society that imposed itself on them by violence, power plays, and even religion....The ashes are an exterior manifestation of the innermost attitude of the collective soul of the people: suffering but not despair, acceptance but not fatalism, *aguante* ("endurance") but not passive resignation, joy but not frivolity. And hope beyond immediate expectations.[42]

170

Lent

The season of Lent emphasizes the human need for repentance and conversion. According to European tradition, Catholic Lenten practice has emphasized repentance and penitence. But Hispanics are little interested in self-inflicted sacrifice because many suffer hardship all year long. Nevertheless, the emphasis on conversion, turning away from sin and back to God, is important.

Each Lent the liturgy committee develops an appropriate theme to connect sermons and liturgical decorations. As mentioned in Chapter 5, in 1995, the theme "Break Down the Barriers, Work for Peace" addressed people's need to eliminate the obstacles blocking their more intimate union with Jesus. The following year, the committee placed in the sanctuary a large heart painted on a white cloth surrounded by the words "Jesus Is Calling; Let Him Enter Your Heart." Guide sheets were distributed for weekly prayer and reflections in the home, as well as a picture of Jesus knocking at a door, symbolizing his desire to enter their hearts. Sunday preaching focused on different ways people close their hearts to Jesus. The connection between the church preaching and home reflections was mutually enriching and helped people participate in a common effort to grow in their faith and life as a community.

Palm Sunday

In the Hispanic community, *Domingo de Ramos*, Passion Sunday, is the most well-attended Sunday of the year. It is the first day of Holy Week, the liturgical high time for Christians. As with ashes, sacramental palms attract many Mexicans who rarely attend church services. Most people take them home as religious symbols to adorn their home throughout the year. The liturgy begins with people gathering in front of church, often in the cold, to receive their palms and join in a procession around the block. They sing and wave their palms on high, welcoming Christ as their king into their community and personal life just as the crowds had received him into Jerusalem shortly before his death. Hispanics love processions;

171

they demonstrate the public nature of their faith and integrate the sacred and secular, authenticating the latter's holiness and enhancing its value. Processions also dramatize people's sense of being on a journey, walking side by side, forming a human chain, symbolically illustrating the very thing they profess: a people moving in unison toward a common destination. God accompanies them on their pilgrimage to eternal life, recalling the exodus of the Jewish people and their journey to the Promised Land.

Good Friday and the Via Crucis Viviente

Mexicans empathize with Jesus' suffering and death, undoubtedly because they experience them so vividly in daily life. Traditional Christian theology has also effectively taught them the redemptive nature of Christ's suffering and death, almost to the exclusion of his triumphant resurrection. On Good Friday, they celebrate not only that Jesus died for them and thereby won for them eternal life, but they also join their sufferings with his in order to participate in his work of redemption. In most Latin American countries, the celebration of Good Friday surpasses the other liturgical days of the Triduum, Holy Thursday and Saturday's Easter Vigil.

Holy Thursday has traditionally focused more on the exposition of the Blessed Sacrament than on the dramatic liturgy reenacting Jesus washing his apostles' feet and his institution of the Eucharist. St. Pius V staff washes people's feet, circulating in the congregation while the priests and deacons wash the feet of twelve parishioners gathered at the altar. The service also emphasizes the Eucharist by distributing first communion to teenagers prepared in the catechetical program. While some people maintain the Mexican custom of visiting six churches during the night to pray before the Blessed Sacrament, many abandon it in Chicago either because few churches are open or because people fear traveling about the city late at night. The liturgy committee continues the Mexican tradition of distributing unconsecrated bread after Mass as a symbol of sharing the Eucharist with those at home. Because Mexicans remember the custom of covering statues with purple-colored cloth during Lent, the parish also obliges them in Holy

Week, even though the Church discontinued the ritual in the 1960s. Maintaining these traditions helps people living in an alien land feel at home in their church.

In the late 1970s, Catholic parishes in Pilsen organized a living Way of the Cross on Good Friday. Representatives from local parishes choreograph this colorful and dramatic pageant, selecting actors for the parts of Jesus, Mary, Pilate, the apostles, Veronica, Roman soldiers, and Simon of Cyrene, and maintaining an elaborate wardrobe. Participants take their commitment seriously, meeting monthly throughout the year to prepare both spiritually and technically for the dramatization.

Early Good Friday morning, the dramatization begins with the Last Supper, Jesus' arrest, and the scourging at the pillar in a church basement at the east end of the neighborhood. An overflowing crowd gasps as Judas betrays Jesus. When the Roman soldiers strip Jesus of his garments, scourge him, and place the crown of thorns upon his head, people weep openly. A Roman centurion on horseback then leads a procession, guided by a police escort, down the neighborhood's main street, cleared and swept earlier by city trucks. The people accompany Jesus, who walks, stumbles, and falls under the crushing weight of the cross for a mile and half until he reaches Calvary, a hill specially constructed for this event in a park on the neighborhood's west end. At the sound of a ram's horn, the crowd stops at fourteen preselected sites (the traditional Stations of the Cross) for a brief commentary on Jesus' passion and its relationship to the community's struggles for survival. Loudspeakers mounted on a van broadcast the narration, and a parish choir leads nearly 6,000 people in traditional Good Friday songs.[43]

This reenactment is the ultimate liturgy for many Mexicans, not only because it allows them to relive the passion and death of Jesus but also because it dramatizes their own sufferings. Many women closely identify with Mary, the mother of Jesus, because they, like she, feel helpless to save their sons. The procession stops at a tavern where people are urged to mourn the suffering caused by excessive alcoholic consumption; it pauses at a shelter to reflect on the plight of the homeless; it passes a health clinic where the commentator reminds the crowd that many residents cannot afford medical care; it stops at a corner, home to a gang, so people can reflect on the violence and death gangs inflict on the community. Along the way, Mary comes forward to embrace her son, and Simon is dragged from the crowd to help Jesus carry the cross. A few blocks later, Veronica rushes forward to wipe her Savior's face with a towel. After the crucifixion, the body of Jesus is taken from the cross, placed on a litter, and carried on the final leg of the procession to the largest church in the community, where the Archbishop offers the final reflection and closing prayer. In Latin America, a separate dramatic evening service often commemorates Jesus' burial. Elizondo writes:

> The final Good Friday reenactment is the burial service, the last station of the cross. In many parts of Latin America the evening procession with Christ's lifeless body is even more well attended than the *via crucis*. Some might ridicule this popular rite of the burial of Jesus and attribute its popularity to the "morbid" inclinations of the Mexican Americans. But when it is realized that even in death this people is rejected, the quiet, almost clandestine, burial of Jesus takes on a deeper significance for them.[44]

Through this drama, people's lives take on deeper meaning and strength. While walking, they sing and pray together. Christian Base Communities from St. Pius V decorate altars at two stations, helping families connect their lives with the sacred event, claim the neighborhood streets as sacred space, and articulate their struggle against the forces of evil. Indeed, residents recognize the street as more than a commercial strip traversing the neighborhood; it is the place where the passion and death of Jesus are reenacted each year. The procession preserves people's cultural heritage and provides parents an excellent opportunity to teach their children the faith.

Karen Mary Davalos, a Mexican American anthropologist, studied the Pilsen *vía crucis* and concluded: "From the beginning, the event conveyed Mexican Catholic sensibilities, social commentary on local injustices, dramatic reversals of power and authority, the sacralization of space, and acts of cultural recovery."[45] Walking with thousands of others in procession, people sense their union not only with their Savior and his mother but with one another as *el pueblo de fe.* Davalos writes:

> The procession is the moment in which Pilsen and other *mexicanos* forge a relationship as a community, speak in nearly one unified voice against forms of oppression, and join past and present. Moreover, it is the overlay between a specific cultural past or heritage and Jesus' life that is invoked in the present: the procession transcends space and time from Mexico to Jerusalem, Mexico to the United States, Chicago to Calvary."[46]

While the procession is serious and prayerful, it is also festive. People greet one another. Youth walk along with their dates. Parents struggle to control their children as they dart through the crowd. Street vendors sell food—corn on the cob on a stick, smothered with butter, cream, cheese, and chili; *paletas* (popsicles); sliced cucumbers with chili powder; fruit cups; and cotton candy. Some people line the streets, and others sit on porches or hang from windows, waiting for the procession to pass before joining in. The event is a happening, the place to see and be seen by others. Reflecting on it, most people comment on the crowd and how good it is that so many share their faith by walking and praying together. Undoubtedly, the *via crucis* is a more important celebration for people than the official church liturgy of the day. Elizondo observes:

> Never was the distance between the "official" church and the church of the people more evident to me than on Good Friday in Mexico City where there might be as few as 100 persons in a *barrio* church for the official Good Friday services, and as many as 60,000 outside the church, taking part in a living way of the cross.[47]

Although in Pilsen thousands participate in the liturgy on the street, the official and the popular church do meet. In the *via crucis viviente*, church officials walk with the people, and many people visit the church during the day to offer a prayer, to sit in silence and sense their solidarity with their crucified Lord. They pray before the statue of *la Soledad* or *la Madre Dolorosa*, Our Lady of Sorrows, clothed in a black shawl and placed near the altar to assist people who want to draw near to offer their *sentido pesame* (heartfelt sympathy) to the Virgin who lost her son.

At night, the parish celebrates the official Good Friday liturgy, including the solemn reading of the Passion, prayers for the universal church, veneration of the cross, and communion. Although the liturgical reforms of the late 1960s discontinued preaching on the Seven Last Words of Jesus, which for centuries had constituted the core of Good Friday liturgy, parishioners want to preserve it. Consequently, the liturgy committee selects seven lay people to offer brief reflections on each of the words in a totally darkened church. Because adoration of the cross is the most powerful ritual of the evening, it is moved from the middle of the liturgy to its conclusion.

Easter Season

To celebrate Eastertide, parishioners bring fresh flowers to adorn the church altar, and pastel-colored banners are hung from the church rafters. The baptismal font becomes a central focus as each Sunday the priest and deacon walk among the assembly, generously sprinkling everyone with the newly blessed water, symbol of their new life in Christ. Gospel accounts of the resurrection and readings from the Acts of the Apostles lend themselves to preaching on the successful efforts of the first Christians to form community and carry on the work of Jesus. Long focused on the death of Christ, Mexicans gradually learn to appreciate the profound significance of the resurrection for themselves.

During the Easter season, the parish celebrates other important religious events. In May, hundreds of children receive first communion at Sunday liturgies for three successive weeks. These celebrations bring new people to church, usually family members of first communicants who may not be regular churchgoers. The parish always celebrates Mother's Day, distributing corsages to mothers and preparing some women to preach about their maternal vocation. Each Friday night, the Guadalupe Group organizes children to present flowers to the Virgin. Corpus Christi, a major liturgical celebration in many parts of Mexico because of its outdoor procession, could otherwise easily pass unnoticed in the Mexican community.

Harvest Season

In mid-October, the church is decorated in a harvest motif. Although such adornment is typically North American, the elements used—pumpkins, cornstalks, squash, and shafts of wheat—are also appreciated by Mexicans. These symbols help immigrants connect their current urban ritual with their former rural life. The decoration produces a warm and welcoming environment, the harvest hues blending well with the earth tones of the church's interior.

During this season, the parish focuses on a variety of themes, from gratitude for God's gifts to generosity in sharing personal resources with the community. Many parishioners remember how their parents and grandparents, following a biblical tradition, made annual offerings or tithings of 10 percent *(diezmo)* of their income, or harvest, to the priest. The pastor presents the annual parish financial report, and for several Sundays selected parishioners speak about the importance of financially supporting the parish. The harvest season culminates with the celebration of Thanksgiving Day, a holiday only gradually integrated into immigrant family ritual.[48]

Day of the Dead

The celebration of All Saints' Day began in the first centuries of the church to commemorate martyrs. Later the feast included all the deceased united with God but unmentioned in the official church calendar. According to most sources, Pope Boniface IV established the feast of All Saints in the seventh century, and in the ninth century, Pope Gregory III moved the celebration from May to November 1, perhaps in an effort to Christianize Celtic festivities marking the beginning of winter with rituals aimed at warding off evil spirits returning to earth.[49]

In the eleventh century, the Day of the Dead (*día de los muertos*), or All Souls' Day, as it is known outside of Latin America, was established as the annual feast celebrated on November 2 to pray for the dead being purified before entering heaven. For most Mexicans, the day is more significant than All Saints' Day. In Mexico, several days before it, special groups of the dead are commemorated. For the deceased with no survivors on earth, people hang jugs of water and bags of bread from street posts to accommodate their return to earth. On October 28, those who died violent deaths are remembered. The eve of November 1 is reserved for the "little angels," namely, deceased children.

Although attendance at Mass is not required on the Day of the Dead, Mexicans in Mexico consider it a national religious holiday. Their celebration begins the evening before, when families visit at the cemetery to clean the graves of loved ones, some remaining for a nightlong vigil. The next day, families gather in the cemetery to pray and remember their beloved deceased. They bring food to share and, with their children, create a picnic atmosphere, which may be enhanced by strolling *mariachis*. Mexicans find it difficult to sustain this custom in the United States because those living in urban areas reside too far from outlying cemeteries, and in northern states, cold November weather and cemetery regulations prohibit all-night vigils.

When the Spanish brought All Souls' Day to the Americas, they incorporated indigenous beliefs and customs about death. Thus, families erect commemorative altars of the dead in their homes and in cemeteries, creating an artistic tradition of elaborately decorated altars that include an *ofrenda*, or offering, of particular significance to the deceased relatives. To celebrate the first Day of the Dead after his father's death, Roberto Roman traveled to Mexico, where his entire family home was decorated as an *ofrenda* for his father.

Pre-Columbian peoples believed that after death, souls begin a long journey to a new land. On November 2, the dead enjoy a special dispensation to return to earth and partake of the food and drink prepared by their family and placed on the altar together with personal and religious articles and special bread *(pan de muerto)* shaped like the human body.[50]

In Chicago, Clemencia Calderon annually arranges an altar of the dead in the corner of her living room with a crucifix, Bible and candle, photographs of her loved ones, and some of their favorite foods: the peanuts her mother-in-law loved, her uncle's special tequila, and her father's pumpkin seeds. She explains, "Once a year I do this to remember the people I love."[51]

The traditional round, yellow *zempazúchil* flowers, representing the sun, a central deity in ancient Mexico, are arranged around the altar of the dead as if to illuminate the path for the departed souls as they return to rejoin their families. Traditionally, *copal*, a tree resin, is burned as incense, emitting a sweet aroma as its smoke rises to heaven and creates an aura of mystery.[52]

In some parts of Mexico, caricatures of skeletons dancing, playing the guitar, smoking, drinking, playing cards, cooking, and eating reflect that death has not altered the deceased's way of living and is not to be feared. People also make tiny candy skulls of sugar, lemon juice, and cream of tartar, decorate them with bright food coloring, and place them on the altar. All these items, far from being macabre, demonstrate the love and respect of the living for their beloved dead and renew their sense of union with them.

Although altars of the dead are rarely constructed in churches in Mexico, St. Pius V erects one in the sanctuary because immigrants gradually stop erecting altars in their homes and gathering in cemeteries. The altar design varies from year to year and remains standing throughout November as the parish prays for the deceased at Sunday Masses. During the offertory procession, a book with names of deceased family and friends is carried to the altar of the dead where a priest reverences it with incense. People visiting the church often pray for the dead before the altar and leave an offering in their memory.

For several years, the liturgy committee created a commemorative wall for those who had died violent deaths in the neighborhood. The wall, twelve feet long and eight feet high, stands in a corner of the sanctuary, covered with paper cutouts of bricks, each bearing the name and date of a person's death, ninety-six in all in 1996. All but two victims were male, most killed in gang violence. The community responded emotionally, some people bringing flowers and candles as well as photographs of the deceased to place before the wall.

The celebration of the Day of the Dead collides with another originally religious but now secular holiday, Halloween. Because immigrant children are bombarded with Halloween in their schools and in the media, its celebration tends to capture more attention than the Day of the Dead. However, St. Pius V and some schools celebrate traditional Mexican customs to help families feel more at home in the community. A teenager expressed his appreciation when he observed: "Americans don't like to talk about death. In Mexico, it's different. Death is not a bad thing there. For them, death is more like a beginning than an end."[53]

The Mexican Fine Arts Center Museum, located in Pilsen, helps preserve Mexican traditions with its fall exhibition of altars of the dead that incorporate elements from both the contemporary and traditional worlds. Altars have featured a teen murdered in the area, death dealt by drugs, and endangered animals. One altar commemorated the tragically slain Tejano singer Selena with black and white magazine photographs of her and some of her CDs strewn across a red satin cloth decorated with her favorite snacks of popcorn and Diet Pepsi.

Thus, the celebration of the Day of the Dead incorporates many values. Remembering the deceased helps people express their love and appreciation for them and keep them close. The celebration also helps the community deal with death, not as something to be feared but as a natural transition to be welcomed. Because the celebration commemorates ancestors in the context of the family, it also strengthens family unity and tradition.

Thanksgiving

To celebrate Thanksgiving Day, St. Pius V joins the American tradition stemming from shared meals between Native Americans and European settlers with the Mexican tradition of giving thanks to God for *techo, trabajo y salud* (housing, work, and health) on the first day of each month. Mexicans offer three coins, symbolizing their desire to give back to God something for the many blessings received. On this day, many churches in Mexico have adoration of the Blessed Sacrament all day. On this occasion, Mexicans thank precisely the Holy Trinity, whom they refer to as Divine Providence, pictured as the elderly father, the son, and the dove. Thus, they mark time each month with an expression of gratitude. The celebration on Thanksgiving Day at St. Pius V helps them understand the American custom and preserve their own gracious tradition.

The liturgical year, rich in meaning and grace, celebrates faith in culture, and Mexicans have developed a unique way of celebrating the major feasts, lending color, sound, emotion, and excitement. Their traditional celebrations in no way undermine or diminish the official liturgical calendar. Rather, they enrich it by providing a distinct Mexican flavor. When parishes help Mexicans preserve and develop their liturgical celebrations, the latter feel welcome in their own church, proud of their culture, and firm in their faith. These celebrations are enhanced by other Mexican religious beliefs and practices outlined below.

Celebrating Faith and Life Through Sacramentals

Mexicans are generally very religious, devotional, and even pious. Religion is inextricably intertwined with their culture. The United States bishops noted in 1987: "Culture for Hispanic Catholics has become a way of living out and transmitting their faith. Many local practices of popular religiosity have become widely accepted cultural expressions."[54] This religiosity is manifested through sacramental objects, actions, and celebrations.

A Sacramental People

Although some Mexicans rarely attend church, most practice their faith through traditional sacramentals. These sensible objects, symbols, and actions enrich life with variety and color, assuming mystical meanings. Most Mexicans sign themselves with the cross in moments of need or when passing a church. They adorn themselves with medals, scapulars, and colorful rosaries around their necks, carry key rings and wear pins and watches with sacred images, and decorate their homes with religious art.

Pérez-Rodríguez notes:

[These] are tangible expresssions of that characteristic of Hispanic worship which we call "embodied." Such "sacramentals" are very important in our tradition and become the *recuerdo* or remembrance which literally allows the prayer event to be held in one's hands.[55]

People want God's blessing on every aspect of their lives. Each Sunday priests bless dozens of pictures, rosaries, medals, and statues. People ask priests to bless their new home, restaurant, beauty shop, or grocery store. Families come for a blessing before traveling to Mexico and bring their new (and used) automobiles to be blessed. Even though priests conclude each Mass with a blessing upon all, many approach them after Mass for an additional personal blessing, especially on their children. Some Hispanics bring miniature replicas, often made of silver, wood, or wax, of the human body or its parts (hands, arms, legs, and internal organs, such as hearts and kidneys) and leave them by the image of Christ or their favorite saint to request a special healing.[56]

In response to people's interest, the parish opened a religious goods store, which is staffed by two parishioners knowlegeable about Mexican religious traditions who often pray with customers and ask God's blessing on their purchases. They soon discovered people's strong interest in religious books, the best-selling item in the store.

Every day people visit the church, which is open from 7:00 a.m. to 8:00 p.m. It is the community's place to pray, but it is also the *casa de Dios*, the house of God, a holy place where people find consolation *(consuelo)* and hope. Even after the church closes, some people kneel on the front steps to offer a late-night prayer. For some Mexicans, the physical place where they experience

God's saving grace becomes a holy place where they return to nourish their intimate relationship with God.

When Laura encountered difficulties in her first pregnancy, she attended Mass at St. Paul parish in Pilsen. God heard her prayer, and her son was born healthy. From that time forward, Laura participated regularly in St. Paul because there she had received God's favor, even though she lived next door to St. Adalbert parish on the other side of the neighborhood.

Mexicans also value elements of nature, notably flowers and water, as sacramentals. Because they readily bring flowers to church, the parish never purchases them for liturgical decoration. For Christmas and Easter, the staff invites donations of poinsettias or lilies, and soon the church is filled with seasonal plants. In fact, it is nearly impossible to keep flowers out of the sanctuary even during the penitential season of Lent, when liturgical norms discourage their use. For Mexicans, flowers are always in season because they are a sign of their faith and love *(cariño)* for God, the Virgin, and the saints.

When the archbishop asked Juan Diego for a sign from Our Lady of Guadalupe, the Virgin sent roses, symbolizing for indigeneous people not only beauty but truth, goodness, and order in the universe. They, together with the music that originally drew Juan Diego to the Virgin—*flor y canto*—constituted proof of the divinely imspired apparitions. As Elizondo notes: "The beautiful flowers that gave forth the heavenly perfume complete the revelation initiated by the singing of the birds."[57]

In Mexico, where water is not always plentiful, people appreciate its vital gift. As a sacramental, they cannot get enough of it. St. Pius V distributes dozens of gallons of holy water each week. People fill empty milk cartons of holy water to sprinkle around their houses and on their children. They often drink it, believing it has a medicinal effect. Unlike Americans, who when passing the font at the church entrance, wet only the tips of one or two fingers, Mexicans generally douse themselves with water. A parishioner once explained that Mexicans splash holy water not only on their foreheads but also on the backs of their necks to ward off the devil, who might approach from behind. Dousing water on themelves represents their desire to cover themselves and their loved ones more fully with God's blessings.

When the parish was installing a baptismal pool for bodily immersion, the architect questioned placing it behind the altar because people might not readily approach it. The staff assured him that drawing near to water was so natural for Mexicans they would not hesitate to enter the sanctuary, reach down into the pool, and gather water to bless themselves. And so they do.

For Mexicans, the spiritual world is not something hovering beyond the earth but intimately part of it. Powerful spiritual forces, both good and evil, permeate their cosmology, and they look for sacramentals to protect themselves against harmful spirits.[58] Mexicans frequently avail themselves of healers and doctors of folk medicine (curanderos) for cures for what ails them physically and psychologically. Specific ailments, such as empacho (an undefined stomach illness), el mal puesto (a curse resulting from envy), and susto (fright), are among various psychosomatic illnesses that need special healing.[59] Some believe their physical ailments and even misfortunes result from evil spirits or someone who has bewitched them. Their cure may require natural medicines, such as herbal teas and ointments, as well as incantations of a spiritist or witch (espiritistas or brujos).

As good Catholics, most Mexicans know they are not supposed to participate in witchcraft (brujerías) and, consequently, hestitate to mention their involvement to a priest. However, in some instances, for example, when children have trouble sleeping, many parents ask a priest to pray the evangelios (gospels) over them, believing a spirit may be frightening their children at night and a blessing will dispel it. This tradition reflects an ancient custom in which the priest reads a section of the Gospels while praying for the children to sleep in peace. An explanation of dreams and the difficulty children have distinguishing between dreams and reality help some parents understand the nightmares, but in the end, they still want the blessing.

Mexicans commonly believe the spirits of the dead linger in this world to inflict harm, often without apparent motive. Once a couple called a priest to their apartment, where they believed an evil spirit had settled in. Three days earlier, after they had returned from shopping and heard strange noises, they dropped their groceries and fled to a friend's home. They believed a spirit was bothering their small son, who complained of seeing things at night. To protect the boy, on his bedroom floor they arranged a candle, a glass of holy water, and a pair of sandals in the form of a cross. They believed the spirit belonged to a man who had died in the apartment years before.

Upon request, parish ministers bless these apartments but also talk with people about their beliefs. In this case, why would a man's spirit want to bother people he had never met, especially an innocent child? If indeed it were a spirit, why would it act only in one bedroom? Why would any spirit want to stay in this world, given Jesus' promise to welcome it into eternal life with him?

Although these questions help people think more critically about their fears, in the end, a sense of helplessness in the face of greater, unknown forces and traditional beliefs may rule the day. Belief in curses and spirits, common among the poor and powerless, is a direct consequence of low self-esteem, which supports passivity, resignation, and readily concedes power to external forces whether people or spirits.

A Family of Saints and Spirits

Through liturgies at home and in church, Mexican people strengthen and extend their personal and family relationships outward into the community and into communion with the saints. They believe they belong to a world filled with the great Spirit of God and the family of the saints, a world at once visible through signs and epiphanies of a greater invisible and mysterious world. Pérez-Rodríguez notes:

> (T)he center of our life still revolves around the Indian belief in the Spirit....There is, consequently, no individual life but only the one life in which all living things share and struggle to live in harmony....This one Spirit gathers us together into community. And it is this Spirit who is at the center of popular religiosity for the

Hispanic community....It is this Spirit, now baptized, who...becomes *"Diosito* (dearest God)," a God of the home. God becomes *"el niño Dios* (baby God)" of Christmas, needing shelter and protection; and as an adult, becomes the suffering Lord, tortured and crucified...[and] is reflected in Mary: the mother, the grieving woman, and the good neighbor. God is also revealed in the lives of the saints, who are our constant companions and family.

People...view themselves living in a world of spirits, which the Catholic Church calls the Communion of the Saints. Mexicans feel a great affection for the saints, who they believe intercede for them before God. Since they themselves are very physical people, they often touch the images, almost as though they were caressing the saints. Many adopt one particular saint as their favorite; *"ese es mi santo.*"[60]

In Mexico, babies often receive the name of the saint on whose day they are born. Thus, they celebrate the saint's day each year *(el día de tu santo)* on their own birthday, a custom that is disappearing in the United States.[61] Because saints are seen as part of the family, it is no wonder that Hispanics feel threatened when non-Catholic groups challenge their belief in saints, usually invoking St. Paul's teaching that Jesus is the only mediator between humankind and God.

Among all the saints, St. Jude Thaddaeus has become popular among Mexicans in the second half of the twentieth century. Devotion to St. Jude, one of the twelve apostles, developed in the United States around the Great Depression when in desperation people prayed to this "patron of difficult or hopeless cases," and the devotion has since spread to Mexico. Other popular saints include Martin de Porres, *Santiago* (St. James), Martin of Tours, Anthony of Padua, and Thérèse of the Child Jesus ("the Little Flower"). One saint unknown in the United States is Lazarus, a fictitious poor man created by Jesus for a story about final justice for the rich. Lazarus, who represents the poor who will receive justice in eternal life, is seen by the poor in Latin America as their representative and intercessor before God.[62]

One curious favorite saint of Mexicans is the *Niño de Antocha* (the child of Antocha). Dominican priests brought a statue of *Nuestra Señora de Antocha* from Spain to the town of Plateros in Zacatecas, Mexico, during the 1780s. The *Santo Niño*, who sat on the Virgin's arm, became physically separated in the early nineteenth century, acquiring an identity of his own. A legend relates that the child lived in Antocha, a section of Madrid, when the Moors had imprisoned many Spanish Christians. Because the conquerors barred everyone but little children from entering the prison, the prisoners' relatives prayed for God to send someone to visit their loved ones, who needed food, water, and spiritual consolation. One day a child, dressed like the pilgrims of the time, entered the prison carrying a basket of bread and a gourd of water hanging from a staff. The prisoners eagerly received the food and drink and the child's blessing. After all the captives had been served, the child's gourd and basket were still full. In the people's mind, Christ had returned to earth to serve their loved ones.[63] Mexicans' attraction to the *Niño de Antocha* reflects their devotion to the Child Jesus, mentioned above.

Whenever there is a hint of a supernatural phenomenon, Mexican eyes widen with interest; they are quick to investigate and ready to believe. The popular movies *Mi Familia* and *Like Water for Chocolate* captured the mystique of the ever-present spirit world that permeates their experience of food and is evident in omens, manifested, for instance, in the owl's hoot or cloud formations. Many Mexicans in Chicago are moved by media reports of weeping statues or by the apparent likenesses of Christ identified in branches of trees or reflections in windows. On occasion, parishioners bring photographs of clouds and overexposed snapshots that appear to reflect the face of Jesus or the image of the Virgin; for them, these are signs of God's presence.

Priests, unsympathetic or unaware of the differences between Hispanic and Euro-American spirituality, may criticize this response as misguided piety, foolishness, or simply superstition. Gilberto Hinojosa, an author of Hispanic theology,

responded to a priest who decried the weak faith of people flock-
ing to see a weeping statue of Mary:

> For Mexican Americans, the phenomenon was no less
> than an incarnational event, a manifestation of God's
> presence on earth. *La Virgen* was crying for her people
> and their community which was enduring a rash of
> senseless gang slayings and drive-by shootings. To
> *Mexicanos*, the Blessed Mother's weeping was a sign that
> she shared their pain.[64]

The incident reflects the strength of popular religiosity and
argues for a cautious and respectful silence toward ambiguous
phenomena. Ada María Isasi-Díaz writes:

> Hispanics know that we wear our emotions pinned on
> our sleeves, that we express quite readily what we
> believe and feel. Not to feel deeply seems to us to
> diminish our sense of humanity....Those who wish to
> understand Hispanics need to know that our religious
> practices express our close relationship with the divine.
> A personal relationship with God, and the living-out of
> that relationship in day-to-day life, is much more
> important to us than establishing and maintaining rela-
> tionships with church structures and going to church
> on Sundays.[65]

For centuries, Mexican Americans have integrated the supernatural with the joys and tribulations of their daily life. Pérez-
Rodríguez notes:

> Touching the heart of a people means touching their
> spirituality in a tangible, visible way. It means bringing
> all the happiness and pain, laughter and tears, joy and
> sorrow, to God in celebration....Some have called this
> (expression) the "fiesta approach" of popular religiosity:
> fiesta not in the minimalist sense of a party, however,
> but in the sense of gathering all of life's experiences into

the embrace of the moment, be they filled with laughter or moved to tears.[66]

Religious Practices of the Family and Home

Mexicans have developed rites and liturgies to respond to particular personal and social needs while reflecting and reinforcing their faith.

Promesas *and* Juramentos

A common practice among Mexicans is *la promesa* or *manda*, a commitment to a saint, the Virgin, or Jesus to perform a special act, such as saying certain prayers, wearing a religious garb (a scapular or religious habit), or attending Mass on first Fridays of the month. Promises are normally made in return for requests, creating obligations not to be taken lightly. These promises must be kept regardless of whether the favors are granted, and they are, sometimes costly in personal or financial terms. For example, some people promise to make a pilgrimage to the Basilica of Our Lady of Guadalupe in Mexico even though they lack the money for the journey or the legal documents to leave and re-enter the United States. Sometimes people quiz priests about their self-imposed obligation, looking for a dispensation from a promise they can hardly keep.[67]

The effective force of *juramentos* (oaths or pledges) to stop drinking, smoking, or fighting at home indicates the power of people's faith. In the presence of a priest, Mexicans swear before God to cease their harmful behavior for a given period of time, and they generally request a card on which the priest writes the date, duration, and substance of their promise. Although priests usually encourage pledgers to seek professional help to deal with substance abuse, they recognize that *juramentos* do help some people stop "cold turkey." Their success results directly from a strong religious commitment, and many return to renew their commitment after successfully completing their *juramento*.

Novenarios *for the Dead*

In Latin America, the dead are generally not embalmed but interred within twenty-four hours of death. The family has little time to gather, pray, and express condolences. Consequently, the grieving process is extended after burial through a novena *(novenario)* of prayer, generally in the home of the deceased. Friends gather each night to accompany the grieving family in prayer and offer support through an extended grieving process that helps mourners accept the hard reality of personal loss. In Chicago, families often celebrate the *novenario* for people who die in Mexico together with family and friends from their hometown.

Ordinarily, the grieving family arranges a small altar with a picture of the deceased enshrined amid candles, flowers, and some personal effects. Participants kneel as women ministers recognized as *rezadores* (pray-ers) lead the rosary, adding prayers and hymns after each decade, and recite litanies and other prayers, all from memory and sometimes at breakneck speed.

Once, to support a widow and her three children, the community organized a *novenario* in the garage where the father had hung himself. Because the widow owned the property and was unable to move, she wanted the site blessed, and as is frequently the case, she requested a priest to celebrate Mass in the garage on the last night of the novena.

The concluding prayer of the *novenario* involves an "enthronement" of the deceased in the home. The family slowly raises a cross *(levántacruz)*, laid upon a table alongside the deceased's picture, as participants pray for the resurrection. Finally, family and friends share a meal.

Posadas *and* Pastorelas
on the Way to Christmas

To teach indigeneous peoples about the the incarnation of Jesus and to Christianize religious customs, Spanish missionaries in Mexico instituted a novena before Christmas called the *posada*, a Spanish word for lodging, shelter, or inn. This liturgical tradition began in Spain in the sixteenth century when monks carried statues of the Virgin Mary and St. Joseph from monastery to monastery on nine evenings before Christmas. In the late 1500s, Augustinian missionaries initiated the celebration in Acolman, Mexico, to counteract the Aztec religious tradition of sacrificing humans to the god Huitzilopochtli. During the winter solstice, indigenous peoples believed it necessary to nourish the sun with human blood to restore its summer heat. In place of human sacrifice , the missionaries substituted the celebration of the birth of Jesus, who, of course, gave his blood that all might have life.[68]

The *posada* involves both pageant and fiesta aimed primarily at catechizing children. Reenacting the journey of Joseph and Mary from Nazareth to Bethlehem, families gather each night for a procession through the village, or *barrio*, with a young boy and girl dressed as Joseph and Mary leading the way. (Sometimes adults carry statues of Mary and Joseph instead.) Some people carry *luminarios*, traditionally brown paper bags with a lighted candle inside. The crowd closes in behind the children as the prayer leader begins the rosary. The procession stops at a few houses where participants ask for lodging, that is, *posada*, but are denied. They continue until they reach the house designated for that night's reception. When Mary and Joseph knock at the door, the assembled crowd sings the *posada* song, asking for lodging while the host family responds antiphonally from inside that there is no room. When the holy visitors reveal their identity, the hosts swing open the doors to welcome them. The following is the *posada* song with the hosts' response in italics.

In the name of heaven
I ask you for lodging,
because to keep on going
my beloved wife is unable.

This is not an inn;
continue on your way;
I can't open (the door);
You may be riffraff.

Don't be inhuman;
have charity for us
that the God of heaven
may repay you for it.

You may go now
and don't bother us,
because if I get angry
I'm going to hit you.

We are very tired,
coming from Nazareth.
I am a carpenter,
Joseph by name.

I don't care about your name;
let me sleep;
how is it that at night,
she is walking alone?

Asking you for lodging,
kind homeowner,
for only one night,
is the Queen of Heaven.

If she is a queen
who is asking,
how is it that at night,
she is walking alone?

My wife is Mary,
she is the Queen of Heaven,
and she is going to be mother
of the Divine Word.

Are you Joseph?
Your wife is Mary?
Come, pilgrims,
I did not know who you were.

Good people, may God reward
your charity,
and may heaven fill you
with happiness.

Happy this house
which welcomes
the pure Virgin,
the beautiful Maria.[69]

Once inside, an adult talks with the children gathered around the nativity scene about the meaning of Christmas. Then traditional Christmas carols are sung, and the party begins in earnest. As children play and adults converse, food and drink are shared with visitors. The hosts serve *tamales, tostadas,* or *posole* (a hot peasant soup) and hot chocolate, or *atole* (a wheat-based hot drink), to wash them down. To host a *posada* is to welcome people, even strangers, into one's home. One cold winter night, a homeless man joined the *posada* procession on the chance he might find a place to spend the night and some food to fill his stomach. He seemed surprised to be included, especially when the hosts made sure he ate as much as he wanted and later took him to the parish shelter.

After sharing food and drink, the children are blindfolded and armed with a broomstick for hitting a *piñata* swinging by a rope from a nearby streetlight pole. As the children thrash blindly about, onlookers cheer them on. When they finally break the *piñata*, candy rains down and children scramble, piling on top of one another as they gather up as much candy as possible. The *piñata* was originally developed in Mexico by peasants *(colonos)* working in the fields of wealthy landowners. To hold the candy, they originally hollowed out pineapples (thus the name *piñata*, from *piña*) and later made earthenware pots decorated with colored *papier-mâché*. Today *piñatas* are often made of cardboard and decorated with brightly colored tissue paper.

Different interpretations explain the origin of *piñatas*. One political theory claims that it is a symbol of the oppressive landowner; shaping it as a star, a donkey, a clown, or a devil disguised its intended representation. When the *piñata* breaks, his horded riches scatter among the poor. A more religious and probably later interpretation is that the *piñata* symbolizes evil; for example, a seven-pointed star represents the seven deadly sins. The *piñata* is beautiful like sin, and breaking it as difficult as overcoming evil. As Christians fight sin, they struggle in the darkness of faith, symbolized by the blindfold, and swing a stick representing the love that destroys it. The candies raining down from the broken *piñata* symbolize the blessings received for practicing virtue. Unfortunately, few people learn the political or religious interpretations of the *piñata*. For most, it is simply a festive game designed to entertain children.

Before people leave the *posada*, the hosts distribute to the children, if not to everyone, *aguinaldos*, small bags of candy, peanuts, fruit, and a piece of sugarcane, symbolizing the largesse of the festivities. On each of nine nights, the festive ritual is repeated in a different home.

It is more difficult to organize *posadas* in Chicago than in Mexico. The bitter December cold often makes outdoor processions problematic, if not dangerous for children. In addition, unlike the spacious patios of Mexico, the tiny apartments of local residents cannot accommodate a large number of visitors. Nevertheless, some parishioners, principally those involved in Christian Base Communities, maintain this tradition.

On the Sunday within the *posada*, the parish participates in a citywide *posada* at the cathedral in downtown Chicago. The St. Pius V parish staff helped develop the annual event, which originated with the Hispanic community's desire to offer *posada* to all undocumented immigrants in 1986. Four busloads of parishioners join fifteen hundred people from thirty-five parishes in a procession through downtown Chicago to ask for lodging.

The *posada* is a rich tradition that provides catechetical formation for children and reflects important Mexican cultural values—hospitality, faith, joy, community, and generosity. It is inspiring to watch poor families host a *posada;* they are pleased when people partake in festivities in their home.

When fifty people visited Sandra Marines's home, she commented, "I love seeing my house filled with people. The more the merrier." She added, "I love celebrating *posadas* because I love Jesus. I see him as a baby, and I want to have a party for him. I want to see him smile. I would host the *posada* all nine nights if I could." She had prepared a huge kettle of *posole*, and to her satisfaction, there was enough for everyone. Reminiscent of the protagonist in *Like Water for Chocolate*, Sandra commented:

> As I cook the *posole*, I am blessing it, and it multiplies so there is not only enough for everyone but leftovers for people to take home. I love to give everything I have, even if I end up with nothing. All I need are my health and my family; God provides everything else. But, in fact, people help me out. My *compadres* brought chilis, and a friend paid for the fruit for the punch.[70]

Her munificent spirit captures perfectly the true meaning of *posadas*.

For a time, people organized Christmas plays called *pastorelas* in the church hall. Like the American dramas *A Christmas Carol* or *It's a Wonderful Life*, the *pastorelas* are repeated every year without diminishing interest. Modeled on early Christian plays in Greece, they were originally written by Jesuit priests in the fourteenth century to evangelize and conscienticize people about the Christmas story.[71] The central theme has remained constant: the birth of Jesus marks the triumph of good over evil. Although originally serious and even ritualistic, *pastorelas* gradually incorporated humor, satire, and social commentary.

The tradition of celebrating the *pastorela* is usually passed down in certain communities or families, who invest in learning the lengthy scripts and maintaining elaborate costumes. Hundreds of adaptations have developed but usually with the same personages: the shepherds; Bato, the glutton; Gila, a woman representing anger and discontent; Gabriel, the archangel who announces the arrival of the Savior; Lucifer, the devil, who, despite every effort to prevent the birth of the infant God, always loses; and, of course, Mary and Joseph. The shepherds are presented as the contemporary poor and oppressed who are the first to hear the good news of Jesus' birth.[72] Their journey is fraught with obstacles and temptations, playfully represented by the devil, who tries to discourage them from going to Bethlehem by explaining it is too late, too cold, and too difficult.[73]

Unfortunately, *pastorelas* are fading away in the United States because their production requires an enormous commitment of time and energy. St. Pius V has not been able to sustain them, but some groups of young Mexican actors have prepared and presented the dramas to the community.

Posadas and *pastorelas*, parties and plays, prepare for Christmas. While Mexicans might have attended Christmas Eve Mass in Mexico, in the United States most gather with family at home, often eating and drinking traditional foods and beverages until the early morning. Christmas church services at predominantly Mexican parishes attract the smallest attendance and collection of any feast or Sunday of the year, which is, of course, exactly the opposite experience of non-Hispanic parishes.

Some families conduct the traditional home ritual of laying the baby Jesus in the crib *(la acostada del niño)*, an elaborate prayer service based on the rosary and traditional songs. The infant is brought in naked to show he is truly God become one of us, sharing our vulnerability.[74] After a previously selected couple (*padrinos*) rocks the baby in a cloth to sounds of a lullaby, they carefully dress him in elegant clothing. Before ceremoniously laying him in the crib, the *padrinos* place the baby on a tray of hard candy. Participants express their loving affection for the Christ child by kissing the baby and taking a piece of candy, which should be eaten immediately.

Although the liturgical reforms of Vatican II moved the end of the Christmas season forward to the Sunday after the Epiphany, many Mexicans continue to conclude their Christmas celebration on February 2, the feast of the *Candelaria*, known in the United States as the Purification of Mary or the Presentation of Jesus in the Temple. Then they celebrate a ritual of the *levantada del niño* (lifting the baby from the crib), much as they celebrated the *acostada del niño* on Christmas Eve.[75]

On the Epiphany (Three Kings Day), families prepare cakes baked in the form of a wreath, called *rosca de reyes* (the wreath of kings), in which one or more small plastic figurines of the baby Jesus are hidden. People receiving the figurines when the cakes are shared are to host the fiestas to close the Christmas season. Unfortunately, because the immigrant community lacks sufficient people to lead the long prayers and songs at these celebrations, many families are losing the tradition of the *acostada* and *levantada*.

Quinceañeras *as the Gift of Life*

Mexicans celebrate in a special way the fifteenth birthday (*quince años*) of young girls, called *quinceañeras*. The origins of the ancient custom are widely disputed. Some claim it originated in Spain, while others find its roots in Aztec or Toltec cultures, where a ritual presented young women, now biologically mature, for marriage or perhaps human sacrifice to the gods.[76]

Despite the dearth of research on its historical roots, the celebration of *quince años* is generally recognized as the religious and secular celebration of a young girl's rite of passage to maturity, common in many cultures. It is less defined and more broadly conceived than the social cotillion, Jewish *bat mitzvah*, and sacrament of confirmation. Two key anthropological notions are involved: fertility and right order. A young woman's potential for creating life takes on transcendent status for the community, ensuring a right relationship with the creative forces of the cosmos, affirming her own and the community's potential for continuity and victory over chaos.[77]

The significance of the *quinceañeras* ritual has changed over the years and continues to evolve. Icaza notes that in the United States the celebration has acquired greater dimensions and even deeper meaning than in Mexico, reclaiming and recreating ethnic, gender, and religious identity.[78] The festivities help girls reassert their Mexican identity, celebrate their maturity as women, regardless of how available they are for marriage, and recognize themselves as favored children of God, living in a special relationship with Our Lady of Guadalupe, their model and ideal. In addition, the ritual is celebrated as a rite of passage: from childhood to adulthood, from passivity to participation, from recipient to servant. Some pastoral ministers have reinterpreted the celebration as renewing young women's baptismal commitment to service. Although some effort is made to celebrate the *quince años* for boys, it remains strongly tied to women, perhaps reflecting their pivotal role in developing family and popular religiosity.

Karen Davalos interviewed Mexican *quinceañeras*, their families and priests in Chicago and concluded that the form of the celebration varies widely and, in the end, is of little consequence for understanding the meaning of the *quinceañera*. While some families search for the proper way to celebrate the event, in the end, most believe what they experienced in their family is the most authentic tradition.[79]

Although there is no universally fixed ritual, a basic pattern has developed, generally beginning with a Mass.[80] The *quinceañera* enters the church in procession with her entourage. Some have only female attendants or male escorts; others have both. If the girl has a male escort, he is kept at a distance to avoid the appearance of a wedding. Some girls dress elaborately and others simply, most in pastel colors, since white is reserved for brides. After the homily, the young woman renews her baptismal promises, rededicates herself to Jesus and his mother, and commits herself to serve the community. After a blessing for the *quinceañera*, the priest blesses gifts, such as a Bible, rosary, prayerbook, ring, necklace, bracelet, and earrings. After communion, the *quinceañera* offers a prayer and a bouquet of flowers at the altar of Our Lady of Guadalupe.[81]

Some pastors do not celebrate *quinceañeras*, believing they promote early courtship and even sexual activity or that they are only an excuse for parents to throw a party for their daughters. Because some celebrations are extravagant, plunging families into years of debt, they appear to be more focused on impressing friends and family than on celebrating the gift of life. Because of the expense involved, less than one quarter of Mexican families in Chicago (probably fewer in Mexico) celebrate the *quince años* of their daughters in church or with a major fiesta. Nevertheless, the church's refusal to celebrate this ritual, which is embedded in people's tradition, is often perceived by Mexicans as a rejection of their culture.

St. Pius V approaches the *quinceañera* as an opportunity to form young women in the faith, develop their self-esteem, guide them toward service, and involve them in the church. In a historical moment when parents and community are losing many young people, every opportunity to dialogue with them and include them in activities of the larger community makes sense.

Catechists provide a formation program that begins with the girls and their parents clarifying the meaning and purpose of the celebration. This session reveals that parents and daughters often have different ideas and reasons for celebrating the day. Three more classes for the girls and their attendants offer basic catechesis about the vocation of adolescent Christians. After a session explaining the liturgy, a rehearsal in church prepares participants for the Mass.

Because relatively few churches in Chicago offer *quinceañera* services, St. Pius V is inundated with requests that it cannot accommodate individually. Consequently, it offers the service only to families connected to the parish and only to young women who have received their first communion and who have either been confirmed or are preparing to receive confirmation. Because of the parish's limited number of clergy and its restricted time slots for Saturday weddings, the parish offers only two *quinceañera* Masses per month. All the girls interested in celebrating that particular month must choose one of those two Masses, which inevitably means joining more than one *quinceañera* in a Mass. Not having a Mass solely for their daughter discourages some families from participating. This communal practice, however, helps socialize the *quinceañeras* and their attendants, accommodates the parish's limitations, reduces costs for the families, and reinforces the Mexicans' sense of community celebration.

Liturgy and Community

Parish liturgy celebrates the sacred mysteries of old, as well as people's lives today. By presenting their babies at Mass, by including their testimonies, and by providing preaching related to their experience, people's lives are integrated into the liturgy. Liturgy also enters people's lives and communities through Masses on the street and special blessings and rituals in homes and in the community. The following examples demonstrate some other ways St. Pius V takes liturgy into the community.

Resurrecting the Local Neighborhood

In 1990, six neighborhood parishes formed a housing development corporation. To launch their commitment ritually and fully engage the community, parishioners from each participating parish signed a covenant during Sunday Masses to symbolize their agreement to work together for the good of the neighborhood. While people in the pews signed individual commitment sheets, parish leaders signed an eight-foot-high form to be carried from parish to parish.

When Mayor Richard M. Daley came to support the initiative in the presence of a packed crowd in a local church amidst religious songs and prayers, he and other city officials immersed various carpentry tools in a pool of water, symbolizing their baptism and their newborn power to give new life to the community.

Through this ritual the mayor became a godparent of the parishes' efforts.

Blessing a New Home at Posadas

A few days before Christmas 1989, a raging fire destroyed a large apartment building two blocks from the church. Agustina Morales and her five daughters escaped the smoke and flames, but her seven-year-old grandson died in the fire. With the help of her brother and the parish, she bought a small house.

To celebrate her dream-come-true and to thank the community for its support, Agustina hosted a *posada* on the first anniversary of the fire. On that cold December night, several hundred people holding candles gathered in front of her home to pray for the family and sing the *posada* song. Afterward, Agustina invited everyone into her home for *tamales, tostadas,* and hot chocolate. The liturgy had reached into the community to celebrate its struggle for life over death.

Blessing the Site of a Murder

On numerous occasions, people ask that a Mass be offered at the site of a murder. Generally, the victims are young men killed in gang warfare, but sometimes they are innocent bystanders.

One warm summer night, as one gang chased another, shots rang out. The victim was an eight-year-old boy enjoying pizza in the park with his family. Although he survived a bullet to the head, he suffered serious disabilities. Hundreds of people attended the Mass in the park to console his family and reclaim the spot where life and peace had been broken.

Once a son, high on drugs, brutally stabbed and killed his mother. Months later, the neighbors, concerned about the soul of their friend and their own peace of mind, gathered to celebrate a Mass for her in the building where she had lived.

Promoting Peace, Reacting to War

When the United States attacked Iraq in January 1991, blind enthusiasm for war swept the country. With riveted fascination, people watched on television the spectacular displays of "smart" bombs allegedly destroying military targets. As Pope John Paul II publicly criticized the war, St. Pius V dedicated Sunday homilies to the subject of peacemaking. The liturgy committee created an altar of peace in the sanctuary area, decorated with a large dove and rainbow. In a book on the altar, parishioners wrote their intentions and the names of people affected by the war. One Sunday a parishioner and Army reservist about to be sent to the Gulf spoke at the Masses about the hardship the war was causing his family and about his own resistance to being involved in senseless killing. The effect was stunningly powerful.[82]

In 2003, following the lead of Pope John Paul II, the parish again erected an altar to remember all those affected by the Iraq War and distributed posters opposing the unjust preemptive war to all parishioners interested in placing them in their front windows.

Celebrations of prayer and ritual in the community help people relate their daily experience to their faith and to the church. Their faith is not just a personal matter but relies on as well as supports the life of the community.

Liturgy and Secular Life

To integrate liturgy and life more fully, St. Pius V supports different activities on Sundays. This inclusion helps to sanctify and put life's struggles into the context of faith, as well as challenge faith to work for justice. The following describes some of these activities.

Mexican Elections in Chicago

In August 1994, when Mexico was holding its national elections, various Mexican groups in the United States organized mock ballots and polling places where Mexican citizens could cast a symbolic vote to be forwarded later to the Mexican government. The very presence of the polling site in front of St. Pius V caused considerable discussion, helping parishioners question the justice of denying Mexican nationals living abroad the right to vote in their country's election.

Confronting Oppression in Chiapas

In March 1995, the parish became a principal stop for the national caravans organized by Pastors for Peace to transport material aid to needy communities in Chiapas, Mexico. In preparation for each caravan's arrival, parishioners raised money for the diocese of San Cristobal de las Casas in Chiapas. When an associate pastor returned from a delegation of international observers, he spoke at all the Masses about the oppression of indigenous people there. As a result, people donated more money in the second collection for Chiapas than in any other collection in ten years. The incorporation of the suffering of the people in Chiapas into the Sunday liturgy created solidarity between parishioners and their brothers and sisters in southern Mexico. Later, the parish began assisting a poor community in Chiapas each month with both material aid and political advocacy.

Supporting Immigrant People

When the United States began to tighten restrictions on immigrants, Mexican immigrants needed orientation and advocacy. While the parish provided counselors and lawyers, the priests addressed people's concerns in Sunday sermons, emphasizing the biblical imperative to welcome the foreigner. Petition drives in church helped the community oppose unjust legislation affecting immigrants. One such effort helped convince the governor of Illinois not to replicate California's Proposition 187, which limited immigrants' access to public education and health care. Other petitions protested the destruction of public housing apartments without creating alternative affordable units, reductions in municipal mental health facilities, and the extension of the death penalty to gang-related homicides.

Promoting a Healthy Community

Sunday mornings after Masses have become a time for education about a variety of issues. Lawyers speak about immigration issues, and labor advocates address workers' rights. Speakers address health issues, such as the AIDS epidemic, about which the Hispanic community has little knowledge and much fear. Professionals speak about depression and other mental health problems, as well as organizing blood drives, enchancing blood reserves and dispelling fears among Hispanics about donating blood. The parish also regularly sponsors blood pressure and diabetes screenings, free mammograms, and informational sessions about breast cancer and the use of car seats, since Hispanics have the highest death and injury rates for children in car accidents in Illinois.

All these Sunday activities are announced during Mass, and because they are swirling on the periphery of the eucharistic celebration, they highlight the church's commitment to build the kingdom of God and bring the reality of people's lives into the liturgical celebration.

Mexican immigrants are a sacramental people with a rich religious tradition. Their strong faith, often expressed and strengthened through religious practices, can help evangelize the American people. Their home-centered devotions, their integration of the spiritual and the material, their sense of God's loving presence, and their community-oriented celebrations can enrich the faith and culture of people in the United States.

Notes

1. *Puebla*, 913.

2. Sixto J. García, "U.S. Hispanic and Mainstream Trinitarian Theologies," in Deck, *Frontiers*, 90.

3. Orlando Espín, *The Faith of the People: Theological Reflections on Popular Catholicism* (Maryknoll, NY: Orbis Books,1997), 2. He distinguishes between two general Hispanic-American religious worlds: (1) "popular Catholicism," closer to, if not rooted in, mainstream Catholicism, and (2) "marginal religion," further from the doctrine, liturgy, and praxis of universal Catholic life. This chapter considers primarily the first religious world.

4. Peréz-Rodríguez cites Chupungco: "...adaptation to various cultures has been a constant feature of Christian liturgy. Indeed, it is part and parcel of her tradition. The apostles did it, and so did the Fathers of the Church and her pastors far into the Middle Ages. Adaptation of the liturgy to various native genius and tradition is not a novelty but fidelity to tradition." Pérez-Rodríguez, *Popular Catholicism*, 3.

5. Vatican Council II, "Constitution on the Sacred Liturgy," 37, in Walter M. Abbott, SJ, ed. *The Documents of Vatican II* (Guild Press: New York, 1966), 151.

6. Allan Figueroa Deck, SJ, "'Pox on Both Your Houses': A View of Catholic Conservative–Liberal Polarities from the Hispanic Margin," in Mary Jo Weaver and R. Scott Appleby, eds., *Being Right: Conservative Catholics in America* (Bloomington: Indiana University Press, 1995), 99.

7. *Puebla*, 913.

8. Joyce Ann Zimmerman, "Liturgical Notes," *Liturgical Ministry* 7 (1998): 147.

9. *Puebla*, 914.

10. Segundo Galilea, "The Theology of Liberation and the Place of 'Folk Religion,'" *Concilium* 136 (New York: Seabury, 1980): 40–45.

11. Francis and Pérez-Rodríguez, *Primero Dios*, 7–8.

12. Keith F. Pecklers, "Issues of Power and Access in Popular Religion," *Liturgical Ministry* 7 (1998): 138.

13. James L. Empereur, "Popular Religion and the Liturgy: The State of the Question," *Liturgical Ministry* 7 (1998): 109–10.

14. Orlando O. Espín, "Pentecostalism and Popular Catholicism: Preservers of Hispanic Catholic Tradition—Reflections on Popular and Folk Religion," *ACHTUS Newsletter* 4, no. 1 (Spring 1993): 10.

15. Empereur, *op. cit.*, 107.

16. *Ibid.*, 129–30. Allan Figueroa Deck, SJ, Arturo Pérez-Rodríguez, and Mark R. Francis argue strongly for the dominance of medieval Catholicism in the colonial period. See Deck, "Pox," 91. For a comparison of folk religion with Nordic Christianity, see Virgil Elizondo, *Christianity and Culture* (San Antonio, TX: Mexican American Cultural Center, 1975), 124–28, 156–57, as well as William Worth, "Arte Popular Cristiano," *Religiosidad Popular: Las Imagenes de Jesucristo y la Virgen Maria en America Latina* (San Antonio, TX: Mexican American Cultural Center, 1990), 7–14. See also Thomas O'Meara, OP, "Leaving the Baroque," *America* 174 (February 3, 1996): 14, 25.

17. Virgil Elizondo, *"Mestizaje* as a Locus of Theological Reflection," *Frontiers*, 110. *Mestizaje* is discussed at greater length in his book *Galilean Journey*.

18. Bartolomé de las Casas, *Apologética Historia* 1, c. 263, cited in E. O'Gorman, ed., *Los Indios de México y Nueva España. Antología* (México City, 1966), 109–44.

19. Deck, "Pox," 56.

20. Elizondo, *"Mestizaje,"*113.

21. Mark R. Francis, "Building Bridges Between Liturgy, Devotionalism, and Popular Religion," *Assembly* 20 (April 1994): 3.

22. Also, Richard Rodriguez, *McNeil-Lehrer News Hour*, PBS-TV, July 29, 1996.

23. NCCB, "National Pastoral Plan," *Hispanic Ministry*, 68.

24. Pecklers, 139.

25. *Ibid.*, 140. Cites C. Gilbert Romero, *Hispanic Devotional Piety: Tracing the Biblical Roots* (Maryknoll, NY: Orbis Books, 1991), 83–84.

26. Roberto S. Goizueta, *Caminemos con Jesus: Toward a Hispanic/Latino Theology of Accompaniment* (Maryknoll, NY: Orbis Books, 1995), 48.

27. Espín, *Faith of the People*, 4–5.

28. Francis, "Building Bridges." Francis does an excellent job of describing the connection between the official liturgical calendar and what he calls "the Hispanic liturgical calendar."

29. Pérez-Rodríguez, *Primero Dios*, 7.

30. A lively debate on the matter is currently under way in the literature about popular religiosity. Are popular religious practices prior, parallel, or antithetical to the official liturgy? See Robert E. Wright, "Popular Religiosity: Review of Literature," *Liturgical Ministry* 7 (Summer 1998).

31. Mark R. Francis, "The Hispanic Liturgical Calendar: The People's Calendar," *Liturgical Ministry* 7 (Summer, 1998): 129.

32. Mark R. Francis, "Popular Piety and Liturgical Reform in a Hispanic Context," in Pineda and Schreiter, *Dialogue Rejoined*, 169.

33. Icaza, "Prayer, Worship, and Liturgy," in *Frontiers*, 135.

34. A 1985 survey of Hispanic Catholics indicated that 55 percent of those surveyed had never heard of Vatican II. Timothy M. Matovina, "U.S. Hispanic Catholics and Liturgical Reform," *America* (November 6, 1993): 23.

35. Sacred Congregation of Rites, *General Norms for the Liturgical Year and the Calendar*, cited in Icaza, *op. cit.*, 142.

36. Virgil Elizondo writes: "If Ash Wednesday stresses the earthly belonging and present suffering of the people, and Good Friday marks their collective struggles and death, the feast of Our Lady of Guadalupe shouts out with joy the proclamation that a new dawn is breaking: the collective resurrection of a new people. She is not a goddess but the new woman from whom the new humanity will be born. She is herself the prototype of the new creation. She is *la mestiza* (of mixed race), *la morena* (the dark one)....It is important to remember that flowers were the sign that the Virgin gave proof that she was God's messenger. In ancient and contemporary Mexican culture, flowers are a sign of new existence. In many ways, the roses are for Mexicans what lilies are for Europeon and North American Catholics at Easter....Guadalupe is also a *pentecost* event: she opened the way to true dialogue between Europeans and Mexican Indians. She is a symbol of unity, of the universality of the Christian faith. As a *mestiza* she symbolizes two cultures fusing together to make something new." Elizondo, *Galilean Journey*, 43–44.

37. Gilberto Hinojosa, "Prologue," in Dolan and Hinojosa, *Mexican Americans*, 121.

38. *Lumen Gentium: Dogmatic Constitution on the Church*, 52–69 in Abbott, *op. cit.*

39. Gary Moore, "Mariachis Recall Romance of Old Mexico," *Chicago Tribune* (January 6, 1998), sec C, 5. In the United States, *mariachis* have become a primary symbol of Mexican culture, which is ironic because they were considered crude and vulgar when first beginning in the mid-eighteenth century. See Alejandro Riera and Benito Gárcia, "Todo lo que Debe Saber Sobre el Mariachi," *Exito* (September 11, 1997), 47–48; Alvaro Ochoa Serrano, *"El Mariachi Como Elemento de Identidad en el Sur de California,"* paper given at the *Fronteras Fragmentadas* Conference at El Colegio de Michoacán, Zamora, México, October 24, 1997.

40. Moore, *loc. cit.*

41. NCCB, *Hispanic Presence*, no. 120.

42. Elizondo, *Galilean Journey*, 33.

43. Margaret M. Nava, *"Via Crucis:* Way of the Cross in Chicago," *Liguorian* (March 1998): 16.

44. Elizondo, *Galilean Journey,* 42.

45. Karen Mary Davalos, "'The Real Way of Praying': The *Vía Crucis, Mexicano* Sacred Space, and the Architecture of Domination," 9, paper later published in Riebe-Estrella and Matovina, eds., *Horizons of the Sacred.*

46. *Ibid.,* 13.

47. Elizondo, *Galilean Journey, loc. cit.*

48. In 1986, few Mexican residents understood Thanksgiving. Few needy families were interested in receiving donations of turkeys. By 2000, the situation had changed as people looked forward to the holiday and receiving turkeys, many of which were still cooked Mexican style.

49. For valuable history and analysis of celebrations in Los Angeles, see Lara Medina and Gilbert R. Cadena, *"Dias de los Muertos:* Public Ritual, Community Renewal, and Popular Religion in Los Angeles, in Matovina and Riebe-Estrella, eds., *Horizons of the Sacred,* 69–94.

50. Kay F. Turner, "Mexican American Home Altars: Towards Their Interpretation," *Aztlan* 13 (Spring and Fall, 1982): 20–33.

51. Melita Marie Garza and Teresa Puente, "Day to Honor the Dead Lives On," *Chicago Tribune* (November 3, 1995), Sec. B, 1.

52. Some people believe altars should include symbols of the four elements of fire, water, earth, and air: the light of a candle and flowers to help loved ones find their way home; water to quench their thirst on the journey; fruits of the earth for nourishment; and colorful paper cutouts hung from threads above the altar, at once symbolizing endless sky and their heavenly destination.

53. *Ibid.,* 2.

54. NCCB, "National Pastoral Plan," 69.

55. Pérez-Rodríguez, *Popular Catholicism,* 30.

56. These items, called *milagros,* represent a religious custom common in many non-Christian religions dating back to classical Greek times. Martha Egan, *Milagros: Votive Offerings from the Americas* (Santa Fe, NM: University of New Mexico, 1991)

57. Virgil Elizondo, *Guadalupe: Mother of the New Creation* (Maryknoll, NY: Orbis Books, 1999), 76.

58. Paul J. Wadell, CP, "Ethics and the Narrative of Hispanic Americans: Conquest, Community, and the Fragility of Life," in Piñeda and Schreiter, *Dialogue Rejoined,* 138.

59. Hinojosa, "Mexican American Faith Communities," in Dolan and Hinojosa, *Mexican Americans,* 94. For the integration of *curanderismo*

and Catholic faith, see Luis D. León, "'*Soy una Curandera y Soy una Católica*': The Poetics of a Mexican Healing Tradition," in Matovina and Riebe-Estrella, eds., *Horizons of the Sacred*, 95–118.

60. Pérez-Rodríguez, *Popular Catholicism*, 12–13. See also "National Pastoral Plan," 94.

61. Wadell, "Ethics and the Narrative of Hispanic Americans," 139. This change results partly because recent reforms of the church's calendar reduced the number of saints' feast days, and partly because Mexicans in the United States are greatly influenced by local culture to select names based on other criteria. Some immigrants now choose names foreign to their culture, such as Jacqueline, Brian, Kevin, Jonathon, Jennifer, Ashley, Melissa, Kimberly, and Eric.

62. Lazarus's entrance into Mexicans' pantheon of saints comes through the syncretic religious practices of the Caribbean, where native religions mixed not only with Spanish Christianity but with African religions introduced into the area by African slaves.

63. Thomas J. Steele, SJ, *Santos and Saints* (Santa Fe, NM: Ancient City Press, 1974), 70–71. In New Mexico, this child-saint has served as a patron for prisoners and travelers.

64. Hinojosa, "Mexican American Faith Communities," in Dolan and Hinojosa, *Mexican Americans*, 11.

65. Isasi-Díaz, "Pluralism," in Deck et al., *Perspectives*, 26–27.

66. Pérez-Rodríguez, *Popular Catholicism*, 12–13.

67. Hinojosa, "Mexican American Faith Communities," in Dolan and Hinojosa, *Mexican Americans*, 93–94.

68. For a brief history of *posadas*, see Eduardo Pinzon-Umaña, SJ, *En Nombre de Dios, Pedimos Posada: Nueve Noches de Esperanza antes de Navidad* (Ligouri, MO: Ligouri Press, 1995), 15–95.

69. Elizondo, *Galilean Journey*, 36–37.

70. Charles W. Dahm, "Celebrating Christmas with Love and Faith," *El Mensajero* (Winter 1998): 8.

71. A Spanish bishop introduced the idea, and St. Ignatius of Loyola and the Society of Jesus developed it. Historical records date the first *pastorela* in the New World to 1578, but not until the period of Mexican independence in the nineteenth century did it become widespread.

72. Raúl Gómez, "Christmas Among Hispanics," *Liturgy* (Journal of the Liturgical Conference, vol. 12, No. 3): 8. See also Icaza, "Prayer, Worship, and Liturgy," 145.

73. Pablo Helguera, "Pastorelas: De Obra Didáctica a Símbolo de la Navidad," *Exito* (Chicago, November 27, 1997), 19 and 23.

74. Gómez, "Christmas among Hispanics," 7.

75. For Hispanics, February 2 is the feast of the *Virgen de Candelaria*. The feast of February 2 has several names and meanings. First, it is the presentation of Jesus at the temple. The word *candelaria* refers to the "light to the world," mentioned by Simeon in his prophecy of the Virgin's presentation of her son Jesus in the temple (Luke 2:32). The feast also celebrates the presentation, or purification, of the Virgin herself, who as a Jewish women having just given birth, had to present herself to a priest at the temple for purification.

76. Raúl Gómez observes: "In my judgment, the Celtic fertility rites, with their ritual meal and dance, as well as the Mozarabic liturgical rites of passage, suggest that the *quince años* ritual may have a stronger connection to Spain than to Meso-America. Nonetheless, its contemporary expression is like Hispanics: a *mestizaje*, a blend of European, African, and American blood, language, and culture." "Celebrating the *Quinceañera* as a symbol of Faith and Culture," in Davis, *Misa, Mesa y Musa, loc. cit.*, 108.

77. Article without title or source noted.

78. Icaza, *op. cit.*, 141.

79. Karen Mary Davalos, "*La Quinceañera:* Making Gender and Ethnic Identities," *Frontiers* XVI, no. 2/3: 101–27.

80. The most commonly used bilingual text is Angela Erevia, MCDP, *Religious Celebration for the Quinceañera* (San Antonio, TX: Mexican American Cultural Center, 1980).

81. The publication of the Office of Divine Worship in Chicago discourages this practice because "acts of private devotion should not be encouraged" within a public liturgy. This comment reflects the lack of appreciation for the meaning of the ceremony for the family and Hispanic people. Mary Lou Barba, "Celebrating Quince Años: A Report from Austin," in *Liturgy* 90 (Chicago: Liturgical Training Publications, June 1995): 6.

82. On a subsequent Sunday afternoon, the local parishes organized a joint prayer service in the largest church in the area. Children performed a peace dance, and families gave dramatic testimonies of the suffering the war was causing them and their loved ones. Participants then signed a giant postcard to President George Bush asking for an end to the bombing. They concluded the ceremony by joining in procession to the local post office to mail the card signed by all, as well as individual cards addressed to the president.

7.

A Community
of Teaching Ministries

Teaching is central to parish ministry. Every parish is called to teach as Jesus did, to instruct people in Catholic doctrine, and to develop a mature and critical conscience. Parishes serving immigrants with limited academic experience have the added responsibility to help parishioners acquire skills normally learned in schools. St. Pius V offers an extensive religious education program for its burgeoning population of Mexican children and youth, operates a parish elementary school, and provides programs of religious and secular formation for adults.[1]

Religious Education of Children

Until 1986, religious education in Spanish for children not enrolled in the parish school was directed by a volunteer Hispanic couple for approximately forty children, who received first communion after one year. Their formation followed the traditional Mexican format of memorizing basic church teachings and prayers. Most parishes in the United States had long abandoned this approach, a practice still popular in parts of Mexico, where it is commonly referred to as learning the "doctrine." In 1986, a Dominican Sister, Margaret McGuirk, arrived at St. Pius V to diversify and expand the program. By 1998, 850 children were enrolled in a two-year program. Because Sister Margaret had seen Catholics convert to pentecostal and evangelical churches, she developed a catechetical program that incorporated the following positive aspects of non-Catholic churches.

The Centrality of Jesus Christ

Fundamentalist churches are less concerned than the Catholic Church about elaborate, abstract theological concepts. They emphasize Jesus Christ as personal Lord and Savior; his life and teachings are the core of their catechesis. Mexican immigrant children entering St. Pius V frequently know little about Jesus; many cannot recount a story of his life. Sr. Margaret observed that the *Catechism of the Catholic Church* does in fact emphasize the centrality of Jesus Christ as Savior and clearly teaches that the transmission of the Christian faith consists primarily in proclaiming the person of Jesus.[2] St. Pius V thus began focusing its weekly catechetical lesson on the Gospel reading assigned for each Sunday, a lectionary-based catechetical method that focuses on the Good News of Jesus' life rather than church doctrine. Each story or teaching offers insights into the person of Jesus.

Hands on the Bible

Fundamentalist churches put the Bible in people's hands, and almost all teaching emanates directly from the scriptures. Many Hispanic Catholics are amazed how fundamentalist missionaries, ordinary people like themselves, visit their homes and expound at length on a biblical passage. Although Hispanic Catholics love the Bible, most have never studied it. Because they rarely see their priest carrying a Bible or citing a biblical text, some are easily misled to believe that priests are unschooled in the scriptures.

Proclaiming the Word of God at weekly worship has always been the center of the church's formation. Early Christians followed the Jewish custom of weekly reading and reflecting on a portion of the sacred texts in sequential fashion, thus forming the lectionary, which is the church's curriculum. But over the years, the tradition of commenting on the weekly scriptural readings gave way to teaching ecclesiastical rules and regulations. In years past, the Catholic Church discouraged laity from reading the Bible in order to avoid its misinterpretation. Instead, catechisms

211

with doctrinal summaries and prayers for children and adults to memorize were created.

After Vatican II, this doctrinal approach lost favor, and in its place more integrated religious texts were developed around specific doctrinal, sacramental, and biblical themes, such as creation, God, reconciliation, Eucharist, church, sacrament, the Ten Commandments, and prayer. Although sacred scripture was included, its use was not extensive until the 1980s, when the lectionary-based catechetical approach gained favor. This method, selected by St. Pius V as the most appropriate way of incorporating Mexican culture and popular religiosity in church teaching, includes several key points.

First, the Bible is at the heart of Catholic tradition. Each Sunday after a reading of the scriptures, the priest delivers a homily explaining the text and applying its message to people's lives. Through his exposition, the faithful develop, albeit unconsciously, a Catholic approach to the scriptures. Catholics may not be able to quote chapter and verse from the Bible, but they have a general understanding of its content and its meaning for their Christian life.

Second, the Bible, presented in lectionary format, is easier for people to understand than lessons focused on doctrine. Mexican immigrants relate easily and enthusiastically to biblical stories about God's people and Jesus' life because of similarities to their own experiences. They learn how God's people experienced poverty and oppression and lived as foreigners in a strange land. They learn that biblical stories are written for the poor and from the point of view of the poor. Hispanic immigrants read the Bible with insights born of their unique experience. Putting the scriptures in their hands is like offering them living waters for which they thirst.

Third, lectionary-based catechesis is integrally linked to liturgy. On Sundays, catechists first help children reflect on the day's scriptures in their respective classrooms. The children then gather in the church basement to celebrate the first part of the Mass, a children's Liturgy of the Word. In the classrooms, children craft a symbol representing the day's theme, drawing or cutting out sheep, hearts, hands, stars, palms, crosses, salt, light, water, rocks, and so on. Catechists continually focus on images that help children learn who Jesus is: shepherd, teacher, healer,

friend, savior, king, child, missionary, and prophet. A few catechists preach during the children's liturgy, connecting the readings, images, and the children's lives. After the preaching, children
pray for their needs and then proceed upstairs, entering the
church during the presentation of bread and wine at the altar,
where they sit facing the assembled congregation.

Fourth, the program facilitates parental involvement.
Because parents hear the same readings and homilies during
Mass, they are able to share the lessons with their children. Some
parents accompany the children to their Liturgy of the Word in
order to experience their lively exchange with the catechist-
preacher. Children in their second year of formation make their
first reconciliation, together with their families and the community, at two parish communal reconciliation services celebrated
during Advent and Holy Week. In May, they receive first communion amidst family, friends, and parishioners at different
Sunday liturgies. To prepare for these sacraments, they attend
special classes on Saturday mornings, in which some parents also
participate. It should be noted that lectionary-based catechesis
allows families to enter the program easily, not feeling lost or
needing to catch up.

The Spanish Language

Teaching religion to children whose first language is Spanish
is more important than is often realized. The choice of language
is more a matter of selecting a cultural system of communication
that conveys deeper meaning than of deciding what language a
child understands. The language mothers use with their children
is the language of love; it bespeaks the stability and depth of history and tradition. Children associate this language with their primary caregiver. Hispanic immigrant children usually learn their
second language, English, in school, where the setting is formal
and academic, something foreign and non-religious. To speak
about God in the language of the heart conveys a feeling of love,
enhancing understanding and faith. Pope Paul VI noted:
"Evangelization loses much of its force and effectiveness if it does

not take into consideration the actual people whom it addresses, if it does not use their language, their signs and symbols, and if it does not have an impact on their concrete life."[3]

Having chosen lectionary-based catechesis, the next task was to find a fully bilingual children's lectionary program. Because no such text was available in Spanish in the United States until the mid 1990s, Sister Margaret selected *Seasons of Faith*, from Brown Publishers, and obtained permission to translate it.[4] It organizes children into pre-school, primary, and intermediate groups, thus providing more familial groups of students. Hispanic brothers and sisters, although of different ages, like to attend class and study together. Moreover, because the text was written for a rural community, it incorporates images from nature familiar to many Mexican immigrant children. The resource guide follows the methodology of Christian Base Communities, which differs from the traditional classroom approach based on detailed lesson plans. By following the process of "see, judge, and act," participants begin by telling their story, listening to God's Word, and then applying it to their lives.

The Empowerment of Local Leadership

Fundamentalist churches attract many Hispanics because they promote Hispanic leadership, quickly entrusting them with responsibility. The advantage of Hispanic leaders in a Hispanic community cannot be overestimated. Because these leaders speak the people's language and understand their lives, they are warmly received and tend to promote inculturated evangelization. In the Catholic Church, on the other hand, Hispanics are drastically under-represented at all levels of leadership. In 2000, in the Archdiocese of Chicago, only a dozen of 835 diocesan clergy were Hispanics. Many parishes teach catechism to Hispanic children only in English, automatically limiting catechists to English-speaking adults. This arrangement practically assures that Hispanic culture will not influence religious education.

Recruiting catechists is not easy in an inner-city, working-class Hispanic neighborhood because people lack time for service or feel insufficiently prepared, particularly if they have difficulty reading and writing. Consequently, St. Pius V trains catechists "on the job." To recruit catechists and provide young children with teenage role models, the parish developed the position of catechist assistant for those who feel unprepared but interested in assisting children. By accompanying catechists, assistants learn how to be catechists themselves. Because the lessons are dialogical, assistants join with the children in "telling stories," modeling for them love for their faith and commitment to service. In contrast to many traditional catechetical programs in which each grade has a different theme and teachers prepare lessons independently, catechists prepare their classes together, usually on Friday nights and Saturday mornings. Because they themselves share the material, they are energized to share their faith and speak from their own experience when they teach the children.

Clemencia Calderon, an immigrant mother of ten children, had dedicated her entire life to her husband and children. When most of her children were reared, she wanted to reach beyond her family and become a catechist for small children. Despite all her parenting experience, she was unsure of herself. During the weekly preparations, Clemencia gradually discovered that she was excellent at sharing her history. Her rich experiences of life were harvested, and she soon realized she had insight and wisdom to share. Through her catechetical ministry, Clemencia developed a greater awareness of herself as a mature and independent woman and began providing leadership to other catechists. After a few years, she developed the confidence to speak in front of a large assembly of children, and when she gave a reflection to the parish on Mother's Day, she proved herself an articulate preacher and role model for many mothers in the community.

Younger, more educated women also benefit from being catechists. Patricia Hernandez, a young woman who grew up in St. Pius V and graduated from DePaul University, wrote:

> My Catholic faith has been a source of comfort and hope for me as long as I can remember. My parents, grandparents, aunts, and uncles were my first catechists and those responsible for introducing me to Jesus. I

clearly remember the crucifixes in every bedroom in my house, learning to say my prayers, attending Mass every Sunday, and celebrating Our Lady of Guadalupe. As pleasant as these memories sound, my faith was not always as strong as today. As I grew up, things that once fascinated me slowly lost their charm. I grew tired of reciting the old prayers and participating in the same Sunday rituals. As I questioned myself, my faith became less fulfilling. When I entered high school and then college, my time became scarcer. At the same time, I wanted to fill the void forming in my soul. Because I wanted to relive the wonders of my childhood, I volunteered as a catechist, trying to give back something to my community. When I started working with the children, I had no idea what was in store for me. As I planned my lessons and tried to make the material interesting, I discovered I was becoming interested. The children had lots of challenging questions that I once had but was afraid to ask. They helped me revisit them and eventually find answers. And by participating in the children's liturgy I found a refreshing change of pace at Mass. I had thought I was going to enrich the lives of children as their catechist, but instead they taught me about faith.[5]

Through their participation as catechists many women and a few men grow and blossom as persons and as leaders in their community.

Conserving and Celebrating Popular Religiosity

Catechesis is not accomplished by a single catechist, and faith is not developed primarily through official teaching. Rather people's religiosity in the family and community, including devotions, prayers, and festive celebrations, at once expresses the faith and preserves and transmits it from one generation to the next.

Because Mexico is arguably the most Catholic country in the world, it is not surprising to find among its richly diverse cultures a treasure of religious customs. Indeed, the culture of the people supports their faith. When Mexicans move to the United States, they experience an alien culture, largely devoid of popular religiosity, which gradually erodes their beliefs and practices. Not only is there a separation of church and state, but religion in general is a private matter between the individual and God. In contrast, the Hispanic practice of faith is more communal and is often expressed in periodic formal and informal fiestas. Religious holidays are times for social events and public demonstrations of faith. People readily talk about their faith and God's work in their lives. Miracles—God's extraordinary intervention in their lives—are expected and openly discussed. In the United States, Mexicans must work hard to sustain their faith. St. Pius V parish, through its religious education program, attempts to build on the strengths of American culture while preserving the wealth of Mexican popular religiosity.

Lectionary-based catechesis lends itself well to the public expression of faith because, following the liturgical calendar, it provides the thematic structure for popular religiosity, making faith visible through concrete sacramentals. As mentioned above, each week the children develop a symbol reflecting the teachings of the Sunday scriptures. The parish also organizes dramas for the children to perform for one another. As children reenact stories from the Bible each year, they not only learn their faith but create a learning tradition.

Several years after making his first communion, Rudy Lozano Jr. visited Sister Margaret. When she appeared not to remember his name, he blurted out, "You remember me; I was the prodigal son."

The first pageant of the catechetical year is celebrated on Mission Sunday in October. To celebrate God's love for children around the world, children wear hats from different countries and learn that God sent Jesus to save everybody and that because Jesus is their brother, they are brothers and sisters with everyone.

On the Sunday nearest All Saints' Day, November 1, the saints are presented as God's friends who provide examples of following Jesus. Their stories tell of love, goodness, and heroism. Over the years, the parish has accumulated a wardrobe that families use to dress their children as saints for the Sunday liturgy.

For the feast of Our Lady of Guadalupe, children also dress in costume. Girls wear green, white, and red, the colors of the Virgin of Guadalupe, while boys dress like Juan Diego. At the children's Sunday liturgy, the children dramatize the apparitions of the Virgin and Juan Diego's response.

Because the time before Christmas is so hectic, and because Mexicans are accustomed to enthusiastically celebrating Three Kings Day, the catechetical program celebrates both the pre-Christmas novena of *posadas* and Three Kings Day on the Saturday before Epiphany. Children dress as angels, shepherds, and wise men for a pageant of the nativity story. Afterward, all gather in the church basement for a traditional *posada* party, complete with *piñatas* and *aguinaldos*.

On a Saturday in early spring, catechists organize A Day in the Life of Jesus, presenting a pageant depicting life in Israel at the time of Jesus. Children dress as scribes in flowing robes, with shawls covering their heads. After reading the scriptures, the children enter a room arranged like a village market in Israel. The catechist teams, dressed in Jewish costumes and uniforms of Roman soldiers, receive the children under tents, where they learn to weave and play ancient games, make unleavened bread and letter a scroll, construct a toy cart and fashion clay figures. A magician and a storyteller also entertain the children, and live roosters and a goat enthrall all who draw near to pet them. To conclude their visit, children learn a Jewish dance and share refreshments.

On Palm Sunday, the children dramatize the story of Jesus' passion and the Way of the Cross in the church basement, as catechists provide the lighting, costumes, music, and staging. After Jesus carries the cross across the stage and is crucified, he rises triumphantly from the tomb amidst smoke from dry ice and flashing lights. These pageants provide opportunities for children and catechists to interact and enjoy one another in the process of catechesis, and also preserve the rich and diverse traditions of a Catholic people in a new land.

Faith in Family

St. Pius V tries to educate people in the faith in the context of family, often a difficult approach. Although the reception of first communion is a priority for most families, some parents fail to recognize themselves as the best teachers of the faith for their children. They might drop off their children at church on Sunday and return later, unaware of the counterproductive message they give their children by not participating. While many feel unprepared to educate their children, they can participate actively in the life of the church and thus provide them an important model of religious involvement. Unfortunately, some parents mistakenly think that once their children receive the Eucharist, they need no additional catechetical formation, because they themselves had received nothing more. Indeed, because most children do not continue attending religious education classes after first communion, their knowledge of their faith is limited.

Most adults have happy memories of their first communion and want their children to enjoy the celebration. The children's preparation is also an opportunity for parents to grow in understanding their faith and to participate more actively in the church, and parents respond enthusiastically to the programs to learn more about their faith. Spanish-speaking parents living in the neighborhood participate in at least eight home meetings of small Christian Base Communities. This requirement provides them with an opportunity to share their faith with a small group of parishioners, and some parents remain active in these communities after fulfilling this requirement. Those who speak only Spanish and live outside the neighborhood gather either on weekday evenings or Sunday mornings to participate in ten classes in formation of their faith. For a time, English-speaking parents participated in a program of "home catechesis," studying the catechism at home with their children.

Because recently arrived immigrants are somewhat reluctant to venture very far from their homes and may be unaware of cultural and recreational opportunities available in the city or surrounding areas, catechists at St. Pius V organize family excursions on Sunday afternoons. Catechists accompany families on trips to such places as the botanical gardens, zoos, or Chicago museums. The family events celebrated in the context of the catechetical program help the family welcome learning about their faith as family.

Always Missionary

St. Pius V expanded its catechetical program to include outreach to developmentally disabled children and indigenous children in Guatemala, efforts that enriched the catechists and the program in general. In an inner-city community, many developmentally disabled children are hidden away in small apartments and are rarely seen. Because some immigrant families are ashamed of their children's condition, mistakenly believing they are somehow responsible for their children's disability, and because few programs exist in Mexico for special children, parents tend not to bring developmentally challenged children to church for religious instruction.

Working with the archdiocesan office of Special Religious Education for the Disabled (SPRED), St. Pius V inaugurated the first parish program for special children in Spanish in the Archdiocese. The parish's first catechist trained in this method, Rocio López, organized a parish center that works with fifteen to twenty children, some from neighboring parishes, and in which each child has a personal catechist. The children are prepared for the sacraments in a way that depends less on words than on loving relationships and the use of the senses. Catechists use play dough, finger painting, candles, bread, and music to teach basic elements of the faith. The experience proves rewarding for catechists, as well as enjoyable and life-giving for the children.

Each week SPRED catechists use a different symbol for prayer to help the children express themselves and share their feelings. One week, when an autumn leaf had been chosen, Lupita, who had been unable to express her feelings about her father's recent death, shared what had happened to her father and how sad she felt. The catechists also teach the children different bodily movements to help them learn about their faith. When Ricardo, who rarely speaks, came home from SPRED, he ran to his mother and showed her with gestures how he prayed in a new way.

Often special education children are either overly protected or so distrusted they are not allowed to assume ordinary household chores. Such was the case with Maria. In SPRED, however, Maria arranged flowers, set the table, cared for plants, and washed and dried dishes. What a surprise her mother received when she started washing dishes at home. After they receive first communion, some children return to the program because they so enjoy the sessions and the friends they make.

After hearing about the massacres of indigenous people in Guatemala in the mid-1980s and after receiving an invitation to develop catechetical programs with them, the parish catechists, under Sister Margaret's direction, launched a parish missionary effort. They spent several summers working in the highlands of Alta Vera Paz, donating their time and resources to assist a small indigenous community tucked away in a mountainous jungle.

A few years earlier, Sister Margaret had initiated a catechetical program for Kaqchiquel orphan children in Santa Apolonia, Chimaltenango, one of the many orphanages constructed after the military's massacres of 440 rural communities in the early 1980s. The catechists, working among children who been traumatized by violence, used the methodology developed by SPRED. They brought educational materials to stimulate the children's senses and imagination and trained local women to work one-on-one with the children, beginning with simple visual and tactile objects. They taught the children to play recorders and the marimba, the national musical instrument of Guatemala. They taught the women developmental games and organized reflections on scripture and prayer during which they heard many accounts of torture and murder. Although their hearts were saddened by the stories of people's suffering, much of their time was filled with joyous laughter.

A second project in Guatemala was initiated by Rocio López in Yalpemech, a small, isolated village lacking electricity and water. Refugees of the Kechi tribe who had returned from exile in Mexico had built the community. The catechists constructed a day-care center and spent three summers training women to work with children. As with most missionaries to Central America, the catechists returned physically exhausted but spiritually renewed by the faith and struggle of the indigenous poor. Their enthusiasm and testimony helped to encourage other St. Pius V catechists and give them a broader vision of their shared ministry. Reaching out definitely strengthened the parish program.

In conclusion, a catechetical program in a Hispanic parish should develop a culturally sensitive approach to religious education, relating catechetical teaching to general parish life, including participation in Christian Base Communities and Sunday worship. It should strengthen the family by emphasizing the importance of parents' participation in the religious formation of their children, foster the idea of the need for continuous religious formation by requiring parents to participate in some religious formation at the same time as their children, and empower adult members of the community to share their faith and experience with the younger generation.

Ministry to Hispanic Youth

With an average age of twenty-one years, Pilsen's population is the youngest in the Midwest. Repeated assessments of community needs consistently rank youth services as a priority for local residents, and the high rate of high school dropouts coupled with escalating gang activity dramatically demonstrate the need for special attention to youth. Yet ministry to youth in inner-city neighborhoods faces serious obstacles. Few inner-city parishes can afford full-time staff for youth work.

Youth ministry is also difficult. Ministers with experience in Latin America comment that forming youth groups south of the border is much easier than in the United States, where youth seek constant stimulation and entertainment and are more drawn to materialistic concerns of trendy clothes and newfangled gadgets than to working together in the community. In Pilsen, a large number of high school students also work after school, making them unavailable for youth activities. Consequently, it is easier to begin working with youth in middle school (sixth, seventh, and eighth grades) than with high schoolers. If a church or youth center has not developed a relationship with teenagers by the time

222

they reach high school, chances of involving them in a youth program are greatly reduced.

As in many parishes, youth ministry began at St. Pius V by preparing youth for the sacrament of confirmation. After a few years, the parish broadened its focus to training youth for Christian leadership. When the staff realized the importance of beginning with younger youth, they initiated an after-school program. As more children became active, the parish purchased and remodeled an American Legion hall and built a new parish youth center, Casa Juan Diego, staffed by young Hispanic adults.

At some point, a parish must decide which youth its program will target. Most parishes do not attempt to tackle "youth at risk," often a euphemism for youth involved in gangs. (In fact, almost all youth in inner-city neighborhoods are "at risk.") It is extremely difficult to find the resources for and the staff capable of assuming this challenging work. Often, agencies hire former gang members to reach out to the gangs, but their lack of professional formation and lingering ties to gangs create additional problems. The most successful programs seem to involve alternative schools that appeal directly to gang members interested in bettering themselves and finding a job. Some anti-gang programs also provide counseling, whether for drug addiction or gang involvement, but these programs are usually operated by specialized not-for-profit agencies that receive referrals from schools and churches. Once involved, few youth abandon gang activity until they either outgrow it, usually in their mid-twenties, or decide to change their lives, often after serving time in jail. Because most parishes lack the resources and expertise to work directly with gang-related youth and because many parents refuse to allow their children to participate in programs where gang members are involved, parishes commonly take a preventive approach, targeting non-gang youth.

While the St. Pius V staff takes a strong stand against gang-related activity, it always assists members in leaving gangs. Over the years, it has successfully helped teenagers leave their gangs and enter Boys Town, a boarding school in Omaha. One of these young men, initially expelled from the parish youth group because of his gang affiliation, later returned and began volunteering at the youth center before being hired as a gang specialist. With his help, the staff reached out to gang members, particularly younger "wannabes," youngsters who flirt with joining gangs. In 1999, the parish formed a special group for gang-affiliated youth, *Segunda Casa* (Second Home), which met apart from other parish youth to explore their own concerns and consider options other than gangs.

The Christian leadership program at St. Pius V includes components essential to any integrated youth program; namely, the study of the Catholic faith, educational formation, involvement in liturgy, community service, recreational and sports activities, and parental involvement. To be effective, the youth program had to help the youth not only in their struggle with personal but also with cultural identity as Hispanic Americans. The youth program helps them to recognize the benefits of having one foot in each culture and to enjoy their privileged position rather than feeling ethnically out of place. A bilingual-bicultural staff assists the youth in planning and executing traditional Hispanic religious celebrations, which they adapt to their world.

To develop deeper relationships among the youth, the staff organizes participants into small groups guided by young adult animators. On the first Saturday of the month, the groups reflect on topics such as friendship, sexuality, faith, culture, church, and relationships with parents. Through these dialogues, teens learn not only about substantive matters but also about how to recognize their feelings, articulate them appropriately, listen to others, express empathy, and form friendships. Every second Saturday, the teens participate in community service, an important formative experience that enhances young people's self-esteem and helps them discover their talents and interests.

When asked why she liked her service of holding babies of drug-addicted mothers at Cook County Hospital, Alicia responded that she felt good because she was helping somebody who was needy and defenseless. In the end, she realized that the experience helped her feel important and useful and began considering a career in health care.

On third Saturdays the youth gather to reflect on their faith and receive catechetical formation. They study the life of Jesus and the basic teachings of the Catholic Church, relating them to the challenges they face as adolescents. On Sundays the youth participate together in a Mass, proclaiming the readings, taking up the collection, and carrying the gifts to the altar.

A serious challenge facing youth ministers in a solidly Mexican immigrant community is the isolation and limited world-view of teenagers. Because Mexican immigrants arrive unable to speak English and often without legal documentation, they fear making a mistake or becoming known by strangers. Furthermore, living in relatively homogeneous neighborhoods, they have little chance to experience other cultures. Upon entering college, many are pleasantly surprised by the ethnic diversity of their classmates and appreciate the distinctive character of their own culture.

Mexican youth also encounter racial discrimination that dis-courages them from venturing out of their communities. Some comment that when traveling outside their *barrio*, they feel strange; people look at them differently. Perhaps security personnel follow them around in a store, suspicious of their intentions. If asked where they are from and they respond "from Pilsen," people often treat them like gang members. Consequently, many teens fear leav-ing their local community. Juan, a young man flirting with gangs, declined an invitation to visit downtown Chicago, noting that he was perfectly happy never to leave the neighborhood.

This reticence to learn more about the world, usually passed from parents to children, is exacerbated by the tendency of many Mexican parents to overly protect their children. Youth ministers sometimes have difficulty convincing parents to allow their chil-dren to participate in overnight retreats or out-of-town trips that help the youth discover the world beyond their *barrio* and gain confidence in themselves.

Weekend retreats to Indiana, and even night visits to enter-tainment centers around the city, build solidarity among youth and broaden their horizons, as do trips to Mexico to assist in building houses for the poor and adventures to Colorado "to meet the wilderness." Participants always return enthusiastically committed to work harder to involve their peers in the youth program.

The after-school program provides tutoring, training in art and music, sports, martial arts, photography, computers, and folk dance. Many parents are relieved that in an area riddled with gangs and violence their children are enjoying healthy, safe, and formative recreation. Many are unavailable, or lack the interest, to accompany them in their activities. Some, however, do contribute by driving youth to events, chaperoning activities, and preparing snacks after school. All parents of youth in the leadership program must take classes aimed at improving their parenting skills, after which they tend to participate more actively in the center. In 2003, fifteen of the more active parents formed a parents' council to help guide the program, support the children, involve more adults, and learn leadership skills.

Although the challenges are many, youth ministry in the Mexican immigrant community is rewarding. As children progress through school, enter higher education, and obtain good jobs, the staff celebrates its success. When former participants return to serve as mentors to the next generation of teenagers, the staff knows that their hard efforts are bearing fruit. In 2003, twenty young adults, mostly single people and graduates of St. Pius V's catechetical and youth programs, formed a new group, Youth in Action, to share their life experiences together, support one another in their daily challenges, reach out to other young adults, and provide service to the community.

Education in the Parish School

St. Pius V parish school was founded as an elementary school for girls in 1872 and later added a commercial school for young working women. In 1967, the school curriculum was revamped to emphasize personalized learning for 270 girls and boys in an elementary school that includes preschool and kindergarten. In the 1960s, Hispanic children began replacing Euro-American students. In 1983, Sister Erica Jordan, OP, arrived as principal, and during her fifteen years of leadership the school flourished, developing new directions and a strong faculty, enhanced by her successor, Nancy Nasko.[6]

The school faculty developed a philosophy, professing that education is a critical means to personal and social liberation, that each person is responsible for creating the world, that parents must collaborate with teachers for the good of their children, that nonviolence is an essential Gospel value, that education is about the fearless search for truth, and that good communication skills enable people to work together to transform society. Because the philosophy also professes a fundamental respect for students, school discipline includes the participation of students, and teachers relate to them in ways that demonstrate the value of each person, as well as the common good. Children are taught to see the connections between their choices and the consequences of those choices for themselves, the community, and the world. They learn self-respect and responsibility because their teachers allow them to choose between right and wrong.

The teachers work as a team, gathering weekly to plan curriculum, coordinate school events, and review ways to implement the school philosophy. They share responsibilities for the school curriculum, liturgies, celebrations, and extracurricular programs. Together they develop methods appropriate to the different developmental stages of Hispanic children, forging a strong sense of identity with and loyalty to the school. All choose to teach there for a significantly lower salary than they could earn in a public school. While frequently exhausted by working with children and families facing difficult social, economic, and cultural conditions, the teachers are energized by working together and are strengthened by the faith and values of the families they serve.

St. Pius V students face enormous challenges, including reading English well. Research has definitively demonstrated not only the importance of reading books from an early age but also the importance of parents reading with their children. Because many parents do not read or write English, and often not even Spanish, they have difficulty assisting their children with homework. Consequently, the school adopted a special reading program, "Read to Win," which vigorously encourages students to read, both in Spanish and English, because reading will have a positive impact on their overall academic achievement. In a six-week period in 1997, 262 students read more than 10,000 books/chapters, or approximately 1,000 books/chapters per grade. "The more you read, the easier it gets," commented one seventh grader. Although children take books home to read, each day the entire school, including the principal and school secretary, reads for fifteen to twenty minutes.[7]

Emotional and physical loss is also a major problem for immigrant children. Research reveals that in the United States one in six children experiences the loss of a parent, either through death, separation, or divorce. In a poor, immigrant community, the situation is worse. It is not uncommon for parents to arrive in the United States first, leaving their children with their grandparents in Mexico, a practice that often seriously scars children with insecurity, distrust, and resentment. Some children experience the tragic death of a sibling or cousin because of rampant gang violence, while others grow up in an environment laden with traumatic domestic violence or sexual abuse. These problems often result in a painful adolescence and an adulthood crippled with drug and alcohol addictions, and difficulties in forming respectful, lasting relationships. For many children, the school is the only place they can turn to for help. They need to talk.

To help them, the school instituted "Rainbows for All God's Children." Through this program, children learn to express their feelings, develop coping mechanisms (including relying on God as a friend and protector), and find peace to enjoy a productive and happy life. Once a week they participate in small groups after school for activities, guided by teachers and teachers' aides trained to help the children realize they are not alone.

Promoting Justice and Peace

Gospel principles and the Catholic Church's teaching on justice and peace permeate the entire curriculum and demeanor of the school. "For me, teaching is a ministry, and justice and peace are integral elements of this ministry," explains Nancy Nasko. To illustrate, she offers the example of World Day for AIDS, when her students removed all the art in their classroom in solidarity with AIDS victims and wrote about the epidemic. "In their essays, written for people with no knowledge of AIDS, they explained why they removed the decorations. They did all this so respectfully I was moved to tears."[8]

In faculty meetings, teachers grapple with many difficult social issues, such as war, violence, racism, and sexism. During the 1991 Gulf War, the teachers hammered out their own position, careful to show concern for the lives of soldiers and civilians on both sides. They held reflections in all classrooms and a prayer service in church for the entire school. When students spoke, many tearfully expressed their desire for the war's end. While the service took place, the pastor was participating in a demonstration in downtown Chicago, where he was arrested for civil disobedience. After coming out of church, the students conducted their own antiwar protest, walking up and down the major avenue fronting the school waving placards calling for an end to the war. Later the students wrote letters to President Bush, asking for a peaceful resolution to the conflict.

Peacemaking and nonviolence are reflected in all aspects of the school: administering discipline, which emphasizes personal responsibility; fostering appreciation of diversity; respecting the dignity of children and their ability to resolve problems through dialogue; reflecting with students on the violence in the neighborhood and developing alternatives to it; promoting leadership among students by helping them "find their voice" in leading the school in prayer and their classmates in discussions, and by encouraging them to speak out against any injustice.

Violent behavior and language are unacceptable. Students learn to deal with anger in a peaceful manner. Each class has a round table where students in conflict dialogue about differences, and if students resort to violent behavior or language, they must write a letter to their teacher to explain what happened, how it affected others, and what would have been a more peaceful way of handling the situation.

Some students, particularly boys, are fascinated by gangs. Many are pressured to join their ranks. Parents and teachers developed a policy of zero tolerance of gang-related activities: no colors, hats, clothing, language, signing, or lettering associated with gangs are allowed. Unfortunately, the school has had to expel a few students for gang-related activity, usually when there is insufficient parental involvement.

For example, after Jorge's father died, his mother remarried. Soon Jorge's stepfather was disciplining him by hitting him, something Jorge's father never did. Jorge's mother failed to recognize the resentment building up in her son until he joined a gang at age thirteen. Only his mother's commitment to listen to him and deal with the cause of his anger enabled her to keep him in school.

To emphasize peacemaking, the school celebrates Dr. Martin Luther King's birthday by having each class choose a classmate as their best peacemaker. Sister Erica observed: "Of all the awards given at St. Pius V, this one is the most prestigious because it represents most clearly the fulfillment of our mission." In 1998, when presenting eighth grader Randy Castillo his award, his classmate Madeline Tapia said:

> There are peacemakers, the ones who make peace in a violent or potentially violent situation...a voice in the crowd that pleads for us to do the right thing, and stop the insanity of violence. But there is another type of peacemaker. This type is even more important; this peacemaker always manages to see when someone needs help and simply steps in to lend a hand...you never have to ask this person....And this person's smile is one of those rare, real, radiant smiles that can transform your mood in a second. But maybe the most important thing about this peacemaker is his genuine, loving nature that does not "stay inside the lines," but kind of goes all over the place! Randy Castillo is our class peacemaker. And in case you are wondering, he is both kinds of peacemaker.

Nonviolent training and peacemaking make profound impressions on the students. When graduates are asked what was special about their years at St. Pius V, many identify peacemaking. When people visit the school or students take field trips to museums or parks, many outsiders comment about their courtesy and respect.

Each year the school sponsors "courtesy week," when students are taught to treat others with respect. They greet one another in the morning, hold the door open for one another, say "please" and "thank you," ask for permission when entering and leaving a room, do not interrupt others, and speak in a moderate tone of voice. On Friday, each class selects the student who excelled in courtesy during the week.

This training is important for all youngsters but especially for Hispanic immigrant families who sometimes are uncertain about what to require of their children. Mexicans themselves comment that children raised in Mexico are taught manners more effectively there than are children in the United States. Since some parents lack sufficient understanding of what to tolerate or prohibit in their children's behavior, their children begin school with little discipline. They have absorbed much of the impulsive and reactive behavior they see on television and fail to perform common courtesies, such as standing when elders enter the room or responding when spoken to. Parents generally respect teachers as professionals and greatly appreciate their efforts to teach their children simple life skills.

Students also wear uniforms that help them identify with the school and develop pride in it. Teachers instruct them that while wearing the school uniform, they are the school's ambassadors in the community and must therefore be on their good behavior.

Respecting Diversity

The elimination of racism is an important focus for the school. Not surprisingly, the students, who are approximately 98 percent Hispanic, are exposed to racism against African Americans in society at large and in their own community. To counteract it, the school celebrates African American month each February, with special studies on black history and culture. Students study slavery, the civil rights movement, and research biographies of famous African Americans, whose portraits are displayed prominently in the school. When Sister Erica was leaving her position as principal, she felt particularly proud when a student encouraged her to continue to "follow your train like Harriet Tubman," a reference to Tubman's work on the underground railroad that saved thousands of African American slaves.

In 1994, the school focused on indigenous people. Teachers incorporated contributions of indigenous people into their teaching and asked students to reflect on historical developments in the United States from the point of view of Native Americans. The students spent a complete semester on the social history of Mexico and Central America, two areas scarcely mentioned in traditional textbooks.

Now, instead of observing Columbus Day as a holiday, the school takes off another day. On Columbus Day, renamed "International Day of Indigenous Peoples," students attend school and focus on the accomplishments of indigenous peoples. Special attention is given to Cesar Chavez, the Mexican American founder of the United Farm Workers. Sessions on Native American culture are held throughout the school. A small museum of Native American artifacts is set up; students learn to draw the Aztec calendar; and Native Americans visit the school to share ancient storytelling, music, weaving, and dance.

Vicky López, a seventh grader, reflected on the day, "Before, all we learned was that Columbus discovered America; now we know he conquered native people. Like Mexicans, they also lived a hard life."

Because many immigrant children experience racial discrimination, cultivating pride in their heritage is important. On the feast of Our Lady of Guadalupe, students gather in church for a special liturgy, reenact her apparitions, and study her significance for Mexicans. Students also study the significance of two Mexican holidays: Independence Day on September 16 and *Cinco de Mayo* on May 5, celebrating them with dramas at a school assembly and a parade through the neighborhood with Mexican flags and patriotic chants. To close the day, students gather in the school playground for some rousing cheers, *Viva México y la Virgen de Guadalupe*, and to share tricolor popsicles representing the Mexican flag.

To counter the destructive tradition of *machismo*, teachers plan a curriculum that emphasizes the dignity and equality of women. Books, videos, and posters of women, especially Hispanic

A Community of Teaching Ministries

women, highlight their significance in history. Women take leading roles at school liturgies and frequently play the part of Jesus or other men while boys assume roles of women. Boys are constantly challenged to respect girls, and girls are encouraged to respect themselves by demanding respect from others.

To build bridges between parents and their teenage children, eighth graders developed ten commandments for themselves and another set for their parents. For themselves, they wrote such things as: Thou shalt wait until parents finish speaking before speaking, Thou shalt communicate with parents, and Thou shalt listen to parents before disagreeing. For parents, the commandments are similar: Thou shalt be open-minded, Thou shalt trust young adults, and Thou shalt have respect for children's privacy.

Surviving the Financial Crunch

The costs of operating a Catholic parochial school rise faster than family income in most large inner cities, causing Catholic schools to serve an increasingly wealthy student population because only relatively affluent parents can afford the tuition.[9] Although six of ten parochial schools in the Pilsen neighborhood closed between 1980 and 2002, as a result of rising costs and declining enrollments, St. Pius V school survived largely because of its excellent academic program, its location on a major thoroughfare, and substantial annual grants from the archdiocese. In 1999, to enhance its service and strengthen its appeal to parents, the school installed computers connected to the Internet in every classroom. Struggling families receive partial scholarships from an endowment fund in return for volunteer service.

In 1998, Matilde and her three children came to St. Pius V in desperation. She had been infected with HIV in Honduras and came to Chicago with her three children for medical treatment. After being accepted into a transitional shelter, she was directed to St. Pius V, where the school obtained outside funding to assist her.

The school continuously looks for ways to assist economically disadvantaged families. For instance, since both parents often work, the school offers an extended-day-care program where children may arrive at 7:00 a.m. and remain until 6:00 p.m. for a modest fee that helps some parents pay for their supervision.

The effectiveness of St. Pius V school is evident. Nearly all graduates study at Catholic high schools, and many proceed to and graduate from college. The National Catholic Educational Association reports that not only do Hispanic students at Catholic high schools have a lower dropout rate than their counterparts in public schools but they are three times as likely to earn a college degree.[10] St. Pius V graduates are proud of their school, and once they are in college, they realize it provided them with a solid academic, moral, and spiritual foundation.

St. Pius V parish maintains programs of religious and secular education for all—children, youth, and adults. In addition to religious education, youth formation, and the parish school reviewed in this chapter, Chapter 6 discussed the Rite of Christian Initiation of Adults; Chapter 8 treats the parish's parenting program; and Chapter 9 outlines the formation of leaders. These programs form critical consciences and instill a spirit of personal and social responsibility. Mexican immigrants' thirst for knowledge about their faith and their new world provide many opportunities for the parish to teach about divine and human truth.

Notes

1. Parts of this chapter were written with the assistance of Margaret McGuirk, OP.

2. *Catechism of the Catholic Church*, 425.

3. *Paul VI, Evangelii Nuntiandi*, 63.

4. Few catechetical resources, including teachers' guides, were fully bilingual. Although texts from South America are written in Spanish, they often do not speak to the American reality, which is a mixture of American, Mexican, and other Hispanics.

5. Patricia Hernandez, "Discover Jesus by Teaching Catechism," *Mensajero* (Winter 1997), 12.

6. The Sisters of Charity of the Blessed Virgin Mary founded the school, and the Sinsinawa Dominican sisters took charge of it from 1980 to 1999.

7. The One-to-One Learning Center introduced the program to St. Pius V, and one of its board members, Cynthia Keller, generously contributes three books for each student each year.

8. Personal interview, May 7, 1999.

9. At the national level, the proportion of family income spent on Catholic schools increased by 60 percent for elementary schools and 200 percent for secondary schools over the thirteen years from 1980 to 1993. In 1980, the average Catholic household made $21,265, and tuition charges for parish elementary schools averaged $490, while Catholic high schools normally charged $980. The average family needed to spend $1,470, or 6.9 percent of their income, to send three children to Catholic schools for one year. Thirteen years later, income doubled to an average of $41,429, but tuition for two students in an elementary school cost $1,591, and secondary tuition for one jumped to $3,220. Thus, the average 1993 family had to allocate $4,811, or 11.6 percent of their income, to send three children to Catholic schools. Of course, for lower-income Hispanics, the percentage would be much higher. Joseph Claude Harris and Cornelius Riordan, "Catholic Education: For Those Who Can Afford It or Those Who Need It?" *National Catholic Reporter* (October 10, 1997), 7.

10. Anne-Marie O'Connor, "Many Latinos Fare Better in Catholic Schools," *Los Angeles Times* (August 3, 1998), 1, 14. Several studies document that Hispanics fare worse than other ethnic groups in Chicago public schools, while the National Catholic Educational Association cites national tests done by the National Assessment of Educational Progress to support its claim that Catholic schools do a better job educating Hispanics than public schools. Keith David Picher, "Hispanics Gain in Catholic Schools," *The New World* (May 26, 1989), 6.

8.

Developing Social Ministries

Parishes in inner-city neighborhoods, particularly in immigrant Catholic communities, are more than a local church—they are general service centers for families. More people call or visit them than parishes in more affluent areas. People come for every kind of need, food, shelter, clothing, health care, and legal aid. To embody the love of God, a parish ministers to them in a compassionate and culturally sensitive fashion.

The Parish as a Center of Social Service

Each week a wide array of people arrive at the parish office. Alfredo came for advice about a summons from the Bureau of Immigration and Citizenship Services (BICS). Estella called because her son had been arrested for turning on a fire hydrant; she needed someone to translate for her in court. Rosa wanted the parish staff to find a contractor to remodel her basement. Juanita asked for a priest to accompany her block club to the alderman's office to convince him to pave their sidewalk. Jose came because the court had ordered him to complete eighty hours of community service for not having car insurance. Letitia arrived because her teenager was out of control, and Francisco needed a lawyer to help his son, who was charged with illegal possession of a gun. The Lopez family came seeking financial assistance to bury their son. Martha wanted to open a beauty salon and needed advice on how to proceed. Susana was desperate because her food stamps had been discontinued. Norma arrived depressed; her husband drinks excessively, and she wanted some *consejos* (advice). Each morning homeless men come in search of food, bus fare, or a change of clothes after spending the night curled up in a dark alley. Frequently families come for furniture and clothing, or perhaps an apartment. When the winter sets in, people seek financial assistance to pay heating and electric bills. Others ask the staff to write letters to obtain an identification card from the Mexican consulate or to assist in processing an application for residency with BICS. Since people stop by to inquire about job opportunities, the staff maintains a list of unemployed persons to recommend to companies looking for workers. Some families call for a woman to live in and wash, clean, cook, and care for children in exchange for room, board, and little pay.

The more service a parish provides, the more life and faith grow in the parish. Rather than a burden, social service is an opportunity to show compassion and build community. Some parishes unfortunately do not want to be bothered with people's problems. Not employing a Spanish-speaking receptionist quickly communicates this message to Hispanic immigrants.

The experience of St. Pius V demonstrates that rather than drain limited funds and sap energies, services for the poor attract resources and strengthen parish life. When a hospital wanted to promote integral health in an inner-city Hispanic community, it began funding three salaries for the social service staff at St. Pius V. Some institutions and businesses also want to support parishes serving the poor. Years before Sammy Sosa hit sixty-eight home runs, he sent an unsolicited donation of $1,000. In 1990, the Greater Chicago Food Depository, a food bank, began donating leftover restaurant food, enabling the parish to operate its soup kitchen at minimal cost. Before a wholesaler of Mexican food products died, he directed his company to continue donating food to St. Pius V after his death because of its service to the hungry. These and many other examples demonstrate how serving the poor actually brings blessings to a parish in the form of valuable resources.

Frequently immigrants traveling across the country ask the parish for money to continue their journey to Florida, Minnesota, or back to Mexico. Although the parish is financially unable to subsidize long-distance travel, some exceptions are made. Victor arrived early one Saturday after traveling from Mexico on freight trains. He walked six miles from the railroad yards to the parish to ask for bus fare to Milwaukee to locate his brother. After working the day in the parish street fair, he had his ticket on a bus, plus a few extra dollars. A week later Victor was back; his brother was in jail on a drug charge. Now he wanted money to travel to California to find his sister. After two days of painting the rectory porch, he was on his way again. Victor was a good man, trying to find a solution to the poverty he, his wife, and children were suffering in Mexico.

Once helped by the church, whether with emergency food or counseling, legal assistance or shelter, people in need are forever grateful. Victor said he would never forget what the church did for him in Chicago. Although every neighborhood has its con artists trying to pry a bit of money from the church with elaborate tales of woe, most parish staffs recognize that Hispanics, unless under the influence of drugs or alcohol, generally tell the truth.

Serving the Spirit, Serving the Body

Over the years, St. Pius V developed a number of services to assist newly arrived immigrants, as well as residents. Each social service ministry creates an opportunity for additional ministry for laity, attracting more volunteers than any other ministry except liturgy and religious education. Although the services increase administrative work for the staff, they also enhance the visibility and effectiveness of the parish as a center of Christian service and attract people interested in participating in a life-giving community.

Los Servidores Sociales

In 1987, parishioners organized a committee called *Los Servidores Sociales* to manage the parish emergency food pantry. Members raised funds through dances and rummage sales to help needy families facing shutoffs of electricity and gas, home evictions, and heavy funeral expenses. The group organized training for their volunteer members to help them make effective and sensitive home visits, assess people's needs, and locate resources. To avoid creating and maintaining dependency among needy families, social service workers ask recipients not for money but to support the parish by participating in its activities, perhaps in Sunday Mass, a Christian Base Community (CBC), or volunteer service. This participation benefits them morally and spiritually and sometimes brings them additional material support.

After a few trips to the parish pantry, Jovita found the courage to talk with a volunteer about her problems with her husband, who refused to get a job and occasionally beat her. The *Servidores Sociales* referred her to the parish counselor, who helped her develop the strength to confront her family's insecurity and her abusive marital relationship. Eventually she became active in two parish groups.

The *Servidores Sociales* organized a parish-wide Christmas giving program of clothes, food, toys, and money donated by families from two suburban sister parishes.[1] For a time, the program ran into difficulties when the clothes did not fit, the food was foreign to Mexican tastes, and some contributing suburban families were afraid to deliver their gifts to unmarked apartments lacking doorbells or hidden in dark hallways. A new model evolved: the Christmas store. The store is organized in the church basement, where needy families choose from a selection of new toys and clothes, some donated, some purchased. Each family chooses a toy and an article of clothing for its children. In addition, each family receives a $50 food coupon, valid at a local grocery store. Sister parishes now contribute money to purchase the toys, clothes, and food coupons.

Families in the neighborhood apply to the store through the parish CBC nearest them. Since the parish could never assist the hundreds of needy families in the area, the CBCs screen the families, accepting those most in need and involved in the parish or community. The program rewards participation and also empowers CBC coordinators, who approve applications.

A Secondhand Store

During the 1980s, charitable agencies, such as Catholic Charities, St. Vincent DePaul, and Goodwill, traditional providers of secondhand furniture and appliances, discontinued their services, owing to high overhead and a decline in quality of donated items—donors seemed to keep them longer and donate them when they were of little use. When the *Servidores Sociales* offered to pick up clothing and furniture, donors called, and soon the parish was making several weekly pickups. Because the church basement proved inadequate to store mountains of clothes and bulky donations accumulated between periodic rummage sales, the parish opened its own thrift shop, *La Tiendita* (The Little Store). Each morning at least a dozen homeless and/or jobless men arrive for clothes at no cost. Needy families can obtain clothing, refrigerators, stoves, beds, sofas, and so on, free of charge. Other residents make a modest donation for their merchandise.

A Kitchen for the Hungry

In 1983, the parish opened a soup kitchen in the church basement, serving approximately 500 hot meals weekly. The parish hired Maria Botello, a parishioner who not only prepares delicious meals but recruits and engages volunteers, mostly mothers in need from the parish. She creates a welcoming environment where volunteers feel at home and grow personally. Food preparation is less a tedious task than a social occasion for them. They gather early over coffee and a tasty *almuerzo* (brunch) prepared from odds and ends in the walk-in refrigerator. Volunteers refuse to use a food processor, preferring the old-fashioned way of chopping vegetables by hand while they converse. Maria, like Mayela Hernandez, her successor, counseled many women on personal and family matters and advocated for them on legal and economic concerns.

When Rita's husband lost his job, she brought her three small children to the soup kitchen and soon was volunteering. Maria gave her extra food to take home and gradually won Rita's confidence. When she learned that Rita's husband beat her regularly, she connected Rita to the parish counselor, who eventually helped her resolve the situation.

Running a soup kitchen is not expensive because many people want to help feed the hungry. One suburban church donates $200 each month, and the Greater Chicago Food Depository contributes packaged food, as well as discarded restaurant food. The parish is also blessed by the regular, generous donations of rice and beans from a tortilla company, *El Milagro*, and bread from several bakeries. Although volunteer parishioners are never lacking, a suburban parish, St. Domatilla, sends volunteers two Saturdays a month to serve food while adding their own cakes and cookies. On another Saturday, parishioners originating from San Luis Potosi, Mexico, purchase, prepare, and serve the food. Porfirio Portales, a member of the group, commented, "This opportunity helps our families work together on a common project, and that way we receive more than we give."[2] The soup kitchen also provides an excellent site for teenagers from local schools and the parish confirmation program to perform community service.

Besides serving a basic human need, social services take on a life larger than themselves. The soup kitchen becomes a symbol of the community reaching out to the needy, a very visible part of the parish, occupying considerable space and time in the church basement. News of parish services to the poor spreads to families in the suburbs, many of whom donate not only clothing but money to support the ministries. Although parishioners are proud their parish feeds the hungry, a soup kitchen is about more than simply feeding the hungry. It inserts the parish into the world of the poor and helps the church respond to the Lord's challenge: "When I was hungry, you gave me to eat; when I was thirsty, you gave me to drink."

Although the soup kitchen serves a good meal for today, what about food for tomorrow? Many people need food for their families. The breadwinner may be sick, lack health insurance, be laid off with no unemployment compensation, or be a mother recently abandoned by her husband and left with her children's hungry mouths to feed. These people find help in the parish food pantry, where volunteers stock the shelves with generous donations and open every Tuesday afternoon or whenever anyone arrives for emergency food—no one is ever denied food. Staff and volunteers visit the homes of those wanting continued assistance and invite them to participate in the parish, as well as in classes in nutrition, hygiene, self-esteem, budgeting, and general life skills.

A Shelter for the Homeless

Because homeless immigrant men reside in the neighborhood, the parish opened a shelter for them, San Jose Obrero Mission, in 1981 and soon thereafter, a smaller shelter for women and children. These shelters were founded by David Staszak, a Dominican priest who served the community for thirty-one years, a man graced with compassion and patience, revered as a sidewalk saint for his generous concern for the downtrodden.

Although the shelters set strict rules for guests, prohibiting firearms, knives, alcohol, and drugs, some local residents criticize them for attracting "undesirable" people to the area. But if the shelters did not exist, the homeless, some mentally and emotionally ill or chemically dependent, would still walk the streets of Pilsen. Shelters provide down-and-out people with a respite until they can transition to a better life.

When Javier arrived from Mexico without any contacts in Chicago, he spent two months working day labor jobs and sleeping at the shelter until he finally landed permanent employment. Eight months later, he had saved enough money to bring his wife and son from Mexico to join him, and commented: "I don't know what I would have done if the mission had not given me the opportunity to get on my feet."

Since the shelter functioned for nearly two decades only at night, many of its residents walked the streets during the day in warmer weather and congregated in the church in colder months. In the early morning hours of winter, when homeless men spill out of packed overnight shelters, they come to St. Pius V, the only church open in the neighborhood, to escape the cold and to rest a bit more before leaving for an employment office, a drop-in center, or the streets. Despite the rules against lying down, talking, and eating in church, it is not uncommon to find twenty men and some women in church, some sitting quietly, others standing by radiators or talking in small groups, at times frightening worshipers as they enter the church to pray. Policing the church is a burden, but given the option of closing the church and excluding homeless people, the staff accepts the aggravation. In fact, St. Pius V has experienced relatively few problems because Hispanics generally respect and care for their church.

Manuel was a middle-aged, alcoholic, and homeless Vietnam veteran who insisted that a long switchblade in his pocket was solely for self-defense. For years, he was ever present in church, always looking out for it, as well as cleaning in the soup kitchen and alerting staff to troublemakers. In the end, Manuel died from exposure one bitterly cold night while sleeping in an abandoned car.

Pastoral ministers in the inner city have many stories about homeless and desperate people, all filled with pathos and sometimes humor. At one wedding, an intoxicated, bare-chested man, a regular visitor at church, berated the presiding priest in a loud voice from the back of church. The priest stopped the service and waited until the organist showed him to the door.

A few people use ingenious methods to steal from alms boxes, the instrument of choice an open coat hanger tipped with a wad of gum to fish bills from the boxes. Arresting such people accomplishes little. Within hours of booking at the police station, they are released and of course never appear for their court date.

A few homeless people, however, are dangerous. One belligerent man, obviously mentally disturbed, repeatedly stole from the vigil light boxes. One day he stole an entire collection box and destroyed it in the alley in an effort to extract money. Another day, while being ejected from the church, he pulled a gun on the music director and pastor. After spending six months in jail for aggravated assault, he returned to the parish. Coming upon the pastor one evening in the church lobby, he grabbed him by the lapels and threatened to hit him. The priest broke his grip, ran to safety in the busy street in front of church, and later that night had him arrested at a shelter, where police discovered drugs in his possession and a warrant for aggravated rape. Despite these problems, the parish's commitment to serve the homeless wins it the reputation of being a refuge for the poor, faithfully reflecting the compassion of Jesus.

A Safe Haven for Women

In 1993, Aida Segura, a young Peruvian just completing an MA in pastoral counseling, became the parish's first pastoral counselor. After speaking at all the Masses one Sunday, she had a full schedule of counselees, challenging the notion that Mexicans are too timid, fearful, or private to seek mental health services. During the following years, under the enlightened direction of Dolores Tapia, the staff expanded to a pastoral counseling team of eight full-time people, as many parents with uncontrollable children, women suffering physical and emotional abuse, and people in troubled marriages came for help.

Not surprisingly, the majority of clients are women, many displaying signs of depression: always tired but cannot sleep; lacking appetite, energy, or desire to do anything; some hearing voices or contemplating suicide. Other women arrive anxious; they have no work or money, live in constant conflict with their spouses or children, and have no one with whom to share their troubles. A dominant pattern involves husbands who are physically or psychologically violent, their aggression often aggravated by alcohol. Unfortunately, their victims often believe they are at fault and gradually slip into a deadly depression. Mexican women feel more comfortable coming to the parish than to secular agencies about these and other family problems, albeit with profound apologies for taking the staff's time. Fearing their husbands, some women visit the office only at times when their husbands will not detect their absence.

St. Pius V assists abused women in a variety of ways. First, it reaches out to them through Sunday preaching. Homilies communicate a liberating message for men and women, denouncing the sin of *machismo* and clarifying frequent misconceptions of ecclesiastical and biblical teaching. For example, although the church teaches that marriage is indissoluble, it requires no one to suffer a violent partner. When Jesus challenged his followers to take up their cross and follow him, he did not mean that women must accept cruel and demeaning treatment from their partners. Furthermore, God is loving and compassionate and not the strict judge and cruel punisher many Mexicans learned about in their youth. Homilies also extol the contributions women make to the family and community and include testimonies of women who have liberated themselves from their abusive spouses. After such preaching, usually more abused women ask the priest for an appointment.

Confession is another avenue for reaching women in need. In private, they may accuse themselves of resentment or anger against their husbands, often telltale signs of domestic violence. Priests encourage them to seek assistance from the parish staff, where they can begin their journey to liberation. A third avenue to women opens at the food pantry, where social ministers detect signs of abuse and refer victims to the parish counselor.

Overwhelmed by abused women seeking help, the parish obtained funding from governmental sources to expand its staff to three counselors, a case manager, a court advocate, two children's and youth counselors, and an assistant counselor. Women receiving counseling named the program H.O.P.E. (*Hay Opciones Para Ella*— There Are Options for Her). In time, the parish also offered counseling for married couples, and as the numbers seeking help increased, the staff formed different support and information groups for battered women, women with alcoholic spouses, children of the victims, people suffering depression, and married couples.

In the women's groups, participants no longer feel alone and unique but supported and strengthened to address the abuse. They learn to be responsible for their problems, rediscovering their personal dignity, self-confidence, cultural values, and religious faith, keys to finding solutions to their personal and family problems.

Each abused woman responds differently. Many struggle to confront their husbands firmly and resolutely, leaving them for a time, only to return later. Some confront and even help their husbands change. Some eventually leave their husbands. Each woman decides for herself what to do and when to do it. Unfortunately, men rarely agree to counseling, leaving the burden of finding a solution to the women. The few men who seek help tend to take action after seeing changes in their wives. They, too, need to recognize their personal worth and the reasons for their abusive behavior.

Norma, married with two children, found more hope at St. Pius V than she ever dreamed she would. She had been sexually abused as a child, and her husband physically and verbally abused her. One day she came to the parish heavily medicated and severely depressed after being released from a hospital where she was treated for injuries inflicted by her husband. After a few weeks of intensive counseling, she entered a women's support group. At first she lacked sufficient confidence in herself to break with her husband. But when a friend of her husband made advances on their daughter, the women encouraged her to separate from her husband. One participant found her a newly renovated apartment; another offered to pay two months' rent; a third volunteered her van to help Norma move; a fourth gave her work in a video store. With so much support (all the women took turns visiting her), Norma finally made the leap into freedom and a new life. The compassionate response of the women, themselves victims of abuse, instilled hope, not only in Norma, but in all women who suffer in silence and solitude.

Counseling of abused women at St. Pius V is notably pastoral rather than strictly clinical. Instead of therapy, women seek counseling that provides information and helps them examine their experience, clarify their options, and make decisions. Counselors are pastoral because they respond to the clients' faith, an integral part of their life and a valuable resource in recovering emotional health. Moreover, women come to the parish expecting faith to play a role in resolving their problem. Because Catholic teaching sometimes has had the effect of oppressing women, counselors emphasize its liberating message: God carefully fashioned them in the divine image and loves them as they are, and Jesus came to convince them of that. Nonpastoral clinical social workers rarely appreciate the importance of faith, either believing it unprofessional to explore it or being unprepared to refer to it. Pastoral counseling also addresses the whole person and not just the dimension of abuse. Consequently, unlike many secular agencies, parish counselors assist the women with housing, jobs, day care and counseling for children, and food.

Moreover, parish services are not restricted to the limited schedule of mid-week office hours but provided when women need them.

Because abused women are often mistreated by police and the courts, the staff may accompany them to file police reports and seek orders of protection. One night after her husband punched her in the face and threatened to kill her, Matilde came to the rectory for help. At the police station when she asked to file a complaint, the attending officer lectured her about the seriousness of her charge and questioned her resolve to follow through with the complaint, noting that the police lack the time to help fickle women who one day file charges and the next day drop them. After the accompanying priest intervened, the officer dutifully wrote up her complaint. Similarly in court, women often need advocates to translate for them and help them understand their rights and options.

As abused women gain strength, the staff encourages them to volunteer in the community. By giving to others, they develop a greater sense of self-worth. Many develop into active volunteers and dedicated parish leaders. One support group decided to become a self-help economic group by producing handicrafts for sale. Then the parish invited them to decorate the church for weddings and *quinceañeras*. Each Saturday a different team arranges the traditional Mexican arches in the aisles and flowers around the altar. For this service they receive a small remuneration that is deposited in a common fund for their individual and group needs.

Each year St. Pius V celebrates International Women's Day with a week of activities. It offers a series of films and talks on domestic violence, and participants share experiences and commentaries and reflect on the gospel text in which some men want to stone a woman caught in adultery. (Instead of condemning the woman, Jesus defends her, challenging the men, "Let the one without sin cast the first stone.") On the final day, participants prepare a luncheon for women volunteers active in different parish ministries where all reflect on stories of struggling women from the past and present.

A Center for Families

Through its counseling, the staff discovered the need for a broader response to family mental health concerns. Families are the life-giving cells of society and the foundation of economic, social, and religious institutions in the community. Families earn wages, nurture youth, care for the ill, participate in civic activity, and teach faith. Unfortunately, many families are plagued with marital strife and intergenerational conflict. Symptoms manifest themselves in chemical addiction, domestic violence, and poor academic performance (including high rates of school dropout and gang involvement). Poverty, overcrowding, systemic discrimination, and cultural isolation combine with low self-esteem and poor human relational skills to cripple Pilsen families. Moreover, parents and children are caught in a cultural transition which exacerbates the usual marital and intergenerational struggles. Immigrant parents want their children to embrace Mexican culture, while children are anxious to blend into American society. Furthermore, parents often work long hours and spend little time with one another and their children, prompting youngsters to find support elsewhere.

How to respond to these family needs? Initially, St. Pius V provided pastoral counseling, but the number of families needing help convinced the staff to develop preventive efforts. Thus, parenting courses are offered to help parents learn to set limits, affirm and confront, communicate with and discipline their children. Facilitated dialogue between parents and children produces amazing results. Teens explain how they feel unsupported and unappreciated, and parents detail how they feel ignored and disrespected. The classes also become a channel for developing new ministries. While some participants bond together, forming support groups, others speak at Sunday Mass to encourage other parents to take the classes. Some formed a committee to promote family life, organizing a parish dance for families on Mother's Day to raise funds for activities, such as a summer family picnic.

A few, like Silvia, are trained to teach the classes.

I wanted to understand the reasons for my reactions to my children. At first my husband did not accompany

me, but he began to attend when he realized the classes
were helping our marriage and family. Now I understand better. I don't shout so much, and when I don't
follow the family rules, my children remind me; they
also help me more. I have grown a lot. I also understand
teenagers better now, and when I saw men in the class
struggle to express their feelings, I understood my husband and my father better. I was so happy with the
course I took it three times. Then the staff asked me to
teach part of a class. I thought I couldn't because I am
just a mother and housewife. I tried and I was able to
give hope to other parents because I had some success in
putting the teachings into practice in my own family. [3]

An Office to Defend Legal Rights

In 1986, the United States Congress passed the Immigration
Reform and Control Act, normalizing the legal status of millions
of undocumented immigrants. Many immigrants did not know
about or understand the offer, and others distrusted it, fearing the
government was tricking them into identifying themselves as
undocumented in order to deport them. St. Pius V staff saw the
need to inform and prepare parishioners to take advantage of the
opportunity. Through talks at Sunday Masses and informational
sessions in the church basement, the staff encouraged people to
apply and worked with a number of lawyers who advised and
processed the papers for the more difficult cases. When the application period ended, the staff wanted to continue offering legal
assistance for immigration problems and other legal concerns,
such as housing, divorce, child custody, and traffic violations.
Thus, when the Chicago Legal Clinic, founded to serve immigrant Mexicans living around the steel mills in South Chicago,
offered to open a branch at St. Pius V, the parish accepted the
offer, opening the Pilsen Legal Office (PLO). When the parishes
in Pilsen began constructing affordable new homes for resident
families, the PLO processed many of the closings for new home
owners. Women trying to free themselves from their abusive

spouses also seek out PLO staff to help them through the painful steps of orders of protection, divorce proceedings, and claims for child support. PLO's excellent reputation and fees based on a sliding scale produce a steady demand for services.

A School for Language

Although a lack of English is often cited as an obstacle to success for Hispanics, during the years covered by this book, the community as a whole greatly increased its ability to speak English. While there are many opportunities to study English in the neighborhood, classes are always full. Consequently, each year the parish organizes classes in English as well as Spanish literacy offered by the not-for-profit organization *Universidad Popular*. The classes involve more than one language. Mary Kosko, a college graduate who contributed a year of community service teaching English, commented, "In our English classes, we include culture and political awareness because immigrants need to learn the customs of this country, just as we need to learn theirs."

A Parish of Volunteers

Because of the heavy demand for social services and because many people who begin as recipients of parish services later become volunteer social ministers, the parish hired a social worker to coordinate services and recruit and train volunteers. Through their service, volunteers grow as persons and learn to work as a team, relate to clients, manage merchandise, and serve the community. As poor as volunteers might be, they nevertheless feel the need to help others. Susana, a mother of seven who struggled with her invalid husband, as well as with her own illiteracy and poverty, is a regular volunteer in the parish soup kitchen. She noted, "I serve here because I enjoy the camaraderie with the other volunteers and the opportunity to help others just as the parish has helped me." This entire dynamic takes on a dimension of evangelization much more significant than simply handing out clothing or serving food.

While generous, some volunteers in poor communities serve with the hope of receiving some compensation. At the secondhand store, they might ask for clothing; at the soup kitchen, some left-overs; and at the pantry, canned goods. The parish also offers low-income parents of students enrolled in the parish school opportunities to work one day a week in a parish program in exchange for a reduction in tuition. Sharing with needy volunteers makes good sense, but it can also lead to criticism from nonvolunteer recipients and create division among the volunteers themselves. Thus, it is important to cultivate among volunteers a spirituality of serving the poor. Each year the parish organizes a day of recollection or sessions in personal formation for volunteers, as well as a luncheon where they are awarded certificates.

Following the teaching of Jesus, social ministry at St. Pius V developed not only to respond to people's material and spiritual needs but also to develop lay ministry. Not every parish encounters the same needs, but every Christian community can move from its ministry of sacramental liturgy into the broader society through ministries that serve people's physical, psychological, and spiritual needs. The diversification and expansion of social services provides parishioners with creative ways of developing new ministries within the church, enriching themselves personally, and strengthening the community. The more service a parish provides, the more its life and faith flourish.

Notes

1. St. Vincent Ferrer and St. Walter.
2. Chuck Dahm, OP, "*Postosinos* Unite to Serve," *Mensajero* (November 1998), 11.
3. Interview published in *Mensajero* (November 1997), 12.

9.

Transforming the Neighborhood

Jesus worked to establish and extend the kingdom of God on earth, a reign of justice, peace, and love. He lifted up the downtrodden and welcomed outcasts, challenged the rich to share with the poor, denounced discrimination against women and foreigners, healed the sick, and reconciled sinners, all the time disobeying unjust religious and civil laws. He founded a community of followers, the Catholic Church, charging them to complete his prophetic mission to renew the face of the earth.

This mandate has been reinforced in the twentieth century by a theological movement known as liberation theology, a perspective developed in Latin America in the 1960s that emphasizes the power of God working for the holistic liberation of every individual and society. It views God's grace working actively in human nature, empowering and guiding people to complete the work initiated in Creation and advanced by Jesus. Corporal works of mercy, like feeding the hungry, visiting the sick and imprisoned, consoling the afflicted, and participating in political action to transform unjust economic systems, help shape a new world. In his encyclical letter *On the Development of Peoples*, Pope Paul VI supported this incarnational perspective by calling on Roman Catholics, "without waiting passively for orders or directives, to take the initiative freely and to infuse a Christian spirit into the mentality, customs, laws, and structures of the community in which they live."[1] This chapter examines how the faithful in St. Pius V and other parishes in Pilsen put their faith into action, garnering wisdom and power to create a healthier community.

Obstacles to Community Involvement

Most Mexicans come to the United States with a number of ideological and cultural obstacles to understanding and/or accepting an active political role for themselves. Some reasons for their reticence follow.

The Kingdom of God Is in Heaven

If one asks, "Where is the kingdom of God?" recently arrived Mexican immigrants are likely to respond, "In heaven." Instead of being taught that the kingdom of God begins here and now, only to be completed at the end of time,[2] Mexican Catholics listened for centuries to priests preach that the kingdom of God awaits them only in the bliss of the afterlife. The order of things on Earth, although harsh, should be accepted, for life on Earth is ordained by God as a time of trial to prepare for the next life. Few understand the Christian's responsibility to build God's kingdom now. Jesus' own struggle for justice is viewed primarily as a manifestation of God's compassion for the poor and oppressed rather than a challenge to imitate his service to others and society as a whole. Jesus' death has been spiritualized as an obedient sacrifice necessary to wipe away the sins of the world and open the gates of heaven rather than as the consequence of a prophetic struggle for justice.

Suffering and Poverty Are Good

For centuries priests taught that suffering quietly and patiently is a virtue, a way for people to "pay" for their sins, draw closer to the suffering Christ, and thus merit a higher place in heaven. Thus a woman may tolerate her alcoholic husband's abusive behavior, believing she must accept "the cross" God has given her. Moreover, erroneous exegesis based on classist ideologies led to distortions of biblical teachings. For example, accepting poverty and injustice is bolstered by Jesus' directive not to aspire to riches, his statements that those "last in this life" will be first in the next, and that people should turn the other cheek when offended. Some claim that Jesus taught that poverty is part of the divine order when he said, "Blessed are the poor for theirs is the Kingdom of God." Some rationalize that the poor are closer to God because they are more dependent on the divine and less distracted by riches. When parishioners reflected on oppression in three periods of history: the New Testament time of Jesus, the Spanish colonization of the Americas, and the United States today, all condemned the unjust treatment of the poor in earlier historical periods, but many justified poverty today because of society's economic need for the poor. "If there are no poor, who will pick the crops, wash the dishes, and sweep the floors?"

Politics Is Bad

For many Mexicans immigrants, the word "politics" is synonymous with corruption. Their experience of politicians in Mexico has soured them on involvement in politics in the United States, and hearing about politicians in Chicago who deceive, manipulate, and steal only confirms this opinion. Because many do not perceive the political system as serving their needs, they see little reason to get involved and feel powerless to influence governmental decisions affecting their lives. Many Mexicans also withdraw from the political arena because it is contentious, divisive, and therefore "un-Christian."

Limited Expectations

Most Mexican immigrants enjoy a higher standard of living in the United States than they had in their homeland. Consequently, they are relatively satisfied and not easily aroused to protest. Their housing is often better than in Mexico. They have more appliances, more clothes, and more disposable income here, and many are eligible for welfare, which is practically nonexistent in Mexico. Also, the police are less corrupt, and judges are not as easily bribed; medical attention is more or less available for the indigent; and although the cost of living is higher, wages are proportionately higher. Once when I suggested to a destitute family that they return to Mexico where at least they had family to lean on, the father replied: "Padre, here, in the United States, no one starves to death. Here, you can at least go to church, and they will give you food. In Mexico, there is nowhere to go for help."

Mexican Citizens Forever

Since Mexico borders the United States, many immigrants frequently travel back and forth, reinforcing their identity as Mexicans and as visitors in the United States. Although a wave of anti-immigrant sentiment and new legislative restrictions on immigrants in the mid-1990s motivated many to apply for citizenship, few abandoned their identity as Mexicans. Although relatively few Mexicans return to live in Mexico, many plan to live there in the not too distant future. Consequently, for most, getting involved in community affairs is a low priority. Although many first-generation Mexican Americans and their children identify more with the United States, most of them are still slow to get involved in socio-political issues.

Powerless To Make a Difference

Many Mexican immigrants see themselves as insignificant and powerless. Virgil Elizondo notes that they have interiorized a sense of inferiority and worthlessness imposed by the Spanish conquest and centuries of subsequent oppression.[3] A history of domination and defeat nurtured a spirit of resignation and apathy, producing a consciousness characterized by tendencies to fatalism.[4] As small farmers and common laborers in their own country, they had little influence in community affairs, and now as foreigners in the United States, they consider themselves even more impotent. Their limited facility in English exacerbates their sense of powerlessness. Moreover, undocumented people, unaware of their civil rights, fear community involvement might draw attention to them and jeopardize their residency here. Some fear traffic court, believing the police might deport them, or if they are mistreated by police, lawyers, landlords, or store clerks, they have no recourse but to accept the abuse.

In addition, because recently arrived Mexicans are among the most poorly paid workers, many work ten to twelve hours a day and Saturdays and Sundays, leaving little time for evening and weekend meetings about community affairs. Also, when families advance economically, they often move out of the neighborhood, searching for better housing and schools, producing a turnover in population that further hinders political involvement. All these reasons help explain why Mexican immigrants are not more actively involved in the political arena.

Parishes and Social Change

Mexican immigrants are, however, concerned about their community, especially about conditions affecting their children. Although most realize their economic situation has improved and that they are hired for their high productivity and trustworthiness, they recognize they are near the bottom of the social-economic ladder. Their schools, overpopulated and underfunded, lack the resources and quality teaching offered to children in other communities. Their housing is rundown and overcrowded, yet they feel helpless to defend themselves against abusive landlords and the forces of gentrification. They know the city provides inferior services to their communities, especially regarding garbage pickup, street cleaning, and street and sidewalk repair. They realize that despite the high proportion of young people in Pilsen, they enjoy less open park space than other neighborhoods and that police often disrespect and sometimes abuse them. These challenging conditions transform some immigrants, usually those living in Chicago for a longer period of time, from passive to active players in their workplaces and communities, while others retreat into passivity. St. Pius V works with Mexican immigrants to raise their political awareness, informing them of their rights, helping them unite to resolve common problems and work for social transformation. The following pages examine some of these efforts.

Community Organizing

Building on the accomplishments of Saul Alinsky, who launched a new style of organizing in Chicago neighborhoods in the 1940s and 1950s, professional organizers came to the Pilsen neighborhood in the early 1960s. They organized people in existing institutions, primarily churches, to form a broadly based community organization, Pilsen Neighbors Community Council (PNCC), that would consolidate sufficient power to effect social, economic, and political change around issues of concern to the general population. They argued that democracy in the United Sates was in danger because its mediating institutions, namely churches, labor unions, independent political organizations, and other voluntary associations, were becoming less effective owing to declining membership and involvement, leaving individuals and families vulnerable to the exploitive designs of corporate and governmental entities.[5] Community organizers in the 1960s convinced local parishes to financially support these new community organizations, to open their parish halls for their meetings, and to identify leaders to work on issues selected by residents at annual conventions. Rather than organize people directly inside the church community for the immediate benefit of the church congregation, organizers focused on neighborhood issues.[6] In the 1970s, however, community organizations modified their strategy. To garner more power, they began to focus less on building their own organizations and more on strengthening the parishes by organizing their constituencies, an approach called "church-based organizing."[7]

Community organizers try to unite people in order to empower them to act in their own self-interest and for the good of the community. Since the community lacks financial power, it must organize to build people-power. Talking about or using power frightens some people, who think it contradicts the leadership modeled by Christ, the suffering servant. Pastors may reject it because they believe power fosters conflict and divides the community, even though they themselves operate from a position of power. In fact, power is morally neutral, its moral value depending largely on its intended purpose and the means used to achieve it.

PNCC organizing efforts produced many improvements. Its most famous battle and notable accomplishment was building the neighborhood's first public high school, Benito Juarez. Hispanic residents had long wanted a local high school so their children would not have to travel outside the neighborhood to attend predominantly African American schools. PNCC led the fight to obtain the land and funding for the school, which was overcrowded the day it opened in 1975. In the late 1980s, PNCC also organized the drive that eventually produced a new multimillion-dollar municipal technical school in the neighborhood's West End. Despite these accomplishments, PNCC failed to develop strong leaders for the parishes themselves.

Community Organizers and Leaders

Every parish faces the challenge of finding and developing lay leaders to carry out its ministries and activities, and frequently community organizations compete with pastors for them. Community organizations have a specific strategy for developing leaders. Usually, with the pastor's permission, organizers interview existing parish leaders, inviting those with the greatest potential to work on social issues. However, because organizers realize that pastors are reluctant to lose their best leaders to nonparish activities or possible burnout, they usually look for new people with leadership potential, people with multiple personal relationships or the ability to develop them.

They train these people to extend these relationships to other influential or potential leaders by getting to know them through relational meetings (one-on-ones). In these forty-five-minute sessions, leaders assess people's self-interest and challenge them to act on their values and beliefs. Because these sessions aim to build relationships of mutual trust and concern, leaders share part of their own history and interests, noting commonalities of experience and vision. To motivate people to get involved, they appeal less to logical arguments or people's altruistic instincts than to people's self-interest, assessing also whether they have enough anger or feeling about their concerns to act on them. These relational meetings are the nuts and bolts of organizing, because they build personal, as well as professional (the politically correct term is "public"), relationships that unite people, cementing the foundation of people-power. In this way, organizers and leaders work their way through the community, learning about people's interests and discovering and incorporating new talent in an ever growing base of power for the organization.

In church-based community organizing, organizers usually appeal to clergy by offering to strengthen their parish. Although they offer to help develop resources and train new leaders, they rarely raise funds or recruit people for more than the work of community organizing itself. Their leaders learn to identify winnable issues, speak in public, run meetings, relate to the press, challenge city officials, and develop a public persona. They also learn how to make an "issue" out of a "problem," that is, take a general concern, such as inadequate housing, and make it concrete by building two new homes. They "cut" (define) an issue in such a way that it can be successfully acted upon, addressing one "winnable" issue at a time. They also learn about power, how to analyze it, create it, and use it for the purposes of the organization. In short, the training amounts to a school of public life, empowering parish leaders to work in the community and engage in constant self-reflection and evaluation.[8]

As the largest parish in Pilsen, St. Pius V was the backbone of institutional support for PNCC. Many of PNCC's conventions were held in the church hall, and at different times, St. Pius V's priests served as presidents of PNCC's board of directors, while parish leaders participated in setting the organization's agenda. However, after relatively brief involvement, parish leaders tended not only to abandon participation in PNCC but in the parish as well.

Although most Alinsky-style organizations cast their work in the context of biblical liberation, they do little to nourish this spirituality among their leaders. Thus many complained about lacking time for their families, being disillusioned with the lack of democratic procedures, or being unsuited for confrontational activity. Community organizers argued that if participants are unwilling or unable to act with sufficient anger or to dedicate significant time to the organization, they are unsuited for leadership. When leaders reduced their commitment or left the organization, organizers, rather than helping them discern their future, abandoned them and recruited replacements. Thus instead of strengthening the parish, the community organization siphoned off parish leaders and alienated them from parish life. Rather than build community, which is what a parish is all about, it fostered a one-dimensional concept of parish leaders, people impassioned about social issues who recruit like-minded people into an organization that wields power in the political realm.

Catholic parishes sell themselves short if they do not challenge and involve all parishioners, regardless of their stage of social commitment, to work consciously and conscientiously for the kingdom of God. This approach is critical in a Mexican community because people bring a unique experience of church, society, and politics. Consequently, leadership formation must involve more than practical training in running meetings, speaking in public, conducting one-on-one relational meetings, and analyzing social structures of power. It should offer broad-based formation that focuses on personal growth and social commitment, including reflections on self-esteem and training in communication, all in the context of faith. Such a process works more slowly and is less univocal in its definition of leaders than the Alinsky method, but it is more respectful of people at different stages of personal development and social commitment and, in the end, more effective in building community.

A model of leadership common among Mexicans is "clientelism," that is, leadership based on patronage. Under this system, leaders ensure support by distributing resources to followers. Clientelist leaders accumulate power in order to secure their positions rather than to empower others. They discourage new leaders, often destroying competitors with rumors, and they guarantee the status quo by ignoring or rejecting new approaches. This system often affects parishes where leaders, ensconced in petty fiefdoms of power and privilege, treat other parishioners as their workers rather than as equals. Their ministry becomes a personal domain, which no one dares to challenge. Other parishioners, believing themselves incapable of leadership, blindly follow their direction or leave the ministry. Because these leaders are usually reliable workers, pastors depend on them, often choosing to overlook their unprofessional conduct, thus supporting a leadership style that inhibits, if not destroys, parish community.

St. Pius V staff continually proposed to PNCC's director that the organization consult people in local parishes about their concerns. For example, before urging people to support the construction of a new technical school and herding them on buses to picket the home of a resistant state legislator, PNCC might prepare reflection sheets about the proposed school for discussions in people's homes. Like many community organizers, PNCC's director did not believe the organization should engage in this educational and consultative process but only mobilize supporters of preselected issues. This attitude mirrors that of Saul Alinsky, who quipped to his friend Monsignor John J. Egan, who had suggested to the illustrious founder of community organizing that he foster some reflection on the religious values of community organization, "You take care of the religion, Jack; we'll do the organizing."[9] Ironically, most community organizers believe that their responsibility is to create organizations with sufficient people-power to effect incremental social-economic change, without necessarily establishing Christian community or always respecting Christian ethical principles.

Not all community organizers would agree with the above characterization of their organizations. Gregory Pierce, an independent consultant for community organizations in Chicago, stated: "Parishes should join such an effort (community organization) if, and only if, the organization can effectively promote community improvements, family stability, leadership training, integration, evangelism, and theological reflection." He and others disassociate themselves from any organization driven by organizers rather than by local leaders and their respective institutions. In the end, the failure of community organizations to be truly democratic is largely the fault of member parishes insufficiently involved in directing the organization.

The Pilsen experience with community organizations taught the churches some valuable lessons:

1. A creative balance must be struck between organizing around self-interests and organizing to create a vibrant community that will last beyond the mobilization of the moment. Building an informed and cohesive community is ultimately more valuable than acquiring additional resources or improving physical conditions.
2. A theology of Christian-based community, as well as the socio-political understanding of how power can be garnered and used to benefit the common good, must undergird and guide efforts to organize a broad-based, representative democracy. The ultimate goal is not the power to accomplish social change, but a strong Christian community that lives the values of God's kingdom.
3. The pursuit of local issues, such as better housing, education, and health care, although important and even urgent, must be viewed within a larger context of ethical standards that place checks and balances on power and curtail the tendency to make the end (common good) justify unethical means. The churches must help leaders understand how their faith must guide their leadership (the model of Jesus).
4. Churches that want to participate seriously and responsibly in community organizing must prepare their parishioners for the rough-and-tumble politics of social struggle, provide them with spiritual and ethical direction, and maintain good communication with their organizing leadership.
5. To avoid creating a new political elite among leaders active in community organizing, churches must develop a strategy for conscientizing and involving the rank-and-file parishioners.[10]

A New Kind of Community Organization

In 1988, several pastors, frustrated with PNCC's unethical practices, failure to develop broadly based leadership formation, and unwillingness to focus on strengthening community, jointly hired a community organizer for their Pilsen parishes. Mike Loftin started by forming an interparochial committee, the Catholic Community of Pilsen (CCP), consisting of two representatives from each parish to work on the principal social issues of concern to the parishes: gangs, neighborhood cleanup, and housing. For Loftin, however, CCP was too dependent on pastors to develop lay leaders. Consequently, within a year the parishes formed the Interfaith Community Organization (ICO), as legally separate from but structurally and morally connected to the parishes. To guarantee a close relationship between the parishes and the new organization, the board of directors was constituted primarily of representatives from the dues-paying parishes. Although three small, mainline Protestant churches and twenty small evangelical churches were invited, only one joined for a short time.[11]

In 1994, ICO merged with the parishes' economic development corporation, the Pilsen Resurrection Development Corporation (PRDC), formed two years prior. The new organization, the Resurrection Project (TRP), was directed by a young St. Pius V parishioner, Raul Raymundo, who explained the name:

> Plain and simple, we wanted a name that means "new life," and new life means creating a healthy community with good housing, solid family relationships, strong economic growth, job and educational opportunities, and positive attitudes. These things surface when we work to build the Kingdom of God on earth. Jesus' resurrection is all about new life, and as a primarily Catholic community, we believe in his life and message. [12]

Because TRP wanted to spend most of its time strengthening the smaller parishes and those with the weakest commitment to organizing, TRP spent little time organizing within St. Pius V. Consequently, the parish hired its own organizer, Megan Reilly, who worked collaboratively with TRP's staff, spending most of her time building relationships with parishioners and organizing members of the parish CBCs to act on social issues.

· The parish staff wanted to involve as many people as possible in selecting and acting on issues. To this end, it developed two courses, one on Christian social commitment and another on building personal relationships. The courses begin by studying the life of Jesus and his commitment to justice. Participants analyze his base of power and the reasons why Jewish authorities crucified him. After establishing that Jesus charged his followers to continue his work of constructing a new order, the courses analyze the world today and the challenges facing Christians. Participants identify injustices affecting their lives and discover that they must build power among themselves to construct God's reign of peace and justice. Their power is generated by developing strong personal relationships with people living in their area so that they can gradually challenge one another to act on their values and beliefs.

Although the courses followed the basic methodology of Alinsky-style training, focusing on building power among people, there were important differences. Because of the importance of faith in the lives of Mexican people, the courses included a deeper reflection on the teachings of Jesus and the role of the church, and they targeted not only leaders but all CBC members. They were taught in Spanish to predominantly monolingual Hispanics, which many community organizations refuse to do, insisting that because English is the language of power, leaders must speak and understand it. Third, to involve people in their own formation, the courses emphasized the active participation of all. The courses followed the pedagogical approach developed in the 1950s in Latin America by Paulo Freire, a Brazilian educator who designed participative learning for the masses of relatively uneducated people. Rather than listening to lectures, participants reflected on their experiences and responded to questions that challenged them to deepen their analysis and expand their vision. Dynamics, including dramas and games, kept participants active and interested.

This "liberating" or "popular" education incorporates three key concepts: 1) Everyone is a teacher and a student. The hierarchical relationship of teacher-student is replaced by a more horizontal one of mutual exchange and a shared desire to challenge one another to grow in knowledge and understanding and to develop the skills necessary to be active catalysts of community change. 2) Since people learn more readily about things that concern them, the people's experience rather than texts, are the starting place for learning. 3) Because no education is ideologically neutral, people need to develop critical thinking to analyze their troubled world and strategize solutions. These skills empower people to be subjects, and not just objects, of their history, active, and not just passive, participants in their communities.[13]

As a result of these courses, CBCs began addressing issues such as neighborhood cleanup, gang violence, sidewalk repair, and police protection. Several CBCs also formed block clubs to attract neighbors uninvolved in church activities. Eventually the block clubs formed a neighborhood association coordinated by TRP.[14]

Promoting Economic Development

The constant pressure of large immigrant families on aging housing stock in Pilsen had left many buildings dilapidated. Overcrowding, large numbers of children, and absentee property owners extracting every possible penny from rental units are a formula for deterioration. Leaky roofs, peeling, lead-based paint, cracked electrical wiring, doors that do not close, and sinks and showers that do not drain endanger the health of children and adults alike. To compound the problem, parish staffs believed that if Pilsen residents did not begin to purchase property, they would eventually be pushed out of the neighborhood by developers and real estate speculators marketing the area to more wealthy outsiders. If the community cleaned the streets and alleys and removed the gangs but did nothing about property ownership, the area would soon cease to be Mexican and immigrant; it would be "gentrified." The area's proximity to downtown Chicago and its accessibility to public transportation, recreational centers, the largest

265

medical complex in the United States, and the University of Illinois would easily attract outside investment dollars and make housing too expensive for Mexican immigrants. Thus, parish staffs and leaders chose housing as a top priority for social action.

To encourage home ownership, the parishes initially involved Neighborhood Housing Services to provide services such as low-interest mortgages, home improvement loans, and counseling for prospective home buyers. Subsequently, they formed their own economic development corporation, which later merged with ICO to form TRP. It wanted to create housing affordable to neighborhood residents, and it succeeded beyond its founders' wildest expectations.[15] Fortunately, Mayor Richard M. Daley was then inaugurating a program to help low- and moderate-income families purchase new homes. His "New Homes for Chicago" provided a subsidy of $20,000 for each new home and made available sixty vacant lots in Pilsen. Working with numerous banks to obtain low-interest mortgages, TRP built one- and two-unit homes for families with a combined annual income as low as $18,000. After completing 124 new homes in just seven years in 1999, TRP began constructing twenty-five more homes in the adjacent neighborhood of Little Village. City officials and other development corporations marveled at TRP's ability to market so many homes among residents in a poor neighborhood, and banks were pleased that not a single TRP home buyer defaulted on a mortgage.

TRP attributes its success to the strong commitment of parishes to encourage parishioners to become home owners and to the people's confidence in the church. Priests helped convince residents they could own a home, preaching a message of hope for a healthier community if people would "buy into it" and make it their home. Raymundo explained:

> We realized that it wasn't that people didn't want to buy homes here, it's just that they didn't know how. For several months...we had families going to their parish halls and learning how to buy a home. That really created the market.[16]

Parishioners prequalified en masse for loans from supporting financial institutions. Because there were many more qualified families than available homes, prospective home owners were put on a waiting list, their place on the list determined by an open lottery. At a joyous celebration, Joseph Cardinal Bernardin drew the name of the first family to own a new home. Approximately a third of the new home owners were St. Pius V parishioners.

Another reason for the project's success was the internal strength of the Mexican family. Solidarity among family members enabled them to pool resources to purchase new homes. In 1991, Mario Rodriguez took the first step in realizing his dream by moving to the United States. He landed a landscaping job paying the minimum wage. Two years later he had saved enough to bring his wife, Juana, from Mexico. Their three teenage children soon followed, and within a year the Rodriguez family expanded with the birth of Elizabeth. They lived in a three-bedroom apartment near Chinatown, bordering Pilsen, that they shared with a Chinese immigrant couple who spoke no English, let alone Spanish. When the family joined St. Pius V, they heard about the new homes and applied, even though they thought they had little chance of being approved. Each time someone in the family received a raise, they called to update their application. The family was approved for a special low-interest loan of 4 percent from Citibank, and the city of Chicago paid the closing costs. When they purchased a new four-bedroom house, they could hardly believe it, and their friends marveled at how quickly they had become home owners. Juana enjoyed sitting in her living room and gazing around her new home. Mario Jr., age seventeen, commented, "After sleeping in the living room all my life, I finally have my own room." Mario Sr., who started the whole process, believes he has more than realized his dream, thanks to the Resurrection Project.

Because many immigrant families cannot afford a new home, TRP began rehabilitating deteriorated buildings, in ten years providing more than 160 affordable rental units. By 2004, TRP had generated more than $77 million of direct investment and was managing $25 million in construction, rental renovation, and facility development. It had educated over 1,500 residents through eighty home ownership workshops. In recognition of its efforts, the young organization won numerous awards, including the prestigious Maxwell Award of Excellence, granted to only six economic development corporations nationwide by the Fannie Mae Foundation.[17]

While building and rehabilitating homes, TRP discovered many small Hispanic contractors interested in participating in its economic development. Conversations eventually led TRP to form a business incubator, the Resurrection Construction Cooperative (RCC), which assisted thirty-five small companies in finding jobs, accessing financial capital, estimating bids, establishing accounting procedures, and processing permits, contracts, and other legal documents. Arturo Fernández, president of RCC, commented at the organization's third anniversary celebration:

> The co-op helps us keep jobs in the community, thus generating income for our families and more money for the local economy. It is beautiful to see how we contractors have grown to trust one another and share our knowledge and resources. Together we can do so much more for our community than individually.[18]

Eventually TRP employed one of RCC's companies as its general contractor and others as subcontractors to build its new homes.

Shortly after founding TRP, the parishes purchased a complex of three shuttered buildings that had been St. Vitus parish. After two years of negotiating, during which gangs and drug dealers vandalized the buildings, the archdiocese agreed to sell the complex to TRP for ten dollars—a blessing for the organization, the community, and the archdiocese.

After moving its offices into the old St. Vitus rectory, TRP formed a committee of former St. Vitus parishioners to plan the future use of the school building. Because the people overwhelmingly favored using it for children and youth, TRP raised $1.2 million to rehabilitate the building for a day-care facility, the Guadalupe Family Center, for 208 children from the community. The facility was given a distinctive new appearance, as neighborhood youth painted murals of children at play and the image of Our Lady of Guadalupe in fluorescent colors on the outside walls.

In 1995, to inaugurate the center, Cardinal Bernardin blessed the building, which was filled the day it opened. Raymundo observed, "What could have been an eyesore in the community has become, once again, an anchor."[19] The cardinal shared his joy at seeing a controversial decision to close a parish and school in a poor community turn into a success story.

In subsequent years, as TRP expanded its work into two adjacent neighborhoods, increasing its membership to fourteen Catholic parishes, it developed three more day-care centers to serve the burgeoning Hispanic community.

Social Issues of Life and Death

The Resurrection Project worked primarily on issues identified by the Catholic parishes during a year-long pastoral planning process in 1987. Because people's primary concern was their children, TRP quickly began working on the problem of gangs.

Gang Violence and the Police

Although gang violence is a serious danger and an overriding concern, its elimination, or even reduction, proves illusive. Gang activity in Pilsen, nearly the highest in Chicago, has deep roots in the community. Some families aid and abet gang activity from their homes. Others, by refusing to recognize their children's involvement in gangs, unwittingly contribute to the problem. Because most people fear working directly with youth in gangs and because these efforts are costly and reach a relatively small proportion of youth, producing few visible results, outreach to gangs is practically nonexistent. The common approach is to provide alternative programs for youth, that is, gang prevention activities, which are less threatening and produce more visible results. After reflection, the parishes adopted a dual approach: working with police and creating alternatives to gangs.

Police often play an ambiguous role in the inner city, making collaboration with them complicated and difficult. Although people need them for security, relations between the police and the community, especially the youth, are often strained and plagued with distrust. Because police generally consider themselves more knowledgeable than residents, they sometimes treat them with disrespect and even disdain. Perhaps because most live outside the community, it is not uncommon for them, to blame the people for problems in their community. "If you parents were more responsible, you wouldn't have gangs." Police also tend to deny or overlook their own shortcomings (for example, few officers speak Spanish and some are corrupt) and the mistakes they make (for instance, hassling children unrelated to gangs). When they fail to respond to a 911 emergency call, they sometimes blame residents for not calling the number enough times.

When the parishes were forming ICO (later TRP), the police were restructuring to incorporate community policing, a model promoted in major cities after the 1993 Los Angeles riots. Community policing proscribes that police work closely with residents on issues that concern them. Before community policing was officially implemented in Chicago, TRP organized the community to convince the city's police superintendent to assign six additional officers to walk the neighborhood streets and help with local problems. While some of these officers spoke Spanish and related well to the community, they brought only a small improvement. Other police remained aloof, unconnected, and at times arrogant. Not only were six officers too few, they were not accountable to the community. The collaborative effort was fraught with frustration, as police, operating within a hierarchical organization, responded to their superiors and not to residents. Although TRP wanted the police to concentrate on six "hot spots" of gang activity, the police resisted, claiming they lacked sufficient personnel to focus on even one. They also refused to draft a plan of action because there were too many unpredictable demands on their time. Moreover, even if they developed a plan, for security reasons, they could not share it with the community. When TRP leaders challenged the police to respect and work with the community, the police questioned TRP's ability to represent the community.

To complicate matters, police are frequently transferred from the district, moved from beat to beat, or rotated from shift to shift without any notice to the community, making it difficult for the community to develop effective working relationships with them. During the eighteen years covered by this book, eight police commanders were appointed to the local district, and only one was Hispanic and Spanish-speaking. After the appointment of each new commander, residents had to develop new relationships of trust, convince new officers of the merits of existing projects, and instruct them about the details of the work involved.

On several occasions, the police did take effective action. For example, they targeted the largest gang in the community and worked secretly with some residents to identify, monitor, and eventually arrest thirty-six gang members for attempted sales of narcotics. The action greatly improved relations between police and the community, but had little lasting impact on the gang. Within a year the gang was back working at previous levels of operations.

In another effort, several St. Pius V parishioners, living on a corner where gang members routinely sold drugs at all hours of the day and night, organized to remove the dangerous activity. When police failed to respond to people's repeated calls, residents suspected police involvement. Not until they contacted the head of Chicago's narcotics division, did they see results. While working simultaneously to infiltrate the band of sellers, police staked out the corner from a nearby apartment. Within several months, the gang disappeared, with no explanation from police.

Parishioners and TRP spent much time and energy trying to work cooperatively with the police, but the latter's response was frustrating. The experience was also frustrating because people could hardly evaluate the police's response. Although police presented reports of arrests, these hardly confirmed any reduction in gang activity. Generally, residents measured police activity by counting squad cards entering an area and the number of shootings they heard—imprecise measures at best. In the end, the community's effort accomplished less in reducing gang activity than in helping police improve their image. In one effort, the police promoted an essay/poster contest in local schools. Although the contest produced little contact between police and youth, it helped foster an image of police as caring about young people. Not until the police department had been cultivating community policing among its officers for several years and TRP had expanded and strengthened its block clubs did the police's attitude and behavior begin to reflect greater respect and cooperation.

To deal with gangs, TRP did more than work with police. It organized activities to prevent gang involvement, such as a summer basketball tournament. Each of the thirteen block clubs organized a team, and on Friday nights they played on different blocks. The police supported the tournament with their presence, guaranteeing safety for youth as the tournament moved from one gang territory to another. In the end, the police fielded a team to join in the fun.

Cleaning Up the Neighborhood

Immigrants slowly but surely assume ownership of their neighborhood. Initially treated like unwelcome strangers, they gradually recognize that the community belongs to them and take responsibility for its welfare.

Mexicans are often stereotyped as dirty, but the opposite is true. In Mexico, women commonly sweep in front of their homes, even if the area is made of dirt. Nevertheless, when Mexicans arrive in a large, strange, and rather inhospitable city, many become passive. Moreover, it is difficult for immigrants overcrowded in tiny apartments to keep things clean. The size and number of garbage cans and the once-a-week garbage collections are inadequate for the volume of trash generated by large families. While the city claims it cannot afford more frequent garbage pickup, garbage bins in alleys fill to overflowing, leaving no place for surplus garbage but the ground. Also, since the city refuses to put garbage cans on sidewalks, streets are littered with wrappers from food people eat while walking about. Moreover, the poor regularly scour the alleys rummaging through garbage to find

272

food or aluminum cans to recycle for cash, often spilling trash on the ground. All these practices attract veritable hoards of rats.

Most residents are unhappy about the sordid state of their neighborhood. Consequently, the parishes focused attention on obtaining better city services. In 1991, TRP organized a meeting of 350 people with city officials at St. Pius V church. There the city's chief of sanitation promised, and later delivered, more frequent garbage collection in selected areas of high usage, weekly street sweeping of major arteries, and monthly sweeping on side streets—major accomplishments in a neighborhood historically ignored by city officials.

Cleaning the area also involved removing numerous dangerous abandoned buildings, often havens for gangs or homeless men. Community residents had long felt helpless to deal with these unsightly buildings, not knowing how to identify owners or force landlords to improve them. One parish CBC on a block with several abandoned buildings confronted an owner who was uninterested in fixing up and renting his properties. Neighbors brought the owner to housing court, but because the Chicago housing court strongly favors owners, religiously respecting the rights of private property, the owner easily obtained continuance after continuance. Although residents appeared in court nearly every month for four years, success eluded them. Through their struggles, however, neighbors developed a high degree of solidarity, meeting in one another's homes to pray and plan other activities for their block.

Improving the Quality of Life

The Pilsen parishes addressed a number of other social concerns: improving conditions in a senior public housing building, blocking stores from selling liquor, creating opportunities for better health services, and strengthening family life.

Down the block from St. Procopius parish (six blocks from St. Pius V), a 225-unit public housing project for senior citizens called *Las Americas* presented the community with a challenge. Elderly residents, approximately half African American and half Hispanic, were furious when changes in federal regulations reclassified persons in

273

drug rehabilitation as disabled, thus permitting them to live with the seniors. Many of these drug abusers had not abandoned their bad habits. Drug-related problems, including prostitution, began to plague the corridors and stairwells. When the seniors asked for help, TRP assisted in successfully convincing the Chicago Housing Authority to change its classification of rehabilitated drug abusers and entrust the building to private management, thus solving the problem.

Pilsen had the second highest concentration of liquor-selling businesses in Chicago. In 1989, fed up with drinking on the public way and convinced that alcoholism was destroying families, residents in the precinct surrounding St. Pius V attempted to place a referendum on the local ballot to vote the area dry. However, the owner of the most notorious tavern, accompanied by a husky companion, visited petition signers, convincing nearly everyone to retract their support for the referendum. People had not been sufficiently prepared and united to withstand such intimidation. Despite that setback, residents succeeded in convincing their alderman to pass a city ordinance establishing a moratorium on new liquor licenses for all establishments except restaurants. When new businesses applied for exceptions, TRP organized parishioners to testify at public hearings, convincing the liquor commission to deny the applications.[20]

Another important issue for families in Pilsen is the quality of health care at the local city clinic. In 2000, approximately 62 percent of nonelderly Hispanics in Illinois lacked health insurance, more than twice as many as whites.[21] Obtaining health care is a real challenge for immigrants, especially for the undocumented, who do not qualify for Medicaid or Medicare or earn so little they can hardly pay for health care.

In Chicago, the uninsured poor regularly go to Cook County Hospital, and for less severe problems to a city clinic like the Lower West Side Clinic in Pilsen. More than a hundred women and children crowd into the clinic every morning. The wait for an appointment for low-risk, non-emergency problems may be three months, and on the day of an appointment, patients often wait hours before receiving attention. Furthermore, since the clinic is not affiliated with any hospital, patients are not referred to specific doctors for specialized treatment. What is even more difficult for immigrants to tolerate is the disrespectful manner in which many are treated by the clinic's staff, often by first- and second-generation Hispanics impatient with their lack of English.

Although St. Pius V worked for years to improve service at the clinic, talking with the director, who complained of his lack of authority to make the necessary personnel changes, and conducting workshops for clinic employees on cultural sensitivity, improvements were minimal. Staff at St. Pius V then trained volunteer ombudsmen to assist patients with their difficulties. Although this system worked well, the parish staff could not find sufficient bilingual volunteers to sustain the program.

However, because the clinic continued to concern local residents, TRP began working first with the University of Illinois and then with Cook County Hospital to establish a new clinic in the area, efforts which still have not borne fruit. By 2000, however, it was helping residents obtain health services through KidCare and low-cost clinics subsidized by state funds.

In 1995, Pilsen pastors discussed the need for family counseling and parent education programs in the community. The prevalence of gangs, school dropouts, domestic violence, and alcoholism indicate serious family problems. The priests believed the parishes could be a catalyst for change because Mexican immigrants trust their church. Because no one parish could adequately address such difficult and pervasive problems, the pastors created a new inter-parish project, Family Hope *(Esperanza Familiar)*, at TRP, based on the St. Pius V model of family counseling, parenting classes, and support groups for women and couples.

The community of parishes successfully addressed other important issues that helped improve the quality of life for local residents. They created two shelters for women and children, stopped "fly dumpers" depositing industrial waste in empty lots, blocked the Chicago Board of Education from demolishing twenty-eight homes to build a new school, turned an abandoned lot into a garden and play lot for children and teens, organized Hispanic university students to assist high schoolers in aspiring to and applying for college admission, helped garner support to pass state legislation enabling undocumented students to pay in-state

275

rather than out-of-state tuition at state universities, and launched a campaign that received $3.4 million from the state to convert an old convent into a dormitory for fifty Hispanic university students who commit to service in the community.

In 1998, to address larger issues, TRP joined United Power for Action and Justice, a Chicago metropolitan community organization consisting of 340 local churches, synagogues, mosques, civic organizations, health clinics, and labor unions formed under the direction of the Industrial Areas Foundation. United Power selected as its first major issue the promotion of health insurance for the uninsured in the state of Illinois. Within United Power, TRP helped form a Hispanic Caucus to advocate for specific issues of concern to the Hispanic community.

Ministry and Organization

These efforts are examples of an immigrant community maturing in faith and action. Residents gradually recognize their responsibility and power, and gain the respect of other residents and public officials as they struggle to build a healthy community. Nevertheless, the area remains a port of entry, a neighborhood in perpetual transition, constantly receiving newly arrived immigrants and losing established residents as their economic situation improves. As a result, the community faces the permanent task of educating and incorporating new families into the struggle. Some pastoral and organizational principles can be extracted from this experience:

1. Churches in the inner city are often the only voluntary institutions through which people can find their collective voice for self-development and renewal.
2. Continuity of pastoral leadership over a long term is crucial to the success of the church's mission in the wider community. The stability of a pastor enables the community to gather and sustain momentum. Each time a new pastor is assigned, a new vision develops,

current leadership hesitates and sometimes withdraws, and different priorities are established.

3. Understanding and accepting Mexican culture contribute greatly to the effectiveness of pastoral ministry by helping people feel at home in their church.

4. Churches can utilize their Judeo-Christian ethical tradition to help people understand the need for organizing political power and using it to promote justice.

5. Faith-based community organizing helps develop a more informed, active, and spiritually motivated community. Inspired by faith, people more readily find their own self-interest fulfilled in the material and spiritual well-being of the whole.

6. Community organizing built upon the institutional membership of many parishes helps create a large membership with greater human and financial resources and, thus, greater power.

7. Dioceses greatly enhance faith-based community redevelopment through appropriate grants of property and funding. Church buildings no longer needed for worship can be renovated into centers for much-needed community services.

8. The Resurrection Project dramatically demonstrates a holistic approach joining the coordinated efforts for affordable housing, economic development, improved education for children and adults, safe streets, leadership formation, and the strengthening of families, churches, and the broader community.

The CBCs of St. Pius V provided much grassroots support, if not the leadership, in most of these successful efforts. The people put their faith into action, forged a greater unity among themselves, and strengthened their organization, TRP. Raul Raymundo commented:

> We wanted to achieve two things at the same time: to promote the tangible and the intangible assets of the community. By focusing on the tangible assets (geo-

graphical location, churches, stores, and homes), we showed people what was positive about our neighborhood. Then, by promoting the intangible assets (culture, language, faith life, and spirit), we began building a healthy community.[22]

The people's faith, appreciation for community, and ethos for democratic action replaced a combination of deference to so-called experts and public authorities and futile complaints about how bad things are. A "new person" emerged in this process.[23] Raymundo noted:

> Three things make this organization unique. First, the parishes and lay people are the owners. They have tremendous commitment and energy. Second, a very talented staff of both community and non-community residents work here because they believe in the mission of the organization. Third, we've created a relationship with fund providers and partners who believe in our vision of creating a healthy community by challenging people to act on their faith and values.[24]

Notes

1. Pope Paul VI, *On the Development of Peoples*, 81.

2. See Benedict T. Viviano, OP, *The Kingdom of God in History* (Wilmington, DE: Michael Glazier, 1988) for a discussion of the evolving notion of the kingdom of God through history.

3. Virgil P. Elizondo, "Mestizaje as a Locus of Theological Reflection," *Frontiers*, 107.

4. Paul J. Wadell, CP, "Ethics and the Narrative of Hispanic Americans: Conquest, Community, and the Fragility of Life," Pineda and Schreiter, *Dialogue Rejoined*, 129. See also Deck, *The Second Wave*, 34.

5. William Droel, "Community Organizing—Empowerment for Human Rights: 25 Years Since the Death of Saul Alinsky," *Blueprint for Social Justice* (October 1997), 3.

6. See Mike Miller, "Organizing: A Map for Explorers," *Christianity and Crisis* (February 2, 1987), 22–30, for an overview of literature and theory about community organizing.

7. Droel, *op. cit.*, 2–3.

8. Alinsky drew a hard line between organizers and leaders, the former typically being staff coming from outside the community and the latter being volunteers residing in the neighborhood. However, in practice, maintaining the distinction between the two is difficult. If an organizer dominates a community organization, it never develops a sense of its own power; on the other hand, if organizers lack power and personality, they hardly motivate people to join together to act. A new generation of community organizers came onto the national scene in the 1980s and 1990s. Many were people of color who tend to see themselves as active participants in a community's deliberations rather than simply outside facilitators. They tend to be more directive and less objective and may promote their own agenda rather than the community's priorities. JoAnn Wypijewski, "A Stirring in the Land," *The Nation* (September 8, 1997), 21–22.

9. Droel, *op. cit.*, 2. In fairness to Droel, he notes that the Industrial Areas Foundation, Alinsky's direct successor, is "explicitly theological and spiritual" in its training and organizing.

10. Charles W. Dahm, OP, with Nile Harper, "St. Pius V Roman Catholic Church and the Pilsen Area Resurrection Project," in Nile Harper, ed., *Urban Churches, Vital Signs: Beyond Charity Toward Justice* (Grand Rapids, MI: Eerdmans, 1999), 172–73.

11. ICO also invited other civic organizations to join, but only the small service organization, *Hermandad Mexicana*, became a member.

12. Jeremy Langford, "Resurrection in Chicago," in Jim Langford, *Happy Are They: Living the Beatitudes in America* (Ligouri, MO: Triumph Books, 1997), 150. This chapter focuses on the person of Raul Raymundo and his Christian commitment to work in this community.

13. Paulo Freire, *Pedagogy of the Oppressed* (New York: Seabury Press, 1974).

14. Janise D. Hurtig, "Hispanic Immigrant Churches and the Construction of Ethnicity," in Lowell W. Livezey, ed., *Public Religion and Urban Transformation: Faith in the City* (New York: New York University Press, 2000), 36–38. Hurtig's chapter compares the work of St. Pius V and the Resurrection Project with that of the Emmanuel Presbyterian Church in Pilsen.

15. The first home financed by TRP was purchased by Agustina Morales, a widow and mother of five daughters who had recently lost her

apartment in a devastating fire in which her grandson had died. See Chapter 6 for her story.

16. *Ibid.*, 152.

17. In 1991, TRP received the Neighborhood Leadership Award from Neighborhood Housing Services of Chicago. In 1993, the Association of Chicago Priests bestowed its award for Outstanding Contributions to the Life of the Church of Chicago. In 1994, the Wieboldt, Woods, and MacArthur Foundations honored TRP with the Achievements in Organizing Award. In 1994, Amoco awarded it the Leader Award in Job Creation and Economic Growth Category; the Local Initiative Support Corporation, Building Owners and Managers Association, Chicago Development Council, and Chicago District Council of the Urban Land Institute granted it the prestigious Non-Profit Community Development Group of the Year Award. In 1998, it won the Fannie Mae Foundation Award for Continued Excellence.

18. Berenice Alejo, "Construction Coop Celebrates Third Anniversary," *Nueva Vida* (December 1998), 8.

19. Langford, *op. cit.*, 158.

20. These successful efforts motivated some parishioners to question the sale of liquor at parish events. Years earlier, the parish council had stopped the sale of beer at summer festivals. Although many had warned of a reduction in financial proceeds, little income was lost and a more familial atmosphere attracted greater attendance.

21. "Health Insurance Coverage and Access to Care Among Latinos," *Coalition News*, Chicago Hispanic Health Coalition (December 2000), 1.

22. Langford, *op. cit.*, 154.

23. Miller, *op. cit.*, 28.

24. Langford, *op. cit.*, 161.

10.

Spirituality, Church, Community, and the Future

The data, images, and recurring themes in this book comprise an ecclesial sociology and a pastoral theology of a Mexican immigrant parish in an urban center of the United States. A community of faith, the parish is a safe haven where immigrants find emotional support, information, and services for their many needs. For example, the promotion of small Christian Base Communities helps immigrants break their fear and isolation, and the incorporation of their devotions, music, and rituals in parish liturgies affirms the value of their faith and traditions and strengthens them in their difficult transition into a new culture. Organizing the immigrant community to more effectively address its specific needs in areas of personal growth, parenting, housing, education, employment, and community development helps them build the kingdom of God that celebrates life while struggling for justice.

The Spirituality of a People

Christianity is too rich to be fully represented by any one monastery or school of thought, by any one age or culture. Distinct spiritualities develop as people live out the Christ-event in different periods of history. Medieval and Baroque figures created famous spiritualities, but the Spirit is always leading believers to concretize their faith. In each time and place, people select different aspects of Christianity, emphasizing some while setting aside others, according to their own experience and needs. The selection and arrangement of Gospel truths into a

281

particular configuration are influenced by history, as well as by the contemporary social and cultural context. Thus, spirituality is a way of understanding life, encompassing biblical interpretation, dogmas, church organization, liturgy, and ministry; it is faith and doctrine in praxis.[1]

What are some elements of the spirituality of a Mexican immigrant parish in the United States? Certain themes or elements are constant and predominant. They emerge from historical experience in Mexico, from small Christian Base Communities and liturgy, from celebrations of *quinceañeras* and struggles to preserve family, from celebrating sacraments and efforts to combat racism and social alienation. The following points outline major components of this spirituality.

God Gives Everyone Family

For Mexicans, family is of the highest priority because God so willed it. God destined that each person be born into, raised among, and supported and challenged by family. Family is a holy, though imperfect, institution that demands time, respect, loyalty, and sacrifice; it provides identity and meaning, creates obligation, and bestows rewards. Mexicans spend Saturday evenings celebrating with family, and Sundays visiting family members in their homes. Their children are precious, the reason for their immigration to the United States. People live simple lives in order to be able to send money to family in Mexico. If nothing thrills the Mexican spirit more than celebrating life in family, nothing pains their heart more than family conflict and division. People learn their faith at home, long before attending catechism class, because grandmothers and mothers are master teachers of divine wisdom. Domestic rituals, religious art, home altars, and the faith of the elders strengthen the family fabric. Moreover, faith and religion extend the family by establishing new spiritual bonds through *compadrazgo* created in the celebration of the sacraments of baptism, confirmation, first communion, and matrimony.

Human Identity Is Incomplete without Community

Strong community life characterized indigenous populations. Private property and hierarchy scarcely existed, and culture
and faith tightly bound people into *el pueblo*. Mexicans see themselves as integral parts of the whole, which gives them meaning
and definition. They love crowds, which remind them that they
are part of something bigger than themselves. Even though many
non-Hispanics prefer a "private" ceremony of baptism, Hispanics
tend to want the whole congregation to witness the baptism of
their children. Immigrant families from the same town join
together to fund public works back home. *El pueblo* embodies a
certain mystique: it is worthy of respect, in need of solidarity and
compassion, wise in distinguishing right from wrong, courageous
in spirit, and unstoppable if united. To invoke "the people" is to
invoke the holy, the sacred, and consequently Mexicans respond
enthusiastically when the church unites people as children of the
one true God and brothers and sisters of Jesus Christ. *El pueblo*
also involves a certain egalitarian and democratic character.
Ordered under duly selected leaders, *el pueblo* includes and
respects each individual, even the poorest, as God's creation. As
baptized Catholics, they are full members of the Catholic Church
and every particular parish, regardless if they are registered
parishioners.

Spiritual Concerns Outweigh Material Possessions

Traditionally, material things hold little value for Mexican
immigrants. They tend to spend little money on clothes, house
furnishings, and even cars. Their homes are simple, almost spartan. They much prefer spending their limited funds on fiestas,
gifts, contributions to the family back home, or for travel to visit
relatives in Mexico than on material possessions for themselves. A
simple lifestyle comes easy to most because they have never had

much and have been taught that one's treasure is in the heart. Simplicity of life also helps them feel close to God and one with *el pueblo*. Their insistence on sacrifice for family and community counters the forces of immediate gratification and indulgent individualism. In the United States, they are generally surprised and chagrined when their children embrace a consumerist materialism foreign to their culture.

Hopeful Strangers in an Alien Land

Mexican immigrants feel like foreigners, exiles far from their homes. Frequently they refer to themselves as "a pilgrim people." Isasi-Díaz writes, "I am caught between two worlds, neither of which is fully mine, both of which are partially mine."[2] They experience a difficult life, most born into and subjected to poverty. Once in the United States, they encounter discrimination that reinforces a sense of inferiority inherited from generations of oppression. Consequently, they easily relate to the sacred, the Holy One, as the almighty force who can liberate them individually and as a people. They see the world from the perspective of the poor and oppressed, readily relating to the Exodus story of Jewish liberation from slavery. While the Protestant ethic, preaching that religious faith and practice produce economic success, permeates American culture, Mexicans view religion as a prophetic call to solidarity with the poor and a force for social change. They have nothing to lose and everything to gain from a more equitably organized society. Indeed, marginality and oppression are the roots of their popular religiosity. During certain historical periods, Christianity counseled resignation to worldly suffering in the hope of achieving a heavenly reward. Consequently, many Mexicans, although dissatisfied with their lot in life, are somewhat resigned, even fatalistic, about their situation. History has made them a "long suffering" people. Difficulties, however, do not weaken their trust in the goodness of God and their hope for a brighter future. Their overwhelming love and affection for children reflect their confidence in and commitment to building a better life for them.

God Is Present in Daily Life, Intervening Directly in This World

God is present, permeating daily life and making each day and everything in it holy.[3] The world is fundamentally sacred, and God watches over every person, making things happen, sometimes for the good, sometimes permitting evil. Consequently, neither miracles nor tragedies are rare events. One only needs faith to see God working wonders but also to solve most of life's problems. Finding a lost child, landing a job, or recovering from an illness, all result from God's loving and direct intervention. When all hope appears lost, whether in poverty or sickness, amidst marital or family problems, prayer and trusting faith will offer a solution. Indeed, strong faith in God is the key to a happy and successful life. As they say, *"Primero Dios."* But God also tests people, challenging their faith to grow. While loving God, people should maintain a healthy fear of God. Everything they do, whether good or evil, will be rewarded or punished, whether here or in the hereafter, by this Just Judge who sees and weighs all.

Mexicans resist the dichotomy between the sacred and secular. God is present in this world in countless ways, and because they are a physical people, they can reach out and touch God through myriad sacramentals: water and candles, medals and rosaries, icons and statues, incense and song, processions and meals. These sensory objects and actions not only remind people of but also connect people to God. Ritual celebrations involving the presentation of newborn babies, baptisms, *quinceañeras*, blessings of homes, vehicles, religious articles, and children provide assurances of God's loving presence. Although this sacramental view is expressed externally, it reflects a profound inner faith, producing a devotionalism, sometimes quite emotional, that can be confused with superstition, superficiality, or excessive sentimentality if not understood correctly.[4]

285

The World Is Filled with Spirits

Mexicans live in a world inhabited by many spirits, both good and evil. Their favorite saints are not only their special advocates in time of need but part of their family, their inner circle of friends. Their deceased family and friends are also not far away. Each year they celebrate their close proximity on the feast of the Day of the Dead, arranging a table, an *ofrenda*, lavish with favorite foods, drinks, and remembrances to draw them near for a family visit. Time and space are experienced in a nonlinear way so that past and present intertwine; those who have died are still present, and the other world is transparent in everyday events. This perspective makes connecting one's life with the communion of saints an easy step. Evil spirits are also busy working in this world, sometimes harassing and harming them with mysterious misfortune. In this mystical worldview, the forces of good and evil, often plainly visible, sometimes revealed in dreams, struggle for supremacy. Holy water, a priest's blessing, a prayer for a favorite saint's intervention, or even witchcraft help protect from harm.

Jesus Is Lord and Brother

Apart from being God and from having unlimited power, Jesus is human like us. He had a mother who carried him in her womb and suffered through his persecution and death. Mexicans see Jesus as their brother and savior, a human and divine person who shares their struggles. He welcomed the immigrant, forgave sinners, healed the sick, defended the poor, and denounced injustice. His suffering and death are particularly relevant to them, as their history almost always involves poverty and discrimination. Sorrowfully but proudly, they walk with him in the *via crucis* and listen to his Seven Last Words on Good Friday.[5] They decorate their homes with realistic images of his crucified body, pictures of his tortured face streaming with blood, and icons of his compassionate, sacred heart. They tenderly caress and kiss images of the baby Jesus during the Christmas season, which remind them of

Christ's loving innocence and vulnerability. Because Jesus is like them, he is accessible, approachable, and one with them.[6]

Guadalupe Reveals the Feminine Face of God

Mary, the mother of Jesus, is a dominant and pervasive figure in the cosmic vision of Mexicans. While truly human and historical like her son, she usually meets Mexicans as the Virgin of Guadalupe. No liturgical feast day surpasses December 12, the anniversary of her appearance to Juan Diego and to the Mexican people. No religious symbol is more common and proudly displayed than her icon, originally imprinted on his humble cloak. As a compassionate, understanding, and loving mother, she watches over and protects her children against harm. Her *mestizo* character, dark skin, and love for the poor and oppressed endear her to the majority of Mexicans, imparting a dignity long denied. Her intimate relationship with her son, Jesus, endows her with nearly divine wisdom, mercy, and power. For Mexicans, she reveals the feminine face of God, as described by the Latin American bishops:

> Having firmly and lucidly decided to evangelize in depth, to go to the very roots of our people and their culture, the church turns to Mary…with her we are dealing with a feminine presence that creates the family atmosphere, receptivity, love and respect for life; a sacramental presence of the maternal features of God; and a reality so deeply human and holy that it evokes from believers supplications rooted in tenderness, suffering, and hope."[7]

Life Must Be Frequently Celebrated in Fiestas

Mexicans are a festive people, frequently gathering friends, family, and community to celebrate life and God's blessings. While

Euro-Americans tend to celebrate when something is achieved or completed, Mexicans tend to celebrate life itself, and any time is appropriate for a fiesta. They want to celebrate life even in the face of struggle, disappointment, sickness, or death.[8] Elizondo writes:

> Fiestas are not just parties. They are the joyful, sponta-
> neous, and collective celebrations of what has already
> begun in us, even if it is not recognized by others or
> verbalized by ourselves…In the fiestas, we rise above
> our daily living experiences of death to experience life
> beyond death.[9]

Mexican celebrations include *misa, mesa,* and *musa* (Mass, table, and muse—meaning sharing prayer, food, and artistic performance).[11] Prayer and liturgy celebrate people's relationship with the divine while sharing food celebrates their relationship with other human beings. Mexicans prepare special dishes, for different, liturgical seasons, such as for Christmas: *tamales, bunuelos,* and the hot drink *champurrado;* for Epiphany: *rosca de reyes,* a wreath of cake baked with one or more small images of the baby Jesus inside; for Lent: *capirotada,* a baked dish of stale bread with raisins and nuts soaked in a mixture of sugar and cinnamon; for the Day of the Dead *(Día de los Muertos): pan de muerto,* bread baked in a human form. Artistic expression, including music, song, dance, costume, and poetry, are essential components of festivities, celebrating their relationship with beauty and nature, where God is ever present. When the Chicago Symphony Brass Ensemble offered to play a joint concert with a noted Mexican folk group at St. Pius V, the parish staff knew instinctively that a successful evening had to include prayer, food, and dance, in addition to music. Thus, the evening began with a prayer and the concert in church and concluded with food and dancing in the church basement, for a perfect evening of celebration.

Whereas Americans constantly focus on the future, Mexicans tend to celebrate the moment. They thank God daily for another day of life. Their emphasis on the present may even give the impression that they lack ambition or are uninterested in progressing personally. Their concern for the moment is born of economic poverty that obliges people to concentrate on surviving day to day. Mexicans' profound respect for people and their concern for the spiritual dimension of life also motivate them to focus on people in the here and now. If someone crosses their path, such as unexpected visitors, they take time to talk, even if it means missing a previous commitment, and a short visit is difficult for them to understand. While planning and saving for the future make sense, they prefer celebrating the present. The future, with the grace of God, will care for itself.

Generosity, Compassion, and Hospitality Are God-like Virtues

Because life is a gift, Mexican immigrants are forever thankful to God and believe that, consequently, graciousness is their way of life. They constantly demonstrate compassion for others more needy than themselves. When asked to help bury the dead, fund a transplant, or assist victims of an earthquake, they generously share what little they have, apologizing for not being able to give more. Like the widow of the Gospel, they share a greater portion of their resources with those in need than do the rich. They receive recently arrived immigrants into their tiny apartments and gladly welcome visitors in their homes, treating them royally. When visitors are introduced at Sunday Mass, people enthusiastically welcome them with applause. Their desire to include everyone in the celebration of *posadas* reflects their interest in being inclusive. In meetings and parties, they pray for those unable to attend, and truly, their joy is incomplete until everyone is present.

Humbleness Is Born of a Sense of Unworthiness, Inferiority, and Guilt

Mexicans tend to be indirect in their communication and hesitant to share their ideas and feelings. Low self-esteem often underlies this lack of candor. As a *mestizo* people, they have been taught that their ideas and feelings are confused, mistaken, or at best, unimportant. The Catholic Church's teaching about sin and its historical discrimination against indigenous people helped create a sense of unworthiness, conditioning people to hesitate to speak their mind, apologize for asking for anything, and excuse themselves for not doing better. When complimented for an achievement, Mexicans are often incredulous. They are also careful not to offend and to avoid confrontation for fear of causing conflict and division.[11] Best to leave things alone. This reserve and respect create a sense of formality uncommon in the United States. Thus, Mexicans often address one other as *señor* and *señora* long after they have met, and people related by *compadrazgo* normally refer to one other by their titles of *compadre* or *comadre* rather than by their first names.

The Theology of a Church and Its Ministry

The theology of church at St. Pius V is different from that in sixteenth-century Spain and nineteenth-century Mexico. Its ecclesiology is the gift of Vatican II that promoted the concept of the church as the people of God, incorporating diverse cultures, elevating lay ministry, reintegrating the sacred and the secular, and encouraging involvement of the church in the world. Vatican II also emphasized the importance of the local church, not as an organizational or administrative sub-unit of a diocese but as the church in miniature. "As such, a parish has the same nature and mission as the church universal."[12] Accordingly, the church should respond directly to local needs. The Council recommended adaptations to different cultures, including changing the liturgical language into people's vernacular. By emphasizing the right and obligation of every baptized person to participate in ministry, it sparked an explosion of lay ministries, involving today approximately 30,000 people in the United States, more than all the priests serving in parishes and dioceses across the country.[13] It taught that the world is not alien, evil, or even secular, but filled with the Spirit from which the church must learn. Although part of this world, the church is called to transform it from within, righting injustice, fostering equality, and fashioning peace. In short, the parish is an instrument for creating the kingdom of God in the personal, social, and political realms. This understanding of parish counters a clericalism that supports priests' monopoly of ministry and relegates laity to passive and subservient roles.

Although the teachings and spirit of Vatican II are present today in the promotion of the local church, liturgical renewal, lay and wider ecclesial ministries, and involvement in and service to the world, interests and ideologies opposed to Vatican II threaten the heart of Hispanic parishes by curtailing liturgical diversity, baptismal identity, and ministerial commitment. The parish is hamstrung by excessive control by central authorities, distant from and unrelated to local life and its challenges. Parish life is crippled by a sharp division of the world into secular and sacred, by a sacral isolation of the priest from the people, or by a characterization of the laity as ignorant, profane, or inactive. The repression of lay ministry and the exaltation of an autocratic, arrogant, and even lazy priesthood go together. All these forces threaten the life of a vibrant parish.

Ministry at St. Pius V not only respects people's culture but works to enhance its strengths. The number and nature of its programs, ministries, activities, liturgies, and groups are defined by the personal and social needs of parishioners. The parish facilitates personal development and community life by preparing laity for ministries ranging from volunteering in a secondhand clothing store to serving as catechists, from organizing fund-raising events to serving as eucharistic ministers, from coordinating a Christian Base Community to planning liturgy, from preparing food in the soup kitchen to visiting the sick, from training altar servers to organizing neighbors to clean up their street, from accompanying youth in the confirmation program to ushering at Mass, from working to build new homes in the neighborhood to preparing *quinceañeras*.[14]

The expansion of ministries also requires the organizational structure within a parish to coordinate the various ministries so that they all work together for the common good. The promotion and supervision of ministries are important functions of the staff, which each year assesses newly created ministries and the new people involved. The staff also evaluates how ministers are growing personally in their self-esteem, understanding of church, performance of ministry, ability to cooperate with others, and spirituality. The body of ministers thus grows in numbers, strength, and coordination.

A review of Hispanic parishes in the United States reveals a picture of growing numbers. Lay and wider ecclesial ministries will undoubtedly continue to expand as the number of priests declines. In 1999, a Harris poll estimated that while the number of lay ministers expands exponentially, the number of Catholic priests will drop dramatically, from 23,098 in 1998 to 15,136 by 2010. In order to maintain the current ratio of 1.77 priests to a parish, the church would have to close 6,773 of the country's 19,800 parishes. The other alternative is to increase significantly the number of parishes administered by lay personnel. Currently, 2,300 parishes lack a resident priest,[15] a number expected to double over the next two decades. The average priest is now sixty-one years of age, and seminarians are expected to provide only 30 to 40 percent of the needed replacements, without factoring in a growing Catholic population.[16]

Fewer priests and more diversified lay ministries should not curtail the Spirit, or diminish the rigor of service to grace and church. New spiritualities must arise, while proven traditions of discipleship remain, and Mexican immigrants and Mexican Americans have much to contribute to this new creation. This ecclesiology is already taking shape.

The Hispanic Church in the United States

Although the Catholic Church is slowly opening its doors to Hispanics at the diocesan and parish levels, it is important to welcome them in more ways than simply asking them to attend Sunday Mass. Some church leaders seem more interested in

Americanizing them than in evangelizing and incorporating them into ministry, integrating their culture, faith, and ritual into regular religious services. As with any people, they need greater understanding of Catholic faith and renewed conversion to follow Jesus more faithfully, but to evangelize them, the Church must understand and appreciate their history and traditions and involve them in the evangelizing process. As Vatican II states: "Anyone who is going to encounter another people should have great esteem for their patrimony and their language and customs."[17] Their thinking and believing, their needs in community, and their ways of forming community must be taken seriously. They want to participate as equal partners in creating something new, and they believe that what they have to offer, a vision of an oppressed people with strong faith and a rich culture, is of great value. In order to respond to Hispanics, the Catholic Church must be respectfully present to them, inviting them into dialogue, and demonstrating openness and inclusiveness.

Hispanics already know how to be church. They have their own cultures, and spiritualities, their own Catholicism and popular religion, and their own forms of life and community. This Hispanic-American church is rich with traditions that amalgamate to form something new in the United States. Various historical and cultural sources enter into a new combination that reflects who they are. Native American culture contributes belief in a spirit-filled world, rich in signs and symbols, integrally physical and spiritual, and focused on communal celebrations of the tribe. Spanish Baroque Catholicism, the form of Christianity presented to indigenous peoples, graced people with the arts, such as dramatic liturgies, elaborate devotions, abundant decorations, vibrant music, and sculpture and paintings that fill every space.

Hispanics face a clear challenge: preserving their culture in an alien land. Their traditions contrast and collide with aspects of nineteenth- and twentieth-century American Catholicism stemming from Protestant northern Europe. The latter is endowed with its unique devotions, emphasis on private prayer and individual salvation, observance of church legalities, and respect for individual rights and administrative order, brevity, and punctuality. Moreover, xenophobic forces promoting assimilation and uniformity threaten cultural diversity. Today, the promotion of multicultural parishes is often little more than a veiled attempt to assimilate the minority culture into the dominant one.[18] Out of fear or lack of understanding, some Hispanics, especially first-generation immigrants, jettison their heritage without realizing its value for themselves and for their new country. Traditions are abandoned, language is forgotten, life is secularized, and values are reorganized. Hispanic immigrants and their children must want to preserve their faith and culture and work hard to maintain it. Perhaps the sheer number of Mexican immigrants in certain areas of the country, such as Chicago, will create a sufficient mass of population to facilitate this preservation. Indeed, much of what is written in this book describing the Mexican immigrant may not apply to many of their children, who prefer to speak English, drive new cars, move away from family, attend church rarely, and live together without marrying. Ricardo Ramirez, bishop of Las Cruces, New Mexico, has sadly commented that the culture of his (Mexican) people is dying in the United States.

The Mexican community of faith, like the church throughout the country and around the world, expands the range of what the church does and who does it. This ecclesiology mirrors the church described in the New Testament, a church in which people create radically novel ways to fashion something that reflects who they are as a people. The characteristics of the Mexican faith community may differ from those of other ethnic groups. While some ethnic groups might emphasize clean and well-kept buildings, orderly services, and a quiet church where people can pray alone in silence, Mexican immigrants value other characteristics in their church, such as respect for and inclusiveness of different cultures, a warm welcome for families, particularly children, service to and defense of the poor and oppressed, myriad fiestas, and commitment to promote unity among all.

It is important to appreciate the rich culture Mexicans immigrants bring and to assist them in preserving whatever they hope to retain. Their cultural heritage not only sustains them but can enrich all Americans, especially the Catholic Church. The historical fabric of the United States is woven from many and diverse ethnic threads. Mexicans can and should enhance this garment with all of their unique color and texture.

Notes

1. See B. McGinn, "The Letter and the Spirit," *Journal of the Society for the Study of Christian Spirituality* 1 (1993): 1ff.; Thomas O'Meara, "The Spirituality of Ministry," *Theology of Ministry* (Mahwah, NJ: Paulist, 1999).

2. Ada María Isasi-Díaz, "A Hispanic Garden in a Foreign Land," in Letty M. Russell, ed., *Inheriting Our Mother's Gardens: Feminist Theology in Third World Perspective* (Philadelphia: Westminister, 1988), 92.

3. Cited by Carlos Fuentes, *The Buried Mirror* (New York: Houghton Mifflin, 1992), 11. In this regard, Mexican spirituality is like Celtic spirituality. See Joyce Rupp, "Celtic Crossovers: May the Lent of the Irish Be with You," *U.S. Catholic* (March, 2001), 13–17.

4. Mateo Perez, CSSR, "Spirituality in the Ministry to Hispanics," in Robert J. Wicks, ed., *Handbook of Spirituality for Ministers* (Mahwah, NJ: Paulist Press, 1995), 519.

5. Virgilio P. Elizondo and Timothy M. Matovina, *San Fernando Cathedral* (Maryknoll, NY: Orbis, 1998). The authors explain much of Mexican spirituality in the cathedral parish in San Antonio, Texas, including their devotion before graphic depictions of Jesus' passion and death, 20.

6. Matovina, "U.S. Hispanic Catholics and Liturgical Reform," 18–19.

7. *Puebla*, 282. See also Jeanette Rodriquez, "Guadalupe: The Feminine Face of God," in Ana Castillo, ed., *Goddess of the Americas, La Diosa de las Americas: Writing on the Virgin of Guadalupe* (New York: Riverhead, 1996), 25–31.

8. This characteristic is identified by Daniel Gerard Groody, CSC, *Corazon y Conversion: The Dynamics of Mexican Immigration, Christian Spirituality and Human Transformation*, PhD Dissertation (San Francisco: Graduate Theological Union, 2000).

9. Quoted in Moises Sandoval, "Gracias a la Vida," *U.S. Catholic* (October 2000), 30.

10. Icaza, "Prayer, Worship, and Liturgy," in Deck, *Frontiers*, 151.

11. Rodríguez, "Guadalupe," 148.

12. Richard P. McBrien, "The Ecclesiology of the Local Church," *Thought: A Review of Culture and Ideas* 66 (December 1991): 361.

13. Philip Murnion, *New Parish Ministries: Lay and Religious on Parish Staffs* (New York: National Pastoral Life Center, 1992).

14. On lay ministry, see *Together in God's Service: Toward a Theology of Ecclesial Lay Ministry* (Washington, DC: NCCB, 1998), and O'Meara, *Theology of Ministry*.

15. "Costs of Clerical Celibacy Are Rising," *National Catholic Reporter* (September 3, 1999), 32.

16. Arthur Jones, "Entrusting God's Word to the Entire Church," *National Catholic Reporter* (November 23, 2001), 12.

17. Vatican II, *Ad Gentes*, 26.

18. Orlando O. Espin, "A Multicultural Church? Theological Reflections from Below," in William Cenkner, ed., *The Multicultural Church: A New Landscape in U.S. Theologies* (Mahwah, NJ: Paulist Press, 1995); Miguel Diaz, *On Being Human: U.S. Hispanic and Rahnerian Perspectives* (Maryknoll, NY: Orbis, 2001).